T0211253

Practical Computer Vision Applications Using Deep Learning with CNNs

With Detailed Examples in Python Using TensorFlow and Kivy

Ahmed Fawzy Gad

Apress®

Practical Computer Vision Applications Using Deep Learning with CNNs

Ahmed Fawzy Gad
Menoufia, Egypt

ISBN-13 (pbk): 978-1-4842-4166-0
https://doi.org/10.1007/978-1-4842-4167-7

ISBN-13 (electronic): 978-1-4842-4167-7

Library of Congress Control Number: 2018964710

Managing Director, Apress Media LLC: Welmoed Spahr
Acquisitions Editor: Celestin Suresh John
Development Editor: Matthew Moodie
Coordinating Editor: Divya Modi

Cover designed by eStudioCalamar

Cover image designed by Freepik (www.freepik.com)

Distributed to the book trade worldwide by Springer Science+Business Media New York, 233 Spring Street, 6th Floor, New York, NY 10013. Phone 1-800-SPRINGER, fax (201) 348-4505, e-mail orders-ny@springer-sbm.com, or visit www.springeronline.com. Apress Media, LLC is a California LLC and the sole member (owner) is Springer Science + Business Media Finance Inc (SSBM Finance Inc). SSBM Finance Inc is a **Delaware** corporation.

For information on translations, please e-mail rights@apress.com, or visit http://www.apress.com/rights-permissions.

Apress titles may be purchased in bulk for academic, corporate, or promotional use. eBook versions and licenses are also available for most titles. For more information, reference our Print and eBook Bulk Sales web page at http://www.apress.com/bulk-sales.

Any source code or other supplementary material referenced by the author in this book is available to readers on GitHub via the book's product page, located at www.apress.com/9781484241660. For more detailed information, please visit http://www.apress.com/source-code.

Printed on acid-free paper

I dedicate this book to those looking to cause peace to prevail all over the world and laboring to stop further killing of children and innocent people just because of religious racism. For every human should want to restore rights to their proper owners, do good for others seeking the pleasure of Allah, and leave the world better after death.

Table of Contents

About the Author

Ahmed Fawzy Gad is an Egyptian teaching assistant who received his M.Sc. degree in 2018 after receiving his 2015 excellent with honors B.Sc. in information technology from the Faculty of Computers and Information (FCI), Menoufia University, Egypt. Ahmed is interested in deep learning, machine learning, computer vision, and Python. He has worked as a software engineer and consultant for machine learning projects. His aim is to add value to the data science community by sharing his writings and preparing recorded tutorials on his YouTube channel (youtube.com/AhmedGadFCIT).

Ahmed has a number of published research papers. He authored a book published in 2017 titled *TensorFlow: A Guide to Build Artificial Neural Networks using Python* (Lambert, 2017). Ahmed is always looking to share experience with other experts in his fields of interest. You are welcome to get connected with him using LinkedIn (linkedin.com/in/AhmedFGad), Facebook (facebook.com/AhmedFGadd), and e-mail (ahmed.fawzy@ci.menofia.edu.eg).

About the Technical Reviewers

Leonardo De Marchi holds a Masters in artificial intelligence and has worked as a data scientist in the sports world, with clients such as the New York Knicks and Manchester United, and also has worked with large social networks like Justgiving.

He now works as lead data scientist at Badoo, the world's largest dating site with over 360 million users. He is also the lead instructor at ideai.io, a company specializing in deep learning and machine learning training and a contractor for the European Commission.

Lentin Joseph is an author and robotics entrepreneur from India. He runs Qbotics Labs (`http://qboticslabs.com`), a robotics software company in India.

He has eight years of experience in the robotics domain, especially in robotics software development using the Robot Operating System (ROS), Open-CV, and PCL.

He has authored seven books on ROS: *Learning Robotics Using Python* (two editions; Packt), *Mastering ROS for Robotics Programming* (two editions; Packt), *ROS Robotics Projects* (Packt), *Robot Operating System for Absolute Beginners* (Apress), and *ROS Programming: Building Powerful Robots* (Packt).

He has also reviewed three books related to robotics and ROS. The first was *Effective Robotics Programming Using ROS* (Packt), followed by *Raspberry Pi Image Processing* (Apress) and *Raspberry Pi Supercomputer* (Apress).

Lentin and his team were winners of the HRATC 2016 challenge conducted as a part of ICRA 2016, and he was also a finalist in the HRATC challenge from ICRA 2015.

He completed his masters in robotics and automation in India and has had research experience at the Robotics Institute, Carnegie Mellon University.

Acknowledgments

I would like to thank Allah for giving me the knowledge and ability to prepare this book. As <u>Allah</u> says in the Noble Quran in Surah Al-Nahl Ayah 53, "<u>And whatever you have of favor - it is from Allah.</u>" I believe that without his help, this work would not have been possible.

Allah saves me from dangers, secures my heart, and makes me stronger. He granted me success in my different educational levels, as I was ranked top among my colleagues. This reminds me of Ayah 15 from Surah Al-Naml in the Noble Quran, "<u>And We had certainly given to David and Solomon knowledge, and they said, 'Praise [is due] to Allah, who has favored us over many of His believing servants.'</u>"

I am grateful to the Apress team formed by Welmoed, Celestin, Divya, Matthew, Leonardo, Lentin, Sherly, Nirmal, and Joseph for giving me the chance to prepare this work for readers all over the world. This is a milestone in my life.

Thanks to my social media followers for their feedback regarding my work. Your comments greatly encouraged me to go forward.

Thanks to my mother and my family members for doing their best for supporting me after my father's death during my childhood. My teachers played a critical role in building my character. Thanks to everyone who has done good to me throughout my life. I remember you all and ask Allah to do the same for you.

Introduction

Artificial intelligence (AI for short) is the field of embedding human thinking into computers In other words, creating an artificial brain that mimics the functions of the biological brain. Whatever the human can do intelligently is now required to be moved into machines. First-generation AI focuses on problems that can be formally described by humans. Using AI, steps for doing something intelligent are described in a form of instructions that machines follow. Machines follow the human without changes. These features are characteristic of the first era of AI.

Humans can fully describe only simple problems such as Tic-Tac-Toe or even chess and fail to describe the more complicated problems. In chess, the problem can be simply explained by representing the board as a matrix of size 8×8, describing each piece and how it moves, and describing the goals. Machines will be restricted to those tasks formally described by humans. By programming such instructions, machines can play chess intelligently. Machine intelligence is now artificial. The machine itself is not intelligent, but humans have transferred their intelligence to the machine in the form of several static lines of code. By static, it is meant that the behavior is the same in all cases.

The machine, in this case, is tied to the human and can't work on its own. This is like a master-slave relationship. The human is the master and the machine is the slave, which just follows the human's orders and no more.

Embedding intelligent behavior inside chunks of code can't handle all intelligent behaviors of humans. Some simple tasks, such as sorting numbers or playing some games, can be described by humans and then handled by the machine with 100% of human intelligence. However, some complex tasks, such as speech-to-text, image recognition, sentiment analysis, and others, can't be solved by just code. Such problems could not be described by the human as done with chess. It is impossible to write code to recognize image objects such as cats. Such intelligent behavior of recognizing objects simply can't be solved using a static code because there is no single rule for classifying objects. There is no rule to recognize cats, for instance. Even if a rule is successfully created to recognize cats in one environment, it will definitely fail when applied in another. So how can we make machines intelligent in such tasks? This is machine learning (ML), in which rules are learned by machines.

To make the machine able to recognize objects, we can give it previous knowledge from experts in a way the machine can understand. Such knowledge-based systems form the second era of AI. One of the challenges in such systems is how to handle uncertainty and unknowns. Humans can recognize objects even in different and complex environments and are able to handle uncertainty and unknowns intelligently, but machines can't.

In ML, the human is responsible to do the complex task of investigating the data to find what types of features are able to categorize objects accurately. Unfortunately, it is a challenging task to find the best types of features to use. This is the question that researchers are trying to answer for different applications. For example, to diagnose a disease, the expert human starts by collecting data for both affected and nonaffected persons, labels such data well, and finds some types of features that are robust in discriminating between people with the disease and those without it. Such features may be age, gender, blood sugar, and blood pressure. This is a very challenging task because the larger the dataset, the more complex for humans to find features working across all samples.

These days, however, ML models can be trained to identify how to discriminate between the different classes. The ML algorithm is what finds the suitable mathematical function that creates the most robust relationship between the inputs and their outputs.

ML algorithms are not doing everything; the key intelligence is still found in the human expert, not in the machine. The human collects and labels the data, extracts the most suitable features, and selects the best ML algorithm. After that, the ML algorithm just learns what the human has told it. Still, the machine plays an important role in finding the rule by which the inputs are mapped to the outputs.

Usually, ML algorithms trained with data from a certain environment(s) can't work with other environments. This is a key limitation. There are huge amounts of data existing all over the world. Day after day, the data increases and traditional ML techniques are not suitable for its manipulation. For instance, images are complex to describe using a set of engineered features due to the variations even within the same environment. The work (i.e., feature engineering) should be repeated to make the ML algorithm suited to work with other environments.

If the human ability to find good discriminating features decreases as the number of classes increases, we can avoid depending on humans and leave that task for the machine. The machine itself will try to explore the data and find suitable features to discriminate the classes. Just give the machine the data and it will find what features to use in order to make a classifier. This is deep learning (DL). The convolutional neural network (CNN) DL model is the trend for working with large amounts of images.

The field of DL focuses on learning how to draw conclusions from raw data without the need of the in-between step of feature engineering. This is why DL can be practically called "automated feature engineering." It is tiresome in its processing and memory requirements and may take weeks to discriminate between different classes.

This book targets those of tomorrow's data scientists who would like to start understanding the basic concepts of DL for computer vision. Readers should have a basic understanding of image processing and Python. Here is an overview of the chapters.

Chapter 1 selects the most suitable set of features for classifying the Fruits 360 dataset based on a review of some commonly used feature descriptors in computer vision. Such features are implemented in Python. By filtering such features in the preprocessing step, the minimum number of elements are used for classification. This chapter concludes that traditional handcrafted features are not suitable for complex problems. DL is the alternative for working with millions of samples and thousands of classes.

Chapter 2 discusses the artificial neural network (ANN), which is the base of DL models. It starts by explaining how the ANN is just a combination of linear models. ANN architecture is designed for some simple examples by specifying the best number of layers and neurons. Based on both numerical and Python examples, it will be clear how ANN works for both forward and backward passes.

Chapter 3 uses the feature set from Chapter 2 to implement the ANN for classifying a subset of the Fruits 360 dataset. Because no optimization technique is used within the implementation, the classification accuracy is low.

Chapter 4 gives an introduction to single- and multiobjective optimization techniques. It uses the genetic algorithm random-based technique for optimizing the ANN weights. This increases the classification accuracy to more than 97%.

Chapter 5 discusses CNNs for recognizing multidimensional signals. The chapter starts by highlighting the differences between fully connected neural networks (FCNNs) and CNNs and how CNN is derived from FCNN. Based on numerical examples, the two basic operations in CNN, namely, convolution and pooling, will be clear. CNN layers are implemented in NumPy for understanding how things work in detail.

Chapter 6 introduces the TensorFlow DL library, which is used to build DL models for parallel and distributed processing of large amounts of data. TensorFlow placeholders, variables, dataflow graphs, and TensorBoard are discussed based on some examples building a simple linear model and an ANN for simulating the XOR gate. By the end of this chapter, a CNN is created using **tensorflow.nn** module for classifying the CIFAR10 dataset.

Chapter 7 deploys the trained models into a web server for being accessed by Internet users using a web browser. A web application is created using the Flask microframework. HTML, CSS, and JavaScript are used to build the front pages for accessing the web server. The HTML pages send HTTP requests to the server with an image, and the server responds to such requests with the predicted class.

Chapter 8 builds cross-platform applications using the Kivy open source library. By linking Kivy to NumPy, it is possible to build data science applications that work unchanged on different platforms. This removes the overhead of customizing the code for a specific platform. An Android application is created to read an image and execute the CNN layers implemented using NumPy in Chapter 5.

To benefit from the projects created, it is preferred to push them online for other people to use and benefit from. An appendix discusses how to package Python projects and distribute them into the Python package index (PyPI) repository.

Before starting, let's take a brief overview of the Python environment used in the book.

All code in the book is implemented using Python. Because native Python is complex for handling images, multiple libraries are used to help to produce an efficient implementation for applications across the chapters.

At first, native Python could be downloaded from this link (`www.python.org/downloads`). The book uses Python 3. Just install the version of Python that is suitable for your system. The next step is to prepare all libraries required across the entire book. Rather than installing individual libraries, it is recommended to use Anaconda Python distribution. It is available for download from this link (`www.anaconda.com/download`). It supports Windows, Mac, and Linux and packages more than 1,400 data science libraries. A list of all supported packages can be accessed from this page (`https://repo.anaconda.com/pkgs`). By just installing Anaconda on your machine, all of the supported libraries will be ready for use. This is helpful to avoid the challenges of preparing the Python environment.

The required libraries in this book are NumPy, SciPy, Matplotlib, scikit-image, scikit-learn, TensorFlow, Flask, Werkzeug, Jinja, Pickle, Pillow, and Kivy. All of these libraries, except for Kivy, are supported by Anaconda. Later in this chapter, we will see the function of each of them. Note that such libraries can be installed easily. After installing the native Python, we can use the pip installer to download and install a library based on this command: "pip install <lib-name>". Just type the name of the library. Some installations are not straightforward and might change if the system changes. Thus, we can't cover the different installations. For such reasons, Anaconda is better than installing each library individually. Let's discuss the libraries needed.

Python supports a number of built-in data structures: list, tuple, dictionary, set, and string. Unfortunately, no data structure provides flexibility in data science applications.

These data structures support working with different data types at the same time. The same data structure might contain numbers, characters, objects, and more. String is an exception, in which only characters are supported. Moreover, string and tuple are immutable, which means it is impossible to change their values after they are created. Dictionary adds a key to each item. Saving image pixels using a dictionary requires adding a key to each pixel which enlarges the amount of data saved. Set is restricted to just set operations and images are not restricted to just such operations.

Talking about images, which are the main concern of the book, list is the suitable data structure. It is a mutable data type that is able to hold matrices. Unfortunately, working with lists makes the process complex. We have to make sure everything is numeric, of a certain specific type because different numeric data types can be saved in the same list. To apply a simple operation such as adding a number to the image, we have to write loops for visiting each element and apply such operations individually. In data science applications, it is recommended to use the tools that make applying the operations easier. There are some challenging tasks to conquer when building an application, and we do not need to add another challenge in programming such tasks.

For such reasons, the NumPy (Numeric Python) library is used. Its basic role is to support a new data structure in Python, which is array. Working with NumPy arrays is simpler than working with lists. For example, using just the addition operator (+), we can add a number to each element in the image after it is converted into a NumPy array. Many other libraries have their functions accept and return a NumPy array.

Some operations are supported inside the NumPy array, but it is not meant to apply operations. The SciPy (Scientific Python) library supports the same operations in the NumPy arrays and more. It also supports working with the n-dimensional NumPy arrays (e.g., images) using the scipy.ndimage submodule. For more advanced operations on images, the scikit-image library is used. For example, image features can be extracted using this library.

After reading the image and applying some operations, Matplotlib is used for displaying the images. It is mainly used for 2D visualization, but it also supports some 3D features.

After reading the images, extracting features, and making visualizations, we can start building ML models using the scikit-learn library. It supports different types of models that are ready for use. Just feed it with inputs, outputs, and their parameters to have a trained model.

After training a ML model, we can save it for later use using the pickle library, which serializes and deserializes the objects. Up to this point, we can build and save an ML model. We then move to building and saving a DL model using TensorFlow. It is the most commonly used DL library, as it supports different APIs that match the needs of professionals and beginners alike. TensorFlow has its own ways to save the trained models.

In order to deploy the trained models, Flask is used. It is a microframework for building web applications. By deploying the trained models to the web server, clients can access such applications using a web browser. They can upload test images to the server and receive the classification label. Flask uses the Jinja2 template engine and WSGI for building the applications. For such reasons, the libraries Jinja and werkzeug must be installed.

In order to build a data science mobile application that runs on-device, Kivy is used. It is a Python library that allows the Python code to run cross-platform. In this book, Kivy is used to build rich data science applications running for Android. The APK generated by Kivy can be used in the market exactly as if it were created normally using Android Studio.

Kivy uses the python-for-android packager, which allows adding the required dependencies in the Android application. Because scikit-image is not supported by python-for-android, images are read using Pillow, which is supported to run on Android devices.

Implementations of the projects are available at this GitHub account: `github.com/AhmedFGad`

CHAPTER 1

Recognition in Computer Vision

Most computer science research tries to build a human-like robot that is able to function exactly as humans. Even emotional properties are not impossible for such robots. Using a sensor, the robot feels the temperature in the surrounding environment. Using facial expressions, it is possible to know whether a person is sad or happy. Even things that seem impossible might eventually only be challenging.

At the current time, a very challenging application is object recognition. Recognition can be based on different types of data such as audio, image, and text. But image recognition is a very efficient way due to the plenitude of information that can be helpful in the task. Thus, it is regarded as the most popular application in computer vision.

There is a massive number of objects existing in the world, and differentiating them is a complex task. Different objects might have similar visual appearance except for subtle details. Moreover, the same object appears differently based on its surrounding environment. For example, based on the light, viewing angle, distortion, and occlusion, the same object appears differently in the image. Depending on the native image, pixels may not be a good option for image recognition. This is because a minor change in each pixel leads to a major change in the image, and thus the system is unable to recognize the objects correctly. The target is to find a set of unique properties or features that do not change even with changing pixel locations or values, as long as the structure of the object appears somewhere in the image. Manually extracting features from images is a big challenge in image recognition. This is why automatic approaches to feature extraction are becoming the alternative.

Because recognition of any object in any environment is complex at the current time, the alternative way is to restrict the environment or the objects targeted. For example, rather than recognizing all types of animals, we can just target a group of them. Rather than working indoors and outdoors, we might restrict the environment to just indoor images.

1

© Ahmed Fawzy Gad 2018
A. F. Gad, *Practical Computer Vision Applications Using Deep Learning with CNNs*,
https://doi.org/10.1007/978-1-4842-4167-7_1

Rather than recognizing objects in different views, we might only work with some views. Generally, creating a narrow artificial intelligence application, while challenging, is easier and has fewer difficulties than general artificial intelligence application.

This chapter discusses how to build a recognition application to classify fruit images. It starts by presenting some types of features that are useful generally with different types of applications and then finds the best of such features for use with our target application. By the end of this chapter, we will find why manually extracting features is challenging and why automatic feature mining using convolutional neural networks (CNNs) is preferred.

Image Recognition Pipeline

Similar to most traditional recognition applications, image recognition is likely to follow some predefined steps, from accepting an input to returning the desired results. A summary of such steps is presented in Figure 1-1.

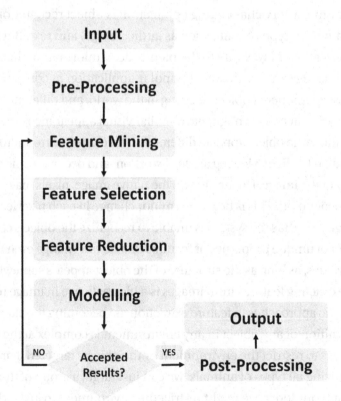

Figure 1-1. *General recognition pipeline*

Sometimes the input image is not suitable in its current form for processing. For example, if we are to build a face recognition application that captures images in a complex environment to recognize the people inside it, then it is preferred to remove the background before starting to recognize the target object. Background removal, in this case, is a type of preprocessing. Generally, any step preceding the actual work is called preprocessing. Preprocessing is a step that maximizes the probability of successful recognition.

After preparing the inputs, we come to the actual work, which starts with feature extraction or mining. This is the critical step in most recognition applications. The target is to find a set of representative features that accurately describes each input. Such a set of features should maximize the probability of mapping each input to its correct output and also minimize the probability of assigning each input a wrong label. As a result, there should be an analysis of the types of features to be used.

The application and the set of features used are related. The features are selected based on the application. By understanding the nature of the application, the type of features required will be easily detected. For an application such as human face detection, what are the features to be extracted? Human faces have skin of various colors, and thus we can determine that skin color is the feature to be used. Knowing that the application is to detect human faces in grayscale outdoor images, low lighting, and in a moving environment helps to select the appropriate features. If you are asked to build an application to recognize oranges and bananas, you can benefit from the fact that oranges and bananas have different colors and thus decide that only color features are enough. But they are not enough to recognize different types of skin cancer, for instance. More work must be done to find the most suitable set of features. The next section titled **Feature Extraction** discusses some features helpful in image recognition applications.

After creating a feature vector holding the features that are likely to be useful in the recognition application, we come to other steps that add further enhancement, namely, feature selection and reduction. The primary goal of feature selection and reduction can be defined as obtaining an optimal feature subset from a set of features that enhances the learning algorithm performance or accuracy by reducing the number of irrelevant, correlated, and noise features. The section titled **Feature Selection & Reduction** discusses the approaches for reducing the feature vector length by removing such features.

Feature Extraction

It is unusual to apply the image in its native form as input to the training model. There are different reasons why extracting features is a better way. One reason is that images, even small ones, have a very large number of pixels, where each pixel is applied as an input to the model. For a grayscale image of size 100×100 pixels, there are 100×100 = 10,000 input variables to be applied to the model. For a small dataset of 100 samples, there will be a total of 100×10,000 = 1,000,000 inputs across the entire dataset. If the image is Red-Green-Blue (RGB), the total number is multiplied by 3. This requires a large memory in addition to being computationally intensive.

Another reason why feature extraction is preferred before training is that the input image has different types of objects with different properties, and we just want to target a single object. For example, Figure 1-2(a) shows an image of a dog from the "Dogs Vs. Cats Kaggle" competition. Our goal is to detect the dog, and we do not care about either the wood or the grass. If the complete image is used as the input to the model, the wood and the grass will affect the results. It is better to just use features exclusive to the dog. It is clear that the dog color is different from other colors in the image, according to Figure 1-2(b).

a   b

Figure 1-2. *Targeting a specific object inside the image is easier when using features*

Generally, successful modeling of the problem is tied to the selection of the best features. The data scientist should select the most representative set of features for the problem being solved. There are different types of features to be used to describe the images. These features can be categorized in different ways. One way is to examine whether they are extracted globally or locally from specific regions in the image. Local features are those such as edge and keypoints. Global features are those such as color histogram and pixel count. By global, it is meant that the feature describes the entire image. Saying that the color histogram is centered at the left region means that the entire image is dark. The description is not just for a specific region of the image. Local features are focused on a specific something within the image such as the edges.

Subsequent subsections discuss the following features:

- Color Histogram

- Edge

  - HOG

- Texture

  - GLCM

  - GLGCM

  - LBP

Color Histogram

The color histogram represents the distribution of the colors across the image. It is usually used with gray images, but there are modifications to use it with color images. For simplicity, let's calculate the color histogram for the 5×5 2-bit image in Figure 1-3. The image has just 4 grayscale levels. The image is randomly generated using NumPy.

3	2	2	0	3
1	3	0	2	2
2	2	2	2	3
3	3	3	2	3
0	2	3	2	2

Figure 1-3. *Two-bit grayscale image of size 5×5*

By calculating the frequency of each grayscale level, the histogram is presented in Figure 1-4. Based on the histogram, it is obvious that the high-frequency bins are located to the right and thus the image is bright because most of its pixels are high.

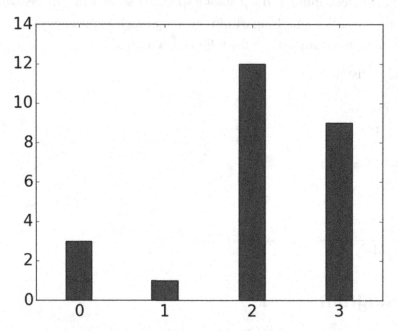

Figure 1-4. *Histogram of a 2-bit 5×5 grayscale image*

Listing 1-1 gives the Python code used to randomly generate the previous tiny image in addition to calculating and displaying the histogram.

Listing 1-1. Histogram for a Tiny Randomly Generated Image

```
import matplotlib.pyplot
import numpy

rand_img = numpy.random.uniform(low=0, high=3, size=(5,5))
rand_img = numpy.uint8(rand_img)
hist = numpy.histogram(rand_img, bins=4)
matplotlib.pyplot.bar(left=[0,1,2,3], height=hist[0], align="center",
width=0.3)
matplotlib.pyplot.xticks([0,1,2,3], fontsize=20)
matplotlib.pyplot.yticks(numpy.arange(0, 15, 2), fontsize=20)
```

The `numpy.random.uniform()` accepts the size of the array to be returned in addition to the lower and higher bounds of the range from which image pixels will be assigned values. The lower bound is 0 and the higher bound is 3 because we are looking to create a 2-bit image. `numpy.uint8()` is used to convert the values from floating-point to integer. Then, the histogram is calculated using `numpy.histogram()`, which accepts the image and number of bins and returns the frequency of each level. Finally, `matplotlib.pyplot.bar()` is used to return a bar graph showing each level on the x axis and its frequency on the y axis. `matplotlib.pyplot.xticks()` and `matplotlib.pyplot.yticks()` are used to change the range of the x axis and y axis in addition to the display font size.

Histogram of a Real-World Image

Let's calculate the histogram on a real-world image as in Figure 1-2(a) after converting it to black-and-white. Both the grayscale image and the histogram are shown in Figure 1-5. It seems that the histogram is mostly concentrated in the left part, which means the image is generally dark. Because the dog's body is white, part of the histogram is located at the rightmost part of the histogram distribution.

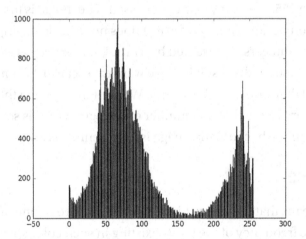

Figure 1-5. *Grayscale image histogram*

Listing 1-2 gives the Python code for reading the color image, converting it to grayscale, calculating its histogram, and finally plotting the histogram as a bar graph.

Listing 1-2. Histogram for a Real-World Image

```
import matplotlib.pyplot
import numpy
import skimage.io

im = skimage.io.imread("69.jpg", as_grey=True)
im = numpy.uint8(im*255)

hist = numpy.histogram(im, bins=256)
matplotlib.pyplot.bar(left=numpy.arange(256), height= hist[0],
align="center", width=0.1)
```

Using the `skimage.io.imread()` function, the image is both read and converted to grayscale using the `as_grey` attribute. When set to `True`, the image is returned as grayscale. The returned image data type is `float64`. To convert it to an unsigned integer that ranges from 0 to 255, the `numpy.uint8()` is used. The image is firstly multiplied by 255 before conversion because `numpy.uint8()` does not rescale the inputs. It just makes sure the numbers are integers represented by 8 bits. For example, applying a number equal to 0.7 to this function, the result is 0. We want to rescale 0.4 from the 0–1 range to the 0–255 range and then convert it into uint8. Without multiplying the inputs by 255, all values will be just 0 or 1. Note that the number of histogram bins is set to 256 rather than 4 in the previous example because the image is represented as 8-bit.

HSV Color Space

Color histogram means that the image pixels are represented in one of the color spaces, and then the frequency of the levels existing in such color spaces are counted. Previously, the image was represented in the RGB color space, which ranges from 0 to 255 to each channel. But this is not the only existing color space.

Another color space that we will cover is HSV (Hue-Saturation-Value). The advantage of this color space is the separation of color and illumination information. The hue channel holds the color information and the other channels (saturaiton and value) specifies the lightness of the color. It is useful to target the color rather than the illumination and creating illumination-invariant features. We will not cover the HSV color space in this book, but it is fine to read more about how colors are generated using HSV. What is worth mentioning is that the hue channel represents a circle with its values ranging from 0 to 360, where a degree of 0 represents red, 120 for green, 240 for blue, and back to red at degree 360. So, it starts and ends at a red color.

For the image in Figure 1-2(a), the hue channel and its histogram are shown in Figure 1-6. When the hue channel gets represented as the grayscale image as in Figure 1-6(a), the red color will be given a high value (white), as shown in the dog collar. Because the blue is given a high hue value of 240, it is lighter in the grayscale image. The green color with a hue value of 140 is nearer to 0 than to 360; thus, it has a dark color. Note that the dog's body, which is white in RGB color space, looks black in the HSV. The reason is that HSV is not responsible for the intensity but just the color. It will be white in the value channel.

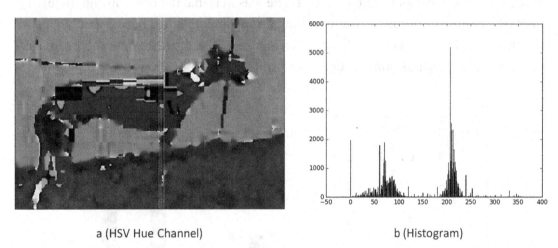

a (HSV Hue Channel)   b (Histogram)

Figure 1-6. *Hue channel of a color image represented in HSV and its histogram*

According to Listing 1-3, the RGB image is converted into HSV color space and its hue channel histogram is displayed.

Listing 1-3. Displaying the Image Histogram Using Matplotlib

```
import matplotlib.pyplot
import numpy
import skimage.io
import skimage.color
```

```
im = skimage.io.imread("69.jpg", as_grey=False)
```

```
im_HSV = skimage.color.rgb2hsv(im)
Hue = im_HSV[:, :, 0]
```

```
hist = numpy.histogram(Hue, bins=360)
matplotlib.pyplot.bar(left=numpy.arange(360), height=hist[0],
align="center", width=0.1)
```

Because the hue channel is the first channel in the HSV color space, it is given the index 0 to get returned.

Features are expected to be unique for different images. If different images have the same features, the results will not be accurate. The color histogram has such a drawback, as it could be identical for different images. The reason is that the color histogram just counts the frequency of colors, whatever their arrangement in the image. Figure 1-7(a) transposed the image in Figure 1-3. Based on Figure 1-7(b), the histograms of the image before and after transposition are identical despite the pixel locations being different.

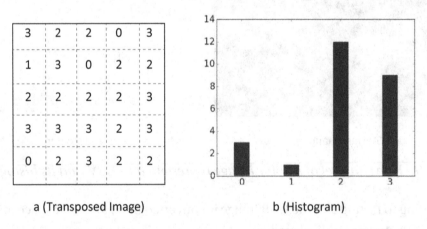

a (Transposed Image)   b (Histogram)

Figure 1-7. *Changing pixel locations does not change the color histogram*

One may think that this is not a problem, as a good feature descriptor should remain persistent even with changes to the image such as rotation and scale. The color histogram is not able to meet this property, as it returns the same histogram even if the images are completely different. To solve this problem, both the pixel intensity and location should be considered to return a more representative feature. Examples of such features are texture features such as GLCM.

GLCM

One of the popular statistical texture analysis methods depends on the second-order statistics extracted from the spatial relationship between pairs of pixels. The most popular of such features are ones extracted from the co-occurrence matrix (CM). One of the CMs is the gray-level co-occurrence matrix (GLCM). Based on its name, it accepts a grayscale image as input and returns GLCM matrix as output.

GLCM can be described as a two-dimensional histogram that counts the number of co-occurrences between each pair of grayscale levels according to the distance between them. What makes GLCM different from the first-order histogram is that GLCM depends not just on the intensity but also on the spatial relationship of the pixels. For every two pixels, one is called reference and the other is called neighbor. GLCM finds how many times two intensity levels co-occur when the distance between them is D and the angle is θ. $GLCM_{(1,3),D=1,\theta=0°}$ refers to how many times the reference pixel with the intensity value of 1 co-occurs with its neighbor with intensity 3 when they are separated by distance D = 1 and angle $\theta = 0°$. When $\theta = 0$, this means they are on the same horizontal line. θ specifies the direction and D specifies the distance in that direction. Note that the reference exists to the left side of the neighbor.

The steps to calculate the GLCM are as follows:

1. If the input image was grayscale or binary, use it directly. If it was a color image, convert it into the grayscale image or use just one of its channels if appropriate.

2. Find the total number of intensity levels in the image. If the number is L, then number these levels from 0 to L − 1.

3. Create an LxL matrix, where both rows and columns are numbered from 0 to L − 1.

4. Select the appropriate parameters of the GLCM (D, θ).

5. Find the co-occurrence between every two pairs of intensity levels.

D Values

Research studies showed that the best values for D are ones ranging from 1 to 10. Larger values will yield GLCMs that don't capture the detailed textural information. So, the results are accurate for D=1, 2, 4, 8, with D=1, 2 being the best. Normally, a pixel is likely to be more correlated with pixels near to it. Decreasing the distance yields better results than higher distances.

θ Values

For a 3×3 matrix, the center pixel has 8 neighboring pixels. Between such center pixel and all other 8 pixels, there are 8 possible values for θ as described in Figure 1-8.

135°	90°	45°
180°	PXL	0°
225°	270°	315°

Figure 1-8. *Values of θ between the center pixel and its eight neighboring pixels*

Because the co-occurring pairs obtained by choosing θ set to 0° and 180° are equal (i.e., $GLCM_{(1,3),\theta=0°} = GLCM_{(3,1),\theta=180°}$), only one angle is sufficient. Generally, angles separated by 180° return the same results. This applies to angles (45°, 225°), (135°, 315°), and (90°, 270°).

Let's start to calculate the GLCM for the previous matrix in Figure 1-3, repeated again in the matrix below, when D=1 and θ=0. Because that image has four intensity levels, then the available pairs when the reference intensity is 0 are (0,0), (0,1), (0,2), and (0,3). When the reference intensity is 1, then the pairs are (1,0), (1,1), (1,2), and (1,3). This continues for 2 and 3.

3	2	2	0	3
1	3	0	2	2
2	2	2	2	3
3	3	3	2	3
0	2	3	2	2

Calculating $GLCM_{(0,0),D=1,\theta=0°}$, the value will be 0. This is because there is no pixel with intensity 0 that is 1 pixel away horizontally from another pixel with intensity 0. The result is also 0 for pairs (0,1), (1,0), (1,1), (1,2), (2,1), and (3,1).

For $GLCM_{(0,2),D=1,\theta=0°}$, the result is 2 because there are three times when the intensity 3 is located 1 pixel away from intensity 0 horizontally (i.e., $\theta = 0°$). The result is also 2 for $GLCM_{(3,3),D=1,\theta=0°}$. For $GLCM_{(0,3),D=1,\theta=0°}$, the result is 1 because there is only one occurrence of the intensity 3 with distance 1 and angle 0 from intensity 0. This is located in the top right of the original matrix.

The complete GLCM is available in Figure 1-9. The matrix is of size 4×4 because it has 4 intensity levels numbered from 0 to 3. The row and column labels are added to make it easier to know which intensity level co-occurs with another.

	0	1	2	3
0	0	0	2	1
1	0	0	0	1
2	1	0	6	3
3	1	0	3	2

Figure 1-9. *GLCM of the matrix in Figure 1-3 where distance is 1 and angle is 0*

The Python code used to return the preceding GLCM is given in Listing 1-4.

Listing 1-4. GLCM Matrix Calculation

```python
import numpy
import skimage.feature

arr = numpy.array([[3, 2, 2, 0, 3],
                   [1, 3, 0, 2, 2],
                   [2, 2, 2, 2, 3],
                   [3, 3, 3, 2, 3],
                   [0, 2, 3, 2, 2]])

co_mat = skimage.feature.greycomatrix(image=arr, distances=[1], angles=[0],
levels=4)
```

13

The `skimage.feature.greycomatrix()` is used to calculate the GLCM. It accepts the input image, distances, angles at which the matrix will be calculated, and finally, the number of levels used. The number of levels is important, as the default is 256.

Note that there is a matrix for each unique pair of angles and distances. There is just a single angle and distance used and thus a single GLCM matrix returned. The shape of the returned output has four numbers as follows:

```
co_mat.shape = (4, 4, 1, 1)
```

The first two numbers represent the number of rows and columns, respectively. The third number represents the number of used distances. The last one is the number of angles. If the matrix is to be calculated for more distances and angles, then specify them in `skimage.feature.greycomatrix()`. The next line calculates the GLCM using two distances and three angles.

```
co_mat = skimage.feature.greycomatrix(image=arr, distances=[1, 4],
angles=[0, 45, 90], levels=4)
```

The shape of the returned matrix is

```
co_mat.shape = (4, 4, 2, 3)
```

Because there are two distances and three angles, the total number of returned GLCMs is 2×3 = 6. To return the GLCM at distance 1 and angle 0°, the indexing will be as follows:

```
co_mat[:, :, 0, 0]
```

This returns the complete 4×4 GLCM, but only for the first distance (1) and first angle (0) according to their order in the `skimage.feature.greycomatrix()` function. To return the GLCM corresponding to distance 4 and angle 90°, the indexing will be as follows:

```
co_mat[:, :, 1, 2]
```

GLCM Normalization

The previously calculated GLCMs are useful for learning how many times each intensity level co-occurs with each other. We can benefit from such information to predict the probability of co-occurrence between each two intensity levels. The GLCM can be converted into a probability matrix, and thus we can know the probability of co-occurrence between each of two intensity levels l_1 and l_2 when separated by distance

D and angle θ. This is done by dividing each element in the matrix by the sum of matrix elements. The resulting matrix is called the normalized or probability matrix. Based on Figure 1-9, the sum of all elements is 20. After dividing each element by that, the normalized matrix is shown in Figure 1-10.

	0	1	2	3
0	0.0	0.0	0.1	0.05
1	0.0	0.0	0.0	0.05
2	0.05	0.0	0.3	0.15
3	0.05	0.0	0.15	0.1

Figure 1-10. *Normalized GLCM matrix with distance 1 and angle 0*

One benefit from normalizing the GLCM is that all elements in the output matrix are in the same scale from 0.0 to 1.0. Moreover, the results are independent of the image size. For example, the highest frequency according to Figure 1-9 of size 5×5 is 6 for the pair (2,2). If a new image is larger (e.g., 100×100), the highest frequency will not be 6 but a larger value such as 2,000. We can't compare 6 by 2,000 because such numbers are relevant to the image size. By normalizing the matrix, the elements of the GLCM are independent of the image size and thus we can compare them correctly. In Figure 1-10, the pair (2,2) is given a probability of 0.3, which is comparable with the probability of co-occurrence from any image of any size.

Normalizing the GLCM in Python is very simple. Based on a boolean parameter called "normed", if set to True the result will be normalized. It is set to False by default. The normalized matrix is calculated according to this line:

```
co_mat_normed = skimage.feature.greycomatrix(image=arr, distances=[1],
angles=[0], levels=4, normed=True)
```

The GLCM is of size 4×4 because we are using a 2-bit image with just 4 levels. For the 8-bit grayscale image in Figure 1-2(a), there are 256 levels and thus the matrix size is 256×256. The normalized GLCM is shown in Figure 1-11. The probabilities are large for two regions. The first one is at the top left (low intensity) as the background has dark colors. The other region is at the bottom right (high intensity) for the dog's body, because its color is white.

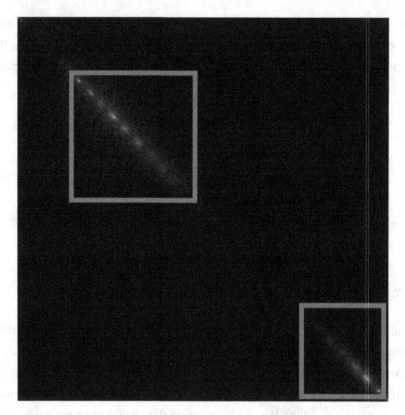

Figure 1-11. *GLCM matrix of a grayscale image with 256 levels with distance 6 and angle 0*

As the number of levels increases, the size of the matrix will increase. The GLCM in Figure 1-11 has 256×256 = 65,536 elements. Using all elements in the matrix in the feature vector will increase its length greatly. We can reduce this number by extracting some features from the matrix, including dissimilarity, correlation, homogeneity, energy, contrast, and ASM (angular second moment). Listing 1-5 gives the Python code required to extract such features.

Listing 1-5. Extracting GLCM Features

```python
import skimage.io, skimage.feature
import numpy

img = skimage.io.imread('im.jpg', as_grey=True);

img = numpy.uint8(img*255)
```

```
glcm = skimage.feature.greycomatrix(img, distances=[6], angles=[0],
levels=256, normed=True)

dissimilarity = skimage.feature.greycoprops(P=glcm, prop='dissimilarity')
correlation = skimage.feature.greycoprops(P=glcm, prop='correlation')
homogeneity = skimage.feature.greycoprops(P=glcm, prop='homogeneity')
energy = skimage.feature.greycoprops(P=glcm, prop='energy')
contrast = skimage.feature.greycoprops(P=glcm, prop='contrast')
ASM = skimage.feature.greycoprops(P=glcm, prop='ASM')

glcm_props = [dissimilarity, correlation, homogeneity, energy, contrast, ASM]

print('Dissimilarity',dissimilarity,'\nCorrelation',correlation,
'\nHomogeneity',homogeneity,'\nEnergy',energy,'\nContrast',contrast,
'\nASM',ASM)
```

One drawback of GLCM is being dependent on the grayscale values. Just a small change in the illumination affects the resulting GLCM. One solution is to build the CM using gradients rather than intensities. Such a matrix is called gray-level gradient-based co-occurrence matrix (GLGCM) . By using gradients, GLGCM is invariant to the illumination changes.

Both GLCM and GLGCM are variant to image transformations. That is, if the same grayscale image is affected by a transformation such as rotation, the descriptor will yield different features. A good feature descriptor should be invariant to such effects.

HOG

GLCM is used to describe the image texture but it can't describe the abrupt changes in image intensities (i.e., edges). Sometimes texture is not the suitable feature to use in a problem, and we have to look for another feature. One category of feature descriptors is used to describe the image edges. Such features describe different aspects of the edges such as edge direction or orientation, edge position, and edge strength or magnitude.

This subsection discusses a descriptor called histogram of oriented gradients (HOG) that describes the edge orientations. Sometimes, the target objects have a unique direction of movement, and thus HOG is a suitable feature. HOG creates a histogram of a number of bins representing the frequency of the edge orientations. Let's see how HOG works.

Image Gradients

There are changes in intensities between every pair of neighboring pixels within the image. To measure that change, the gradient vector for every pixel is calculated to measure how the intensity changes from this pixel to its neighboring pixels. That vector's magnitude is the difference in intensities between two pixels. The vector also reflects the direction of change in terms of X direction and Y direction. For the grayscale image in Figure 1-12, let's calculate the change in the intensity in both X and Y directions for pixel 21 in the third row and the fourth column.

164	43	222	22	58
97	68	50	53	12
91	23	83	21	98
0	88	0	63	162
92	42	32	23	11

Figure 1-12. *Grayscale image to calculate its gradients*

Masks to use to find the gradient magnitude in X and Y directions are in Figure 1-13. Let's start calculating the gradients.

Horizontal   **Vertical**

| 1 | 0 | -1 |

| 1 |
| 0 |
| -1 |

Figure 1-13. *Masks to calculate the horizontal and vertical gradients*

By centering the horizontal mask on the target pixel, we can calculate the gradient in the X direction. In this case, the neighboring pixels are 83 and 98. By subtracting these values, either subtract the left pixel from the pixel to the right or right from left but be consistent across the entire image: the amount of change at this pixel is 98 − 83 = 15. The angle used in this case is 0°.

To get the amount of change at that pixel in the Y direction, the vertical mask is centered at the target pixel. Then, the top and left pixels for that pixel are subtracted to return 63 − 53 = 10. The angle used in this case is 90°.

After calculating the change in both X and Y directions, next is to calculate the final gradient magnitude according to Equation 1-1 and also the gradient direction according to Equation 1-2.

$$Z = \sqrt{X^2 + Y^2}$$
(Equation 1-1)

$$Angle = tan^{-1} \frac{Y}{X}$$
(Equation 1-2)

The gradient magnitude is equal to $\sqrt{15^2 + 10^2} = 18.03$.

Gradient Direction

Regarding the gradient direction, one might say that the direction of change for that pixel is at 0° because the magnitude at the 0° is higher than the vector at 90°. Others might say, however, that the pixel doesn't change at either 0° or 90° but at an in-between angle. Such an angle is calculated by taking both X and Y directions into regard. The direction of that vector is $tan^{-1} \frac{15}{10} = 56.31°$. As a result, that pixel direction of change is at 56.31°.

After calculating the angles for all images, the next step is to create a histogram for such angles. To make the histogram smaller, not all angles are used but just a set of predefined angles. The most common angles to use are horizontal (0°), vertical (90°), and diagonal (45° and 135°). Each angle contributes by a value equal to its gradient magnitude calculated according to Equation 1-3. For example, if the current pixel contributes to the Z bin, it adds a value of 18.03 to it.

Contributing to Histogram Bins

The angle we previously calculated is 56.31°. It is not one of the previously selected angles. The solution is to assign that angle to the nearest histogram bin. 56.31° is located between bins 45° and 90°. Because 56.31° is nearer to 45° than 90°, it will be assigned to the bin 45°. A better way is to split the contribution of that pixel to both of these angles (45° and 90°).

The distance between the angles 45° and 90° is 45°. The distance between the angle 56.31° and 45° is just |56.31° − 45°| = 11.31. That means the angle of 56.31° is far away from 45° by a percentage equal to $\dfrac{11.32}{45°}\% = 25\%$. In other words, 56.31° is 75% near to 45°. Similarly, the distance between the angle 56.31° and 95° is just |56.31° − 90°| = 33.69. That means the angle of 56.31° is far away from 90° by a percentage equal to $\dfrac{33.69}{45°}\% = 75\%$. The value by which the angle adds to a bin is calculated according to Equation 1-3.

$$contribution_{value} = \frac{abs\left(pixel_{angle} - bin_{angle}\right)}{bin_{spacing}}\left(pixel_{gradientMagnitude}\right) \qquad \text{(Equation 1-3)}$$

Where $pixel_{angle}$ is the direction of the current pixel, $pixel_{gradientMagnitude}$ is the current pixel gradient magnitude, bin_{angle} is the histogram bin value, and $bin_{spacing}$ is the amount of space between every two bins.

As a result, the angle of 56.31° adds to 45° a percentage of 75% of its gradient magnitude, which is equal to $\dfrac{75}{100}$x18.03 = 13.5. It adds just 25% of its gradient magnitude to 45° to 90°, which is equal to $\dfrac{25}{100}$x18.03 = 4.5.

A more practical histogram contains nine angles starting from 0° and ending at 180°. The difference between every pair of angles will be 180/9=20. Thus the angles used are 0°, 20°, 40°, 60°, 80°, 100°, 120°, 140°, 160°, and 180°. The bins are not these angles but the center of each range. For the 0°–20° range, the bin used is 10°. For 20°–40°, the bin is 30°, and so on. The final histogram bins are 10°, 30°, 50°, 70°, 90°, 110°, 130°, 150°, and 170°. If an angle is 25°, it adds to the bins it is located between. That is, it adds to bins 10° (by 0.25) and 30° (by 0.75).

By repeating the preceding steps on pixel 68 located at the second row and the second column, the result of applying the horizontal mask is 97 − 50 = 47, which is the gradient change in the X direction. After applying the vertical mask, the result is 43 − 23 = 20. The direction of change is calculated as follows based on Equation 1-2:

$$Angle = \tan^{-1}\frac{Y}{X} = \tan^{-1}\frac{20}{47} = 23°$$

Again, the resultant angle is not equal to any of the histogram bins. Thus the contribution of this angle is split across the bins it falls in between, which are 15° and 45°. It adds 0.27 to 45° and 0.73 to 45°.

For the pixel located at the fourth row and the second column with intensity value 88, the change in in the X direction is 0. Applying Equation 1-2, the result will be divided by 0. To avoid dividing by zeros, add a very small value such as 0.0000001 to the denominator.

HOG Steps

By this point, we have learned how to calculate the gradient magnitude and direction for any pixel. But there is still some work to be done before and after calculating these values. A summary of HOG steps is as follows:

1. Split the input image into patches with aspect ratio 1:2. For example, the patch size might be 64×128, 100×200, and so on.

2. Divide patches into blocks (e.g., four blocks).

3. Divide each block into cells. Cell size within the block is not fixed.

    - For example, if the block size is 16×16 and we determined to divide it into four cells, the size of each cell is 8×8. Note also that blocks might overlap with each other and one cell might be available in multiple blocks.

4. For each cell within each block, calculate the gradient magnitude and direction for all pixels.

    - Gradients are calculated based on the masks in Figure 1-13.

    - Gradient magnitude and direction are calculated according to Equations 1-1 and 1-2, respectively.

5. Based on the gradient magnitudes and directions, build the histogram for each cell. If the number of angles used to constitute the histogram is nine, then a 9×1 feature vector is returned by each cell. The histogram is calculated according to our previous discussion.

6. Concatenate all histograms of all cells within the same block and
    return just a single histogram for the entire block. If each cell
    histogram is represented by nine bins and each block has four
    cells, then the concatenated histogram length is 4×9=36. This 36×1
    is vector is the result of each block.

7. The vector is normalized to make it robust against illumination
    changes.

8. Concatenate the normalized vectors for all blocks within the
    image patch to return the final feature vector.

Figure 1-14 shows a patch from the image in Figure 1-5(a) of size 64×128.

Figure 1-14. *Image patch to calculate its HOG*

Before creating the histogram, the vertical and horizontal gradients are calculated
according to the vertical and horizontal masks. The gradients are shown in Figure 1-15.

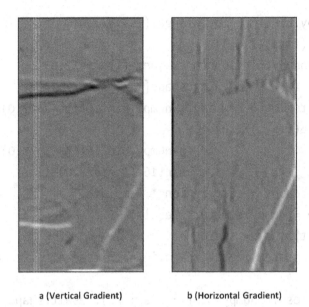

a (Vertical Gradient)   b (Horizontal Gradient)

Figure 1-15. *Vertical and horizontal gradients for the 64×128 image patch*

The Python code used to calculate such gradients is given in Listing 1-6.

Listing 1-6. *Calculating Gradients*

```python
import skimage.io, skimage.color
import numpy
import matplotlib

def calculate_gradient(img, template):
    ts = template.size #Number of elements in the template (3).
    #New padded array to hold the resultant gradient image.
    new_img = numpy.zeros((img.shape[0]+ts-1,
                           img.shape[1]+ts-1))
    new_img[numpy.uint16((ts-1)/2.0):img.shape[0]+numpy.uint16((ts-1)/2.0),
            numpy.uint16((ts-1)/2.0):img.shape[1]+
            numpy.uint16((ts-1)/2.0)] = img
    result = numpy.zeros((new_img.shape))
```

```
for r in numpy.uint16(numpy.arange((ts-1)/2.0,
img.shape[0]+(ts-1)/2.0)):
    for c in numpy.uint16(numpy.arange((ts-1)/2.0,
                           img.shape[1]+(ts-1)/2.0)):
        curr_region = new_img[r-numpy.uint16((ts-1)/2.0):r+numpy.
        uint16((ts-1)/2.0)+1,
                            c-numpy.uint16((ts-1)/2.0):c+numpy.
                            uint16((ts-1)/2.0)+1]
        curr_result = curr_region * template
        score = numpy.sum(curr_result)
        result[r, c] = score
#Result of the same size as the original image after removing the
padding.
result_img = result[numpy.uint16((ts-1)/2):result.shape[0]-numpy.
uint16((ts-1)/2),numpy.uint16((ts-1)/2):result.shape[1]-numpy.
uint16((ts-1)/2)]
return result_img
```

Based on the calculate_gradient(img, template) function, which accepts a grayscale image and a mask, the image is filtered based on the mask and then it is returned. By calling it two times with different masks (vertical and horizontal), the vertical and horizontal gradients are returned.

The vertical and horizontal gradients are then used to calculate the gradient magnitude according to gradient_magnitude() function in Listing 1-7.

Listing 1-7. Gradient Magnitude

```
def gradient_magnitude(horizontal_gradient, vertical_gradient):
    horizontal_gradient_square = numpy.power(horizontal_gradient, 2)
    vertical_gradient_square = numpy.power(vertical_gradient, 2)
    sum_squares = horizontal_gradient_square + vertical_gradient_square
    grad_magnitude = numpy.sqrt(sum_squares)
    return grad_magnitude
```

That function just applies the Equation 1-1 for the previously calculated vertical and horizontal gradients. The gradient magnitude for the patch image is shown in Figure 1-16.

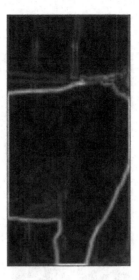

Figure 1-16. *Gradient magnitude based on the previously calculated vertical and horizontal gradients for the 64×128 image patch*

Using the function `gradient_direction()` in Listing 1-8, the gradient direction is calculated.

Listing 1-8. Gradient Direction

```
def gradient_direction(horizontal_gradient, vertical_gradient):
    grad_direction = numpy.arctan(vertical_gradient/(horizontal_
    gradient+0.00000001))
    grad_direction = numpy.rad2deg(grad_direction)
    # Some angles are outside the 0-180 range. Next line makes all results
    fall within the 0-180 range.
    grad_direction = grad_direction % 180
    return grad_direction
```

Note the small value (0.00000001) added to the denominator. This avoids dividing by zero. Ignoring that, some outputs values will be NaN (Not a Number).

Figure 1-17 shows the image patch after being split into 16×8 cells. Each cell has 8×8 pixels and each block has 4 cells (i.e., each block has 16×16 pixels).

Figure 1-17. *Image divided into 16×8 cells*

Based on the previously calculated gradient magnitude and direction, we can just return the results of the first 8×8 cell in the image patch (top-left cell) as in Figure 1-18.

44.41	88.69	91.57	89.74	84.94	84.98	88.62	91.62
0.26	15.95	165.96	63.43	1.97	178.15	173.66	15.26
0.77	29.74	159.44	116.57	2.05	0.0	0.0	168.69
1.02	45.0	161.57	153.43	0.0	0.0	0.0	146.31
0.75	38.66	160.02	135.0	4.4	1.97	172.87	153.43
0.5	36.87	165.96	135.0	4.57	2.05	171.87	53.13
0.25	14.04	0.0	0.0	0.0	0.0	0.0	33.69
179.25	135.0	10.3	26.57	2.29	5.91	35.54	158.96

a (Gradient Direction)

207.19	219.06	219.08	219.	226.88	239.92	249.07	248.1
222.0	7.28	8.25	2.24	29.02	31.02	9.06	11.4
223.02	8.06	8.54	2.24	28.02	30.0	9.0	10.2
225.04	7.07	9.49	2.24	27.0	30.0	9.0	7.21
228.02	6.4	11.7	4.24	26.08	29.02	8.06	2.24
230.01	5.0	12.37	4.24	25.08	28.02	7.07	5.0
231.0	4.12	12.0	3.0	24.0	27.0	6.0	10.82
230.02	5.66	11.18	2.24	25.02	29.15	8.6	13.93

b (Gradient Magnitude)

Figure 1-18. *Gradient magnitude and direction of the top-left 8×8 cell*

The histogram will be created based on the simple examples we previously discussed. There are 9 histogram bins covering the range of angles from 0 to 180. Representing such range using just a limited number of bins makes each bin cover more than one angle. Using just 9 bins, then each one will cover 20 angles. The first bin covers angles from 0 (inclusive) to 20 (exclusive). The second one from 20 (inclusive) to 40 (exclusive), until the last bin that covers angles from 160 (inclusive) to 180 (inclusive). The bin for each range will be given a number equal to the center of each range. That is the first bin is given 10, second bin 20, and so on until the last bin which is given 170. We can say that the bins starts from 10 to 170 with step 20. For each angle in Figure 1-18(a), the two histogram bins it falls within are found. Starting with the top-left element with value 44.41, it falls between bins 30 and 50. That value contributes to both of these bins according to Equation 1-3. The contribution value for bin 30 is calculated as follows:

$$contribution_{value} = \frac{abs(44.41-30)}{20}(207.19) = 0.72 \times 207.19 = 149.28$$

Regarding bin 50, the contribution value is calculated as follows:

$$contribution_{value} = \frac{abs(44.41-50)}{20}(207.19) = 0.28 \times 207.19 = 57.91$$

The process continues for all 8×8 pixels in the current cell. The histogram for the top-left cell is shown in Figure 1-19(a). Assuming that each block contains 2×2 cells, the 9-bin histograms of the three remaining cells in the top-left block marked in bright color in Figure 1-17 are also shown in Figure 1-19. By calculating all histograms for a given block, its feature vector is the concatenation of these four 9-bin histograms. The length of the feature vector is 9×4 = 36.

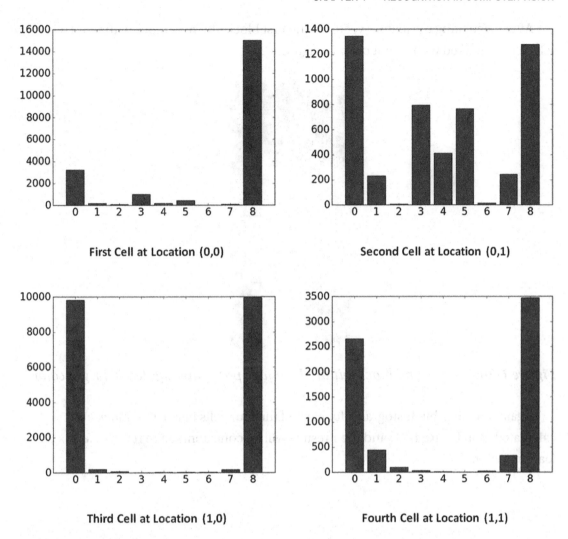

Figure 1-19. *Nine-bin histograms of the four cells inside the top-left block of the current image patch*

After calculating the feature vector of the first block, the next block with four cells is selected as marked with bright color in Figure 1-20.

Figure 1-20. *The second block within the image patch highlighted in bright color*

Again, the nine-bin histograms for each of the four cells inside that block are calculated as in Figure 1-21, and their results will be concatenated to return the 36×1 feature vector.

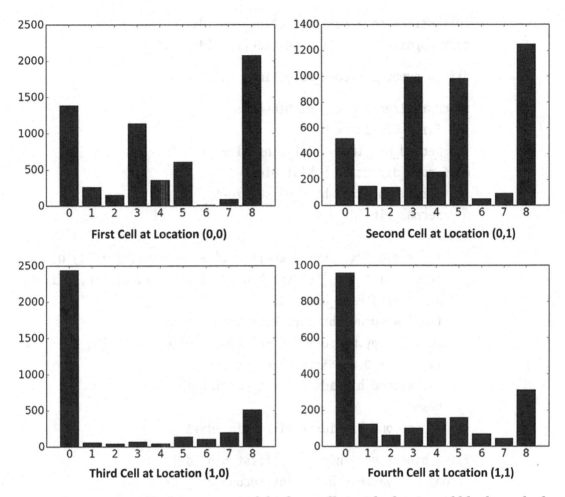

Figure 1-21. *Nine-bin histograms of the four cells inside the second block marked with a bright color in Figure 1-20 of the current image patch*

The histogram of each cell is calculated using the HOG_cell_histogram() function in Listing 1-9. This function accepts the direction and magnitude about a given cell and returns its histogram.

Listing 1-9. Cell Histogram

```
def HOG_cell_histogram(cell_direction, cell_magnitude):
    HOG_cell_hist = numpy.zeros(shape=(hist_bins.size))
    cell_size = cell_direction.shape[0]

    for row_idx in range(cell_size):
        for col_idx in range(cell_size):
```

```
        curr_direction = cell_direction[row_idx, col_idx]
        curr_magnitude = cell_magnitude[row_idx, col_idx]

        diff = numpy.abs(curr_direction - hist_bins)

        if curr_direction < hist_bins[0]:
            first_bin_idx = 0
            second_bin_idx = hist_bins.size-1
        elif curr_direction > hist_bins[-1]:
            first_bin_idx = hist_bins.size-1
            second_bin_idx = 0
        else:
            first_bin_idx = numpy.where(diff == numpy.min(diff))[0][0]
            temp = hist_bins[[(first_bin_idx-1)%hist_bins.size, (first_
            bin_idx+1)%hist_bins.size]]
            temp2 = numpy.abs(curr_direction - temp)
            res = numpy.where(temp2 == numpy.min(temp2))[0][0]
            if res == 0 and first_bin_idx != 0:
                second_bin_idx = first_bin_idx-1
            else:
                second_bin_idx = first_bin_idx+1

    first_bin_value = hist_bins[first_bin_idx]
    second_bin_value = hist_bins[second_bin_idx]
    HOG_cell_hist[first_bin_idx] = HOG_cell_hist[first_bin_idx] +
    (numpy.abs(curr_direction - first_bin_value)/(180.0/hist_bins.
    size)) * curr_magnitude
    HOG_cell_hist[second_bin_idx] = HOG_cell_hist[second_bin_idx] +
    (numpy.abs(curr_direction - second_bin_value)/(180.0/hist_bins.
    size)) * curr_magnitude
return HOG_cell_hist
```

Listing 1-10 gives the complete code used to read an image patch and returns the histogram for the top-left cell in the first block. Note that the code works with grayscale images. If the input image is grayscale it will have just two dimensions. If the input image is color, then it will have a third dimension representing the channels. In this case, just one grayscale channel is used. The number of dimensions of a NumPy array is returned using the ndim property.

Listing 1-10. Complete Implementation for Calculating Histogram for the
Top-Left Cell

```python
import skimage.io, skimage.color
import numpy
import matplotlib.pyplot

def calculate_gradient(img, template):
    ts = template.size #Number of elements in the template (3).
    #New padded array to hold the resultant gradient image.
    new_img = numpy.zeros((img.shape[0]+ts-1,
                           img.shape[1]+ts-1))
    new_img[numpy.uint16((ts-1)/2.0):img.shape[0]+numpy.uint16((ts-1)/2.0),
            numpy.uint16((ts-1)/2.0):img.shape[1]+numpy.uint16((ts-1)/2.0)]
            = img
    result = numpy.zeros((new_img.shape))

    for r in numpy.uint16(numpy.arange((ts-1)/2.0,
    img.shape[0]+(ts-1)/2.0)):
        for c in numpy.uint16(numpy.arange((ts-1)/2.0,
                              img.shape[1]+(ts-1)/2.0)):
            curr_region = new_img[r-numpy.uint16((ts-1)/2.0):r+numpy.
                                  uint16((ts-1)/2.0)+1,
                                  c-numpy.uint16((ts-1)/2.0):c+numpy.
                                  uint16((ts-1)/2.0)+1]
            curr_result = curr_region * template
            score = numpy.sum(curr_result)
            result[r, c] = score
    #Result of the same size as the original image after removing the
    padding.
    result_img = result[numpy.uint16((ts-1)/2.0):result.shape[0]-numpy.
                 uint16((ts-1)/2.0), numpy.uint16((ts-1)/2.0):result.
                 shape[1]-numpy.uint16((ts-1)/2.0)]
    return result_img

def gradient_magnitude(horizontal_gradient, vertical_gradient):
    horizontal_gradient_square = numpy.power(horizontal_gradient, 2)
```

```python
    vertical_gradient_square = numpy.power(vertical_gradient, 2)
    sum_squares = horizontal_gradient_square + vertical_gradient_square
    grad_magnitude = numpy.sqrt(sum_squares)
    return grad_magnitude

def gradient_direction(horizontal_gradient, vertical_gradient):
    grad_direction = numpy.arctan(vertical_gradient/(horizontal_
    gradient+0.00000001))
    grad_direction = numpy.rad2deg(grad_direction)
    grad_direction = grad_direction%180
    return grad_direction

def HOG_cell_histogram(cell_direction, cell_magnitude):
    HOG_cell_hist = numpy.zeros(shape=(hist_bins.size))
    cell_size = cell_direction.shape[0]

    for row_idx in range(cell_size):
        for col_idx in range(cell_size):
            curr_direction = cell_direction[row_idx, col_idx]
            curr_magnitude = cell_magnitude[row_idx, col_idx]

            diff = numpy.abs(curr_direction - hist_bins)

            if curr_direction < hist_bins[0]:
                first_bin_idx = 0
                second_bin_idx = hist_bins.size-1
            elif curr_direction > hist_bins[-1]:
                first_bin_idx = hist_bins.size-1
                second_bin_idx = 0
            else:
                first_bin_idx = numpy.where(diff == numpy.min(diff))[0][0]
                temp = hist_bins[[(first_bin_idx-1)%hist_bins.size, (first_
                bin_idx+1)%hist_bins.size]]
                temp2 = numpy.abs(curr_direction - temp)
                res = numpy.where(temp2 == numpy.min(temp2))[0][0]
                if res == 0 and first_bin_idx != 0:
                    second_bin_idx = first_bin_idx-1
```

```
        else:
            second_bin_idx = first_bin_idx+1
        first_bin_value = hist_bins[first_bin_idx]
        second_bin_value = hist_bins[second_bin_idx]
        HOG_cell_hist[first_bin_idx] = HOG_cell_hist[first_bin_idx] +
        (numpy.abs(curr_direction - first_bin_value)/(180.0/hist_bins.
        size)) * curr_magnitude
        HOG_cell_hist[second_bin_idx] = HOG_cell_hist[second_bin_idx] +
        (numpy.abs(curr_direction - second_bin_value)/(180.0/hist_bins.
        size)) * curr_magnitude
    return HOG_cell_hist


img = skimage.io.imread("im_patch.jpg")
if img.ndim >2:
    img = img[:, :, 0]

horizontal_mask = numpy.array([-1, 0, 1])
vertical_mask = numpy.array([[-1],
                             [0],
                             [1]])

horizontal_gradient = calculate_gradient(img, horizontal_mask)
vertical_gradient = calculate_gradient(img, vertical_mask)

grad_magnitude = gradient_magnitude(horizontal_gradient, vertical_gradient)
grad_direction = gradient_direction(horizontal_gradient, vertical_gradient)

grad_direction = grad_direction % 180
hist_bins = numpy.array([10,30,50,70,90,110,130,150,170])

cell_direction = grad_direction[:8, :8]
cell_magnitude = grad_magnitude[:8, :8]
HOG_cell_hist = HOG_cell_histogram(cell_direction, cell_magnitude)

matplotlib.pyplot.bar(left=numpy.arange(9), height=HOG_cell_hist,
align="center", width=0.8)
matplotlib.pyplot.show()
```

After calculating the feature vector for a block, the next step is to normalize that vector. The motivation to feature normalization is that the feature vector is dependent on the image intensity levels, and it is better to make it robust against illumination changes. Normalization takes place by dividing each element in the vector by the vector length calculated according to Equation 1-4.

$$vector_{length} = \sqrt{X_1 + X_2 + \ldots + X_n} \qquad \text{(Equation 1-4)}$$

Where X_i represents the vector element number i. The normalized vector is the result of the first block. The process continues until returning all 36×1 feature vectors for all blocks. These vectors are then concatenated for the entire image patch being processed.

Based on the preceding discussion, HOG has the following parameters to be specified before its calculation:

1. Number of orientations.

2. Number of pixels per cell.

3. Number of cells per block.

HOG is already implemented in Python in the `skimage.feature` module and could be easily used according to the `skimage.feature.hog()` function. The preceding three parameters have default values that could be changed to meet your goals. If the `normalized` parameter is set to `True` then the normalized HOG is returned.

```
skimage.feature.hog(image, orientations=9, pixels_per_cell=(8, 8),
cells_per_block=(3, 3), visualise=False, transform_sqrt=False, feature_
vector=True, normalise=None)
```

LBP

LBP stands for local binary patterns, which is another second-order texture descriptor. The steps to extract the LBP features are as follows:

1. Divide the image into blocks (e.g., 16×16 blocks).

2. For each block, a 3×3 window gets centered over each pixel.

The selected central pixel $P_{central}$ is compared to each of its surrounding 8 neighbors $P_{neighbor}$ according to Equation 1-5. From the eight comparisons, there will be eight binary digits.

$$P_{neighbor} = \begin{cases} 1, & P_{neighbor} > P_{central} \\ 0, & otherwise \end{cases} \qquad \text{(Equation 1-5)}$$

3. The 8-bit binary code is converted into an integer. The integer ranges from 0 to $2^8 = 255$.

4. Replace the $P_{central}$ value with the calculated integer.

5. After calculating the new values for all pixels within the same block, the histogram is calculated.

6. After calculating the histograms across all blocks, they get concatenated.

Assuming that the block we are currently working on is in Figure 1-12, we can start calculating the basic LBP based on it.

By working on the pixel at the third row and the fourth column, the center pixel is compared to each of the eight neighbors. Figure 1-22 shows the results of the comparison.

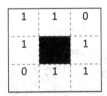

Figure 1-22. *The result of comparing the central pixel to its eight neighbors*

Next is to return the binary code. You can start from any position in the 3×3 matrix but you must be consistent across the entire image. For example, starting from the top-left position and moving clockwise, the code is 11011101. You can either move clockwise or counterclockwise, but be consistent.

After that, the binary code is converted into a decimal by summing the multiplications of each binary by a weight corresponding to its position in the binary code. The result is $128 + 64 + 16 + 8 + 4 + 1 = 221$.

After calculating the binary code for each pixel in the block and returning its decimal, the histogram is created. The process is repeated for all image blocks, and histograms from all blocks are concatenated as in the case of HOG.

This is the basic implementation of LBP, but such a feature descriptor has multiple variations that make it robust against illumination changes, scale, and rotation.

It could be implemented easily in Python using the `skimage.feature.local_binary_pattern()` function that accepts three parameters:

- Input image.

- Number of neighboring points in a circle (P). This parameter helps to achieve rotation invariance.

- Radius of the circle (R). Such parameter helps to achieve scale invariance.

Here is an example of LBP applied to the grayscale image in Figure 1-2(a).

```
import skimage.feature
import skimage.io
import matplotlib.pyplot

im = skimage.io.imread("69.jpg", as_grey=True)
lbp = skimage.feature.local_binary_pattern(image=im, P=9, R=3)
matplotlib.pyplot.imshow(lbp, cmap="gray")
matplotlib.pyplot.xticks([])
matplotlib.pyplot.yticks([])
```

The output image is given in Figure 1-23.

Figure 1-23. *The output of applying LBP over a grayscale image with P-9 and R=3*

Feature Selection & Reduction

Assuming that after a discussion with the experts in a given field, you deduced that features X, Y, and Z are suitable. These features are just selected initially, and there is a probability that some of these features might not be helpful. You decide whether each feature is good or bad based on some experimentation. After training a model based on these three features, the recognition rate is low and something must be changed in the feature vector. To know the reason, you conducted some experiments by training the model for each individual feature. You found that the correlation between feature Z and the target is low and thus decided not to use this feature. Eliminating certain features completely from the feature vector and keeping others is called feature selection. Selection techniques classify the feature as either bad or good. Bad features are eliminated completely while the good features are used exclusively.

In fact, some elements inside each feature might not be suitable for the type of application being analyzed. Assume that a feature X is used within the feature vector and that this feature has a set of 10 elements. One or more of these elements might not be helpful in the task. For example, some features are redundant. That is some features may be optimally correlated with each other, and thus only one feature is sufficient in describing the data and there is no need to use multiple features that work the same. Due to correlated features, there might not exist a unique optimal feature subset. This is because there may be more than one perfectly correlated feature, so one can replace the other and create a new feature subset.

Another type is the irrelevant features. Some features have no correlation with the predictions required and they are regarded as noise. Such features won't enhance but rather degrade the results. So, it is preferred to detect such features and remove them so they don't affect the learning process. Removing just a subset of elements and keeping the others is called feature reduction.

Another motivation behind reducing the length of the feature vector by removing bad features as much as possible is that the longer the feature vector length the more computational time is consumed in training and testing the models.

To classify features as relevant or irrelevant, some metrics are required to show the relevance of each feature with the output classes or how well each feature predicts the desired outputs. Feature relevance is the ability of a feature to discriminate the different classes. After the selection of the metrics, they will be used to create good feature subsets by eliminating bad features. The feature elimination methods are classified into supervised and unsupervised methods. Supervised methods include filter and wrapper, and unsupervised methods include embedded.

Filter

The filter approach adds an additional preprocessing step to apply variable ranking techniques for ranking features based on different criteria calculated for each feature to measure the feature's relevance. These criteria include standard deviation (STD), energy, entropy, correlation, and mutual information (MI). Based on a threshold, the highly ranked features are selected to train the model. The filter methods are very fast and not time-consuming compared to other selection approaches. They are also simple in their calculations, scalable, able to avoid overfitting, and independent of the learning model.

For training different models, the selection is done just once and then the training models can use the selected features. But filter methods have a number of critical drawbacks that affect their performance heavily compared to other approaches to feature selection. The filter/ranking approach doesn't model feature dependencies. It selects each variable/feature independently from the other features/variables in the same subset. A feature is selected when being highly ranked according to the selected criterion. The criterion used for ranking doesn't take into consideration the relationship among multiple features. Ignoring feature dependencies can damage the entire selected subset because features that are significant by themselves in increasing the learning rate are not guaranteed to be so when combined with other features. There are some cases in which useful variables by themselves are still useful when combined together, but this is not always the case.

If the usefulness of two features f_1 and f_2 are x_1 and x_2 respectively, this doesn't mean that their usefulness will be $x_1 + x_2$ when combined together. Also, ignoring feature dependencies makes it prone to redundant and correlated features. This is because there may be two or more features that perfectly satisfy the criterion but each of them is a perfect reflection of all the others doing the same task. So it is not required to use multiples of the same thing; just one is sufficient. Correlation is another form of redundancy in which features may not be identical but are dependent and always work the same (can be represented as two parallel lines). Perfectly correlated variables are truly redundant as they add no additional information. The use of redundant and correlated features leads to a large feature vector, and thus the benefits of feature selection to reduce the feature vector length is not achieved. Filter methods don't interact with the learning model, as they are not relying on the learning algorithm performance due to decoupling the feature selection from the performance. Instead, these just consider a single criterion between the feature and the class label but not information to indicate how well the feature is working with the learning algorithm. A good feature selector should take into account how both the learning algorithm and the training data set interact. Finally, it is not an easy task to calculate the threshold used to classify features as selected or not. All of these reasons lead to the use of other feature selection approaches that overcome these problems.

Wrapper

The wrapper approach is the second approach that solves some of the problems with the filter methods. The wrapper methods try to interact with the learning model by creating a subset of selected features that maximize the performance. The wrapper approach creates all possible subsets of features to find the best subset. The wrapper approach is called so because it is wrapping around the learning algorithm. It uses the induction or learning algorithm as a black box to measure how well the selected feature subset works by training the algorithm with the selected subsets and then to use the one that maximizes its performance. When talking about the wrapper approach, multiple points should be covered well, including selecting feature subset length, creating the feature subset space, searching the feature subset space, assessing the performance of the learning algorithms, stopping search criteria, and determining which learning algorithms to use. The goal of any feature reduction/selection algorithm is to create all possible feature combinations of length L features from an original complete feature vector of length N that maximizes the performance where $<N$. For a normal feature vector length of $=30$, there is a large number of combinations to create subsets of length $L = 10$. For this reason, a search strategy is applied to search for the best subsets with an evaluation function penalizing bad subsets. The objective function, in this case, is the model performance. So, the problem is transformed from a learning problem to a search problem. The exhaustive search is not applicable for such problem, because it visits and train a learning model with all subsets, which is intensive in terms of calculations. So, evolutionary algorithms (EAs) are used to avoid exploring all subsets, and these can be categorized into two classes: sequential selection algorithms (deterministic) and heuristic search algorithms (random).

The deterministic search algorithms are further classified into two categories that are actually pretty similar, namely, forward selection and backward selection. In forward selection, the algorithm starts from a root representing an empty set of features and then adds feature by feature while training the learning model for each change. In backward selection, the root of the search is the complete set of features, and the algorithm then removes features one by one while training the learning model for each change. Examples of such algorithms include sequential feature selection (SFS), sequential backward selection (SBS), sequential forward floating selection (SFFS), adaptive SFFS (ASFFS), and beam search. To prevent the search from being exhaustive, a stopping criterion is added to prevent exploring all possible combinations. The criterion can be a maximum feature vector length for forward selection or minimum length for backward selection. It can also be a maximum performance, so after reaching the selected performance, the search stops.

The second category of search algorithms, random algorithms, are informed searches that use a heuristic evaluation function, generating a heuristic value telling how close each subset is to the maximum performance. Examples of such search algorithms include genetic algorithm (GA), particle swarm optimization (PSO), simulated annealing (SA), and randomized hill climbing. GA will be discussed in detail in Chapter 5.

A question that must be answered is what is the optimal value for L (number of features)? Wrapper methods have different approaches to answer that question. One way is to select a fixed number of features to create the feature vector, and by using combinations, it is possible to get all possibilities to select just L features from N features. But unfortunately, the selected fixed value for L may not be the optimal one and there is no guarantee that the L selected features are the ones that give the best performance for the learning model. So, another way is to make the number of features to be selected variable and dynamically changing. This is by trying a different number of features and selecting the best number of features that maximize the performance as in the sequential selection algorithms. The drawback of making the number of features dynamically changing is adding more and more computational time by creating different features combinations of different lengths and training the model with them. To reduce this time, a criterion can be added to make the learning stop earlier after reaching a target performance or after the number of selected features reaches a maximum length.

Comparing the wrapper approach to the filter approach, there are a number of advantages. The wrapper approach interacts with the learning model as it uses the learning algorithm performance as a metric to select the best feature subsets. It also models feature dependencies, as features are not selected individually or independently from each other, and monitors how combining features together affects the performance. Finally, it is robust against redundant and correlated features. But there are a number of drawbacks to the various wrapper methods. They are time-consuming, as each model has to be trained multiple times. Some models are very time-consuming and may take hours to be trained once. As a result, wrapper methods are not the option for such models. Moreover, wrapper methods are affected by overfitting as the selection is dependent on the learning model and thus can't generalize selected features across different models.

Embedded

Both filter and wrapper approaches to feature selection have their own advantages and disadvantages. The embedded methods try to combine the advantages of both filter and wrapper approaches. Such methods are not time-consuming, as they avoid the retraining of the learning algorithm that is seen in the filter and wrapper approaches. They maximize the performance by interacting with the learning model, as in the wrapper approach. The feature is selected only if it is correlated with the output class labels m. It is called embedded because it works by embedding feature selection within the training step.

Categories of the embedded approach are as follows: pruning, built-in, and regularization (penalization). Pruning methods start by training the learning model with the complete set of features and then calculate a correlation coefficient for each feature. Such coefficients are used to rank the importance of the features according to the model used. High values for coefficients reflect strong correlation. The built-in approach for embedded feature selection calculates an information gain for each feature as in decision tree learning (ID3).

In machine learning (ML), some models are trained very well and can make the correct predictions for any sample in the training data but unfortunately can't make correct predictions for other samples outside the training samples. This problem is called overfitting. Regularization is a technique used to avoid this problem. Regularization is to tune or select the best model complexity to fit the training data while being able to predict unseen samples. Without regularization, the model may be very simple and underfit (can't make correct predictions for both training and testing samples) or be very complex and overfit (correct predictions for training samples but wrong for testing samples). Both underfit and overfit make the model too weak and unable to be generalized to any sample. So, regularization is a way of generalizing the model to predict any sample, whether training or testing.

Regularization

In order to find the best model, the common method in ML is to define a loss or cost function that describes how well the model fits the data. The goal is to find the model that minimizes this loss function. Normally, the objective function in any learning model has only a single criterion, which is maximizing the performance. The regularization approach adds another criterion to the objective function to control the level of complexity, as shown in Equation 1-6.

$$L = \min error(Y_{predict}, Y_{correct}) + \lambda\, penalty(W_i)$$ (Equation 1-6)

Where $Y_{predict}$ is the predicted class label, $Y_{correct}$ is the correct class label, $error(.)$ calculates the prediction error, W_i is the weight for the feature element X_i, and λ is the regularization parameter controlling the model complexity. This parameter is used to control the trade-off between the objective function and the penalty. The penalty is defined according to Equation 1-7.

$$penalty(w) = \sum_{i=1} |W_i|$$ (Equation 1-7)

By changing λ values, the model complexity changes. This is by penalizing some features by setting their weights close or equal to zero. The magnitude of coefficients is a significant factor in determining the model complexity. Feature selection is indirectly achieved by selecting features with high weight magnitudes. The higher the weights, the more relevant is the feature in predicting the correct class. This is why the regularization approach is called penalization.

The goal of the regularization parameter λ is to minimize the loss L and keep it to a minimum. For a very large value for λ approaching ∞, the coefficients must be small and approach zero to make the total value as small as possible. This makes most of the coefficient zero and thus remove them. For a value of $0 < \lambda < \infty$, there will be some coefficients equal to zero, which will be removed, but not many of them equal to zero. What is the best value for λ? There is no fixed value for λ and its value can be efficiently calculated using cross-validation (CV).

Combining the advantages of filter and wrapper approaches makes the embedded approach the most recent research trend for feature selection. It interacts with the learning model because it uses the training model performance as a metric like the wrapper methods, is not time-consuming like the filter methods because it doesn't require retraining the model, and also models feature dependencies to avoid redundant and correlated features. Selecting features while training is efficient in terms of data use, as it is not required to split the data into training and validation sets. However, while features selected by embedded methods do well for the learning model used to select the features, the selected features may be dependent on such model and won't work as well across different models as what is produced with the filter approach.

CHAPTER 2

Artificial Neural Networks

Machine learning (ML) problems can be divided into three categories: supervised, unsupervised, and reinforcement. In supervised learning, a human expert conducts some experiments in a restricted environment and notices their results. The supervised learning algorithm explores the data collected from experiments to map inputs to outputs. For example, a restricted environment might have a robot that wants to go from one side of a small room to another. There are some obstacles in the room that may make the robot fall. The supervisor provides guidance about how to reach the wall without falling. This is done by giving the robot knowledge in the form of examples to help it learn how to pass obstacles. The robot uses this knowledge to increase the probability of passing the obstacle without falling. In such a case, the knowledge of the robot is completely dependent on the human.

In reinforcement learning, the human gives the robot a metric to evaluate its performance. The robot has to maximize this metric to reach its goal. It does not know when to move to the right. Based on the metric, the robot will try different locations to move and calculates the metric. If the robot fell at a given location, then it has to avoid it next time. In this way, the robot will find the way that makes it reach the goal without falling.

Compared to supervised and semisupervised learning, unsupervised learning will not be given the results of the experiments nor a metric. There is no human to guide it at all. This is very challenging.

An artificial neural network (ANN for short) is a kind of algorithm that works in all of these problems. This book only discusses supervised learning using ANN. ANN is a biologically inspired ML model that mimics the operation of the human brain. It is one of the most important topics to be covered when talking about deep learning (DL). Understanding the operation of simple ANNs with few layers and neurons makes it easier to understand how complex models work.

© Ahmed Fawzy Gad 2018
A. F. Gad, *Practical Computer Vision Applications Using Deep Learning with CNNs*,
https://doi.org/10.1007/978-1-4842-4167-7_2

In this chapter, prerequests to learn how CNNs work will be presented. It starts by exploring ANN at a beginner level. Starting by knowing that it is a collection of linear models, you will find that it is not a strange concept at all; in fact, you already know about it. The chapter discusses some concepts related to ANN, such as learning rate, backpropagation, and overfitting. This chapter will help you understand why we need the learning rate in ANNs and whether it is useful or not for training. Using a very simple Python code for a single-layer perceptron, the learning rate value will get changed to catch its idea and notice how changing the learning rate affects the results. It also discusses how the backpropagation algorithm is useful in updating the ANN weights. This chapter also explains overfitting, which is one of the reasons for poor predictions for unseen samples. A regularization technique based on regression is presented by simple steps to make it clear how to avoid overfitting. ANN has a special graph to make interpretation of its results easier. This chapter maps the mathematical representation and its graph and explores one of the points that make beginners struggle, which is how to determine the best number of neurons and hidden layers. Finally, a Python classification example using ANN is given.

Introduction to ANNs

Supervised learning problems are divided into two main categories: classification and regression. Regression outputs are continuous numbers, while classification outputs are categorical labels. Each type of these problems can use either a linear or a nonlinear model. Classification problems can also be divided into binary or multiclass classification problems. All of these types of problems can be solved using neural networks. That is, a neural network can be made to produce continuous or discrete outputs. It can work with binary or multiclass problems and model linear and nonlinear functions. ANN is a general function approximator (i.e., ANN can simulate the operation of any linear and nonlinear functions). ANN is a parametric model that has a set of parameters that are learned from the problem, such as weights and bias. It also has a number of hyperparameters that can be tuned by the engineer, such as learning rate and the number of hidden layers.

ANNs actually consist of linear models that are grouped together to solve complex problems. The next subsection discusses how the basic building block of ANN is actually a linear model.

Linear Models Are the Base of ANNs

The simplest types of models for beginners to start with are the linear models. Of course, everyone knows about linear models, and this makes the next explanation easier. We can start with a simple regression problem in which we are looking to create a linear model for the sample shown in Table 2-1. What is the best linear model to fit such data? Let's see.

Table 2-1. *Simple Regression Problem*

Input (X)	Output (Y)
2	6

"Linear model" means a line that maps each input to its corresponding output. We will start with the simplest linear model, as in Equation 2-1. The model equalizes the input and the output together without having any other parameters in the equation.

After doing that, then we create our first model. One may wonder, where is the training part of building any model? The answer is that this model is a nonparametric model. "Nonparametric" means that the model has no parameters to learn from the data. Thus, no training is required to do the job. Later in this chapter, some parameters will be added.

$$Y = X \qquad \text{(Equation 2-1)}$$

In a regular ML pipeline, after building a model we have to test it. In traditional problems, there will be more samples and the data will be divided into training and testing sets. After training the model, testing starts based on the training data. If it did well on the training data, then we can step through testing it over the unseen test data. This is because if a model is not working well on the data it is trained by, then it will likely to be worse for the unseen data. At all, our example takes us off such work, as it just has one sample and no training required. But the lack of training phase does not mean that there is no testing phase. Let's test our model based on such a sample.

The testing phase checks how accurate the model for predicting the outputs for unseen samples rather than ones using in training. Based on our sample with X=2, when applied to the model it will also return 2. This is because the input always equals the output. The linear model, in addition to the positions of the predicted and desired outputs, is shown in Figure 2-1.

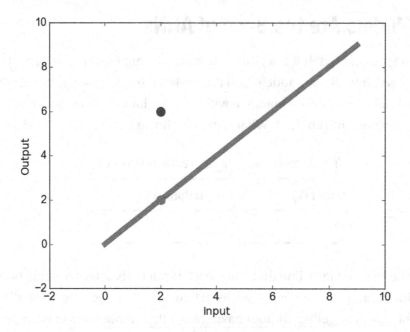

Figure 2-1. *The nonparametric linear model's predicted and desired outputs*

We can simply take the difference between the desired and the predicted outputs as in Equation 2-2. The difference will be $2 - 6 = -4$.

$$error = predicted - desired \qquad \text{(Equation 2-2)}$$

The existence of an error means we have to change something in the model in order to reduce it. Looking back at the model in Equation 2-1, we see that there is no parameter that we could change. The equation just has the input and the output that we could not change. As a result, we could add a parameter a to this equation, which helps in the mapping between the input and the output. Equation 2-3 shows the modified model equation.

$$Y = aX \qquad \text{(Equation 2-3)}$$

Let's say that a has an initial value of **1.5**. The equation is given in Equation 2-3′. Such a linear model is shown in Figure 2-2.

$$Y = \mathbf{1.5}X \qquad \text{(Equation 2-3′)}$$

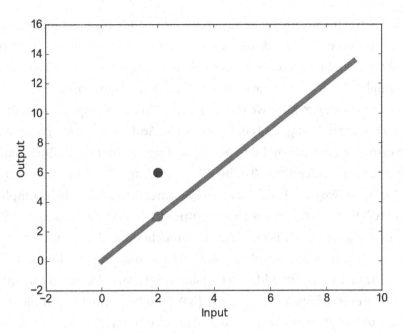

Figure 2-2. *Parametric linear model*

Note that after adding the parameter, the model is now a parametric model. This is because there is at least one parameter to be learned from the data. Now, after building the new model, we could predict the output of our sample. The predicted output is $Y_{predicted} = 1.5(2) = 3$. Then we can measure the error. According to Equation 2-2, the error is $3 - 6 = -3$. Compared to the previous error, it seems that the new model with parameter $a = 1.5$ enhances the results compared to the previous model with no parameter. But there still error in the prediction that we need to reduce.

We can imagine that the first model in Equation 2-1 is actually represented by Equation 2-3, but the parameter **a** is always set to **1**. Comparing the error produced when $a = 1$ to the error when **a = 1.5**, which is **−4**, it seems that the error reduced when **a = 1.5** to be −3. One might wonder how the value −3 is less than −4. The answer is that the negative sign in the error just says the predicted output is lower than the desired output. The amount of difference is the absolute value of the error. That is, an error of **−4** means that there is a difference of 4 between the desired and the predicted outputs and that the desired output is lower than the predicted output because the error is negative. Note that changing the positions of the predicted and desired outputs in Equation 2-2 will change the sign of the error. Let's now return to our problem.

When $a = 1.5$, the results are better compared to $a = 1.0$, and that means increasing the value of this parameter will reduce the error. Thus, we know the direction of change. Let's try using $a = 2.0$. The predicted output will be $Y_{predicted} = 2.0(2) = 4$. The error in this case will be equal to $4 - 6 = -2$. The error reduced more than before.

Based on the previous results, we might deduce a relationship between the parameter and the error. Using $a = 1$, the error is -4. Adding 0.5 to the parameter $(a = 1.5)$, the error got reduced by 1.0 to be -3. Adding another 0.5 to the parameter $(a = 2.0)$, the error got reduced by 1.0 to be -2. So, adding 0.5 to the parameter reduces the error by 1.0. Thus, we could add 1.0 to the parameter to eliminate it completely, and the parameter will be $a = 3.0$. The predicted output in this case is $Y_{predicted} = 3.0(2) = 6$. The error will be $6 - 6 = 0$. The error is now 0 and we reached the best results when $a = 3.0$.

Let's make a change to the sample in Table 2-1 by changing the output of the output to be 6.5 rather than 6 in addition to using a new sample. Based on Equation 2-3 with $a = 3.0$, the predicted output is $Y_{predicted} = (3.0)2 = 6.0$ for the first sample and $Y_{predicted} = (3.0)3 = 9.0$ for the second one. Thus, there is a total error equal to $(6.0 - 6.5) + (9.0 - 9.5) = -1.0$ (Table 2-2). How can this type of error be reduced?

Table 2-2. *Regression Problem with Two Samples*

Input (X)	Output (Y)
2	6.5
3	9.5

The procedure we are following is to change the value of the parameter until reducing the error to 0. Table 2-3 shows the total error for the two values of the parameter. It seems that neither 3.0 nor a value greater than or equal to it eliminates the error. The models corresponding to $a = 2.5$, $a = 3.0$, and $a = 3.5$ are shown in Figure 2-3 along with the desired outputs.

Table 2-3. *Regression Problem with Two Samples*

Parameter	Output (Y)	Predicted	Error	Total Error
3.5	6.5	7.0	7.0–6.5=1.0	2.0
	9.5	10.5	10.5–9.5=1.0	
2.5	6.5	5.0	5.0–6.5=−1.5	−4.0
	9.5	7.5	7.5–9.5=−2.5	

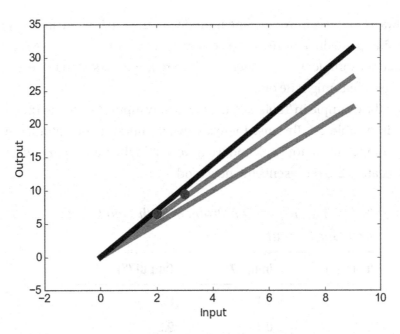

Figure 2-3. *Multiple parametric linear models. The dotted line corresponds to model with a=2.5, starred line to a=3.5, and solid line to a=3.0.*

The truth is that there is no value for the parameter that makes the error equal 0 for our example. We want a value that when multiplied by 2 gives 6.5 and when multiplied by 3 gives 9.5. It is impossible to find such a value. The value of the parameter that satisfies the first sample is $a = 3.25$, while it is $a = 3.17$ for the second sample. Thus, reaching an error of 0 is not possible on the current form of the model. For this reason, the bias plays an important role in solving such situations.

We can add a bias ***b*** to Equation 2-3 as in Equation 2-4. This bias is able to fix our problem.

$$Y = aX + b \qquad \text{(Equation 2-4)}$$

But the problem's complexity now increases. We are trying to find the values for two parameters (a, b). Based on the previous results when $a = 3.0$, the predicted outputs for the two samples are 6.0 and 9.0, respectively. The predicted outputs are less than the correct outputs by 0.5. As a result, the value of $b = 0.5$ is what we are looking for. As a result, $a = 3.0$ and $b = 0.5$ will give an error of 0. This is why the bias is important.

Bias allows us to freely move the linear model on the y axis while increasing the likelihood of fitting the data more than just moving it only on the x axis. Note that it is very useful in our example because there are fewer parameters. When the model has more parameters, bias might be omitted.

Extending the example in Table 2-2, there is a new input Z added to the problem and the new data is in Table 2-4. Because there are two inputs and one output, the previous model in Equation 2-4 will not work and we have to add the new input and its associated parameter. Equation 2-5 represents the new model.

Table 2-4. *Regression Problem with Two Inputs and One Output*

Input (X)	Input (Z)	Output (Y)
2	1.1	6.5
3	0.8	9.5

$$Y = aX + cZ + b$$ (Equation 2-5)

Now, we have to find the best values for the two parameters a and c in addition to the bias b. The same procedure used before will be applied to this problem to find the best values for these variables.

By creating simple linear models, we have successfully learned how the building blocks of ANNs work. ANNs consist of multiple of such linear models that are connected together in order to fit a problem. The following sections will explain how to design a network by connecting linear models together. The next subsection discusses how to draw an ANN for the previously created models.

Graphing ANNs

ANNs are built by connecting multiple linear models together. As the number of parameters required in each model increases, the complete equation of the network becomes too complex. Thus, it is difficult to represent the problem as an equation, but a more simple way is to visualize the network as a graph. The network graph is simpler to understand and design. Here we are going to learn how to build the network graph, starting with a linear model.

ANN is an artificial representation of biological neural networks. We can start by saying that the basic building block in an ANN is the artificial neuron. Previously in this chapter, we said also that the basic block of ANN is the linear model. Thus, we can deduce that the neuron is actually a linear model. As in linear models, the neuron accepts inputs, makes some types of processing such as multiplication and summation, and finally returns an output. Figure 2-4 shows the mapping between the linear model in Equation 2-4 and the artificial neuron. It is noted that all variables existing in the linear model also exist in the ANN graph. This kind of ANN is called a single-layer perceptron.

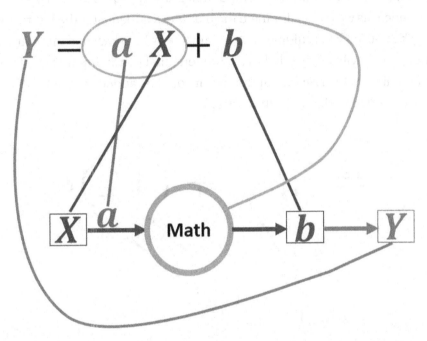

Figure 2-4. *Mapping from a linear model with one input to ANN graph*

We can start from the core of the graph, which is the circle with text "Math". This circle represents the neuron of the neural networks. The neuron is a computational unit, and the type of computation it does is to multiply each input by its corresponding parameter, sum all results, and then return the output that represents the sum of products (SOP). For this reason, the input X is connected to that neuron.

Because each parameter must be associated with its input to calculate the SOP, the parameter a for the input X is written above the arrow connecting it to the neuron. Making each parameter near to its input helps in finding the parameter associated with each input. This is for the inputs and their parameters. The idea might not be clear based on the current example because there is just one input, but it will be clearer later. Let's move to the bias.

A new block is used after the neuron to add the bias **b** to the SOP. After adding **b** to the SOP, the output **Y** is produced. Up to this point, everything works well, but we can still make the graph simpler.

In our previous discussion, we treated the bias differently from the inputs. Each parameter is multiplied by its input, but the bias does not have an input to get multiplied by. We can assume that the bias has an input that is always equal to **+1**. This eases the process too much, as we could eliminate the bias block added after the neuron as in Figure 2-5. The neuron will multiply each parameter by its associated input and treat the bias the same. It will be regarded as a parameter that has an input of **+1**. To make the bias different from the regular parameters, it could be added vertically while other parameters are added horizontally in the graph.

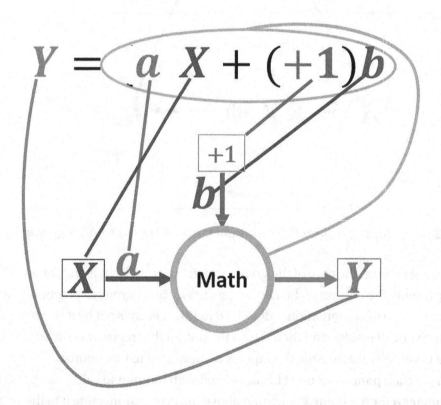

Figure 2-5. *Mapping from a linear model with one input to the ANN graph with bias treated the same as regular parameters by associating it to an input of +1*

Based on the previous example, we know how to graph a linear equation from the neural network perspective. Now, we can work with Equation 2-5, in which there are two inputs. The only change is to add the new input **Z** and its associated parameter **c** to the graph, similar to what we did with the input **X** and its parameter **a**. The new graph is shown in Figure 2-6. The process repeats itself for each new input.

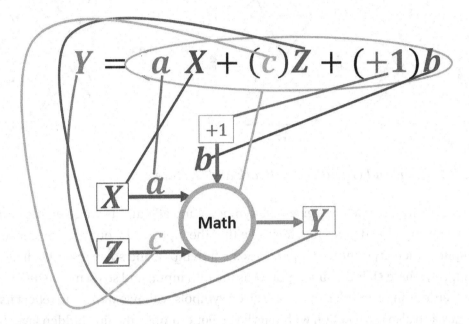

Figure 2-6. *Mapping from a linear model with two inputs to the ANN graph*

In summary, a neuron in an ANN accepts a set of inputs, multiplies each of them by their associated parameters, adds the results of multiplication together, and finally returns the output. In ANNs, neurons are arranged into three types of layers: input, hidden, and output. Such arrangement doesn't exist in biological neural networks but it helps us organize the network. Figure 2-7 shows the architecture of a general fully connected (FC) ANN with such three layers. The network is organized according to the three layers. The network only has a single input and output layer, but it could have more than one hidden layer. Note that neurons within each layer are named according to it. That is, a neuron within the input layer is said to be an input neuron, and a hidden neuron is a neuron within a hidden layer.

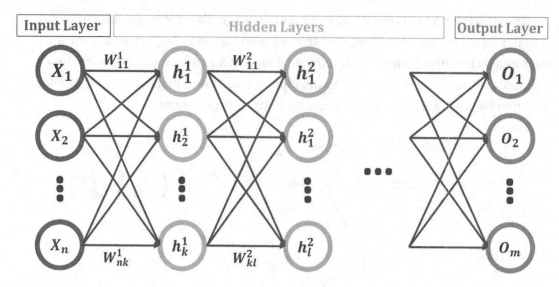

Figure 2-7. *General FC artificial network architecture*

For simplicity, all inputs are given the symbol X and all outputs are given the symbol O with a subscript that defines the index of either the input or the output. The network has n inputs, where X_1 is the first input, X_5 is the fifth input, and so on up to Xn. It also has m inputs, where O_1 is the first input, O_5 is the fifth input, and so on up to Om.

The neurons in the hidden layers are given symbols with two indices to reflect its layer index and also the location within its layer. For example, the first hidden layer has k neurons, where h_1^1 is the first hidden neuron in the first hidden layer, h_5^2 is the fifth hidden neuron in the second hidden layer, and so on up to X_p^r, which is the pth hidden neuron in the rth hidden layer.

Between every two layers, there are a number of parameters that are equal to the multiplication of the number of neurons within the two layers. For example, if the input layer has n neurons and the first hidden layer has k neurons, then the number of parameters required for connecting them is equal to $n \times k$, where the parameter W_{nk}^1 refers to the parameter between the nth neuron in the input layer and the kth neuron in the first hidden layer. This parameter could also be called weights, because each parameter reflects the importance of its associated input. The larger the value of a parameter, the more important its associated input will be.

Up to this point, a basic understanding of ANN is expected, but there is more to know about it. The next sections cover some important concepts about ANN that are critical in the successful building of ANN.

Adjusting Learning Rate for Training ANN

An obstacle for newbies to ANNs is the learning rate. I have been asked many times about the effect of the learning rate on the training of ANNs. Why do we use learning rate? What is the best value for the learning rate? In this section, I will try to make things simpler using an example that shows how learning rate is useful in order to train an ANN. Let's start by explaining the used example.

Filter Example

A very simple example is used to get us out of complexity to just focus on our goal, which is the learning rate. The example is represented by Equation 2-6.

$$Y = \textit{activation}(X) = \begin{cases} 250, & X \geq 250 \\ X, & X < 250 \end{cases}$$ (Equation 2-6)

If the input is 250 or smaller, then the output will be identical to the input. If the input is larger than 250, then it will be clipped and the output will be 250. It works like a filter that only passes inputs below 250 and cuts others to 250. Its graph is available in Figure 2-8.

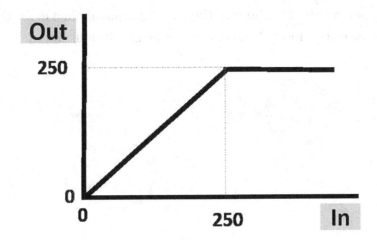

Figure 2-8. *The activation function of the filter example*

The data with six samples is shown in Table 2-5.

Table 2-5. *Data to Train a Network to Filter Inputs to See How Learning Rate Affects the Training Process*

Input (X)	Output (Y)
60	60
40	40
400	250
300	250
-50	-50
-10	-10

ANN Architecture

The architecture of the ANN used is shown in Figure 2-9. There are just input and output layers. The input layer has just a single neuron for our single input. The output layer has just a single neuron for generating the output. The output layer neuron is responsible for mapping the input to the correct output. There is also a bias applied to the output layer neuron with value **b** and input **+1**. There is also a weight **W** for the input.

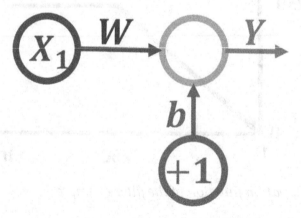

Figure 2-9. *ANN architecture used with the filter example*

Activation Function

Based on the previously discussed networks, we can only approximate linear functions, as in Figure 2-1. But our problem uses a nonlinear function, as in Figure 2-8. How can we use an ANN to represent this type of network? The solution in this example is to use a function such as an activation function in ANN.

ANNs can approximate both linear and nonlinear functions. The way that ANN incorporates nonlinearity in its calculations is via the activation functions. The location of the activation function within the graph of an ANN is after the calculating of the SOP. The output of the neuron in this case will be the activation function output, not just the SOP. This is why the network output is set equal to the activation function output in Equation 2-6.

Python Implementation

The Python code implementing the entire network is given in Listing 2-1. After discussing each of its parts and making it as easy as possible, we will focus on how changing the learning rate affects the network training.

Listing 2-1. Adjusting Learning Rate for Successful ANN Training

```
1   import numpy
2
3   def activation_function(inpt):
4       if(inpt > 250):
5           return 250 # clip the result to 250
6       else:
7           return inpt # just return the input
8
9   def prediction_error(desired, expected):
10      return numpy.abs(numpy.mean(desired-expected)) # absolute error
11
12  def update_weights(weights, predicted, idx):
13      weights = weights + 0.00001*(desired_output[idx] -
            predicted)*inputs[idx] # updating weights
14      return weights # new updated weights
15
16  weights = numpy.array([0.05, .1]) #bias & weight of input
```

```
17  inputs = numpy.array([60, 40, 100, 300, -50, 310]) # training inputs
18  desired_output = numpy.array([60, 40, 150, 250, -50, 250]) # training
    outputs
19
20  def training_loop(inpt, weights):
21      error = 1
22      idx = 0 # start by the first training sample
23      iteration = 0 #loop iteration variable
24      while(iteration < 2000 or error >= 0.01): #while(error >= 0.1):
25          predicted = activation_function(weights[0]*1+weights[1]*
            inputs[idx])
26          error = prediction_error(desired_output[idx], predicted)
27          weights = update_weights(weights, predicted, idx)
28          idx = idx + 1 # go to the next sample
29          idx = idx % inputs.shape[0] # restricts the index to the range
            of our samples
30          iteration = iteration + 1 # next iteration
31      return error, weights
32
33  error, new_weights = training_loop(inputs, weights)
34  print('--------------Final Results----------------')
35  print('Learned Weights : ', new_weights)
36  new_inputs = numpy.array([10, 240, 550, -160])
37  new_outputs = numpy.array([10, 240, 250, -160])
38  for i in range(new_inputs.shape[0]):
39      print('Sample ', i+1, '. Expected = ', new_outputs[i], ' ,
        Predicted = ', activation_function(new_weights[0]*1+new_
        weights[1]*new_inputs[i]))
```

Lines 17 and 18 are responsible for creating two arrays (inputs and desired_output) holding the training input and output data of our example. Line 16 creates an array of the network parameters, which are the input parameter and the bias. They were randomly initialized to 0.05 for the bias and 0.1 for the input. The activation function itself is implemented using the activation_function(inpt) method from line 3 to line 7. It accepts a single argument, which is the input, and returns a single value, which is the predicted output of the network.

Because there may be an error in the prediction, we need to measure it to know how far we are from the correct prediction. For that reason, there is a method implemented in lines 9 and 10 called prediction_error(desired, expected), which accepts two inputs: the desired and predicted outputs. That method just calculates the absolute difference between each desired and predicted output. The best value for any error is for sure 0. This is the optimal value.

What if there is a prediction error? In this case, we must make a change to the network. But what exactly to change? It is the network parameters that must be changed. For updating the network parameters, there is a method called update_weights(weights, predicted, idx) defined in lines 13 and 14. It accepts three inputs: old weights, predicted output, and the index of the input that has a false prediction. Equation 2-7 is used to update the weights.

$$W(n+1) = W(n) + \eta \left[d(n) - Y(n) \right] X(n) \qquad \text{(Equation 2-7)}$$

Where

- η – learning rate
- d – desired output
- Y – predicted output
- X – input
- $W(n)$ – current weights
- $W(n+1)$ – updated weights

The equation uses the weights of the current step **n** to generate the weights of the next step (**n + 1**). This equation helps us understand how the learning rate affects the learning process.

Finally, we need to concatenate all of these together to make the network learn. This is done using the training_loop(inpt, weights) method defined from line 20 to line 31. It goes into a training loop. The loop is used to map the inputs to their outputs with the least possible prediction error. The loop does three operations:

1. Output Prediction.

2. Error Calculation.

3. Updating Weights.

Since we've gotten an idea about the example and its Python code, let us now see how the learning rate is useful in order to get the best results.

Learning Rate

In the previously discussed example in Listing 2-1, line 13 has the weights update equation, in which the learning rate is used. Let's remove the learning rate from that equation. It will be as follows:

```
weights = weights + (desired_output[idx] - predicted)*inputs[idx]
```

Let's see the effect of removing the learning rate. In the first iteration of the training loop, the network has initial values for bias and weight of 0.05 and 0.1, respectively. The input is 60 and the desired output is 60. The expected output of line 25, namely, the result of the activation function, will be activation_function(0.05(+1)+0.1(60)). The predicted output is be 6.05. In line 26, the prediction error is calculated by getting the difference between the desired and the predicted output. The error is abs(60 – 6.05)=53.95. Then in line 27, the weights will get updated according to the preceding equation. The new weights are [0.05, 0.1] + (53.95)*60 = [0.05, 0.1] + 3237 = [3237.05, 3237.1]. It seems that the new weights are too different from the previous weights. Each weight got increased by 3,237, which is too large. But let us continue making the next prediction.

In the next iteration, the network will have this data (b=3237.05 and W=3237.1, Input = 40, and desired output=40). The expected output will be activation_function ((3237.05 + 3237.1(40))= 250. The prediction error will be abs(40 – 250) = 210. The error is very large. It is larger than the previous error, which was just 53.95. Thus, we have to update the weights again. According to the preceding equation, the new weights will be [3237.05, 3237.1] + (–210)*40 = [3237.05, 3237.1] + –8400 = [–5162.95,–5162.9]. Table 2-6 summarizes the results of the first three iterations.

Table 2-6. *Results of the First Three Iterations of Training the Filter Network*

Prediction	Error	Update Value	New Weights
6.05	53.95	**3237.0**	[3237.05, 3237.1]
250	210	**–8400**	[–5162.95, –5162.9]
–521452.95	521552.95	**52155295.0**	[52150132.04999999, 52150132.09999999]
–2555356472.95	2555356422.95	**–127767821147.0**	[–1.27715671e+11, –1.27715671e+11]

As we go into more iterations, the results get worse. The magnitudes of the weights are changing rapidly, sometimes even changing their signs. They are moving from very large positive values to very large negative values. How can we stop these large and abrupt changes in the weights? How to scale down the value by which the weights are updated?

If we looked at the value by which the weights are changing from Table 2-6, it seems that the value is very large. This means that the network changes its weights at high speed. We just need to make it slower. If we are able to scale down this value, then everything will be alright. But how? Getting back to the code, it looks like the update equation is what generates such large values, specifically this part:

```
(desired_output[idx] - predicted)*inputs[idx]
```

We can scale this part by multiplying it by a small value such as 0.1. So, rather than generating 3237.0 as the update value in the first iteration, it will be reduced to just 323.7. We can even reduce this value to 0.001. Using 0.001, the update value is just 3.327.

We can catch it now. This value is the learning rate. Choosing small values for the learning rate makes the rate of weights update smaller and avoids abrupt changes. As the value gets larger, the changes become faster, and this creates bad results.

But what is the best value for the learning rate?

There is no particular value that we can say is the best value for the learning rate. The learning rate is a hyperparameter. A hyperparameter has its value determined by experiments. We try different values and use the value that gives the best results.

Testing the Network

For our problem, using a value of .00001 works fine. After training the network with that learning rate, we can make a test. Table 2-7 shows the results of the prediction of four new testing samples. It seems that results are now much better after using the learning rate.

Table 2-7. *Test Sample Prediction Results*

Input	Desired Output	Predicted Output
10	10	10.87
240	240	239.13
550	250	250
−160	−160	−157.85

Now we are able to understand that learning rate determines the steps by which we move. The larger the step, the more abrupt the changes. We might be near to the best solution and just need to change our parameters a bit to reach it, but omitting or using a bad value for the learning rate gets us away from the solution.

Weight Optimization Using Backpropagation

In the previous section, we used the learning rate to update the weights of the ANN. In this section, we will use the backpropagation algorithm to do that job and deduce how it is better than just using the learning rate. Two examples are used to explain the algorithm numerically.

This section won't dive directly into the details of the backpropagation algorithm but starts by training a very simple network. This is because the backpropagation algorithm is meant to be applied over a network after training. As a result, we should train the network before applying it to catch the benefits of the backpropagation algorithm and how to use it. Readers should have a basic understanding of how ANNs work, partial derivatives, and multivariate chain rule.

Backpropagation for NN Without Hidden Layer

Starting with a simple example, Figure 2-10 shows its network structure, which we will use to explain how the backpropagation algorithm works. It has just two inputs, symbolized as X_1 and X_2. The output layer has just a single neuron, and there are no hidden layers. Each input has a corresponding weight where W_1 and W_2 are the weights for X_1 and X_2, respectively. There is a bias for the output layer neuron with a value of b and a fixed input value of +1.

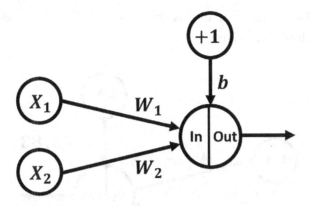

Figure 2-10. *Network structure to train and apply backpropagation*

The output layer neuron uses the sigmoid activation function defined by Equation 2-8:

$$f(s) = \frac{1}{1 + e^{-s}}$$
(Equation 2-8)

Where *s* is the SOP between each input and its corresponding weight. *s* is the input to the activation function, which in this example, is defined as in Equation 2-9.

$$s = X_1 * W_1 + X_2 * W_2 + b$$
(Equation 2-9)

Table 2-8 shows a single input and its corresponding desired output used as the training data. The basic target of this example is not training the network but understanding how the weights are updated using backpropagation. Now, to concentrate on backpropagation, we will analyze a single record of data.

Table 2-8. *Training Data for the First Backpropagation Example*

X_1	X_2	Desired Output
0.1	0.3	0.03

Assume the initial values for both weights and bias are as in Table 2-9.

Table 2-9. *Initial Parameters of the Network*

W_1	W_2	b
0.5	0.2	1.83

For simplicity, the values for all inputs, weights, and bias will be added to the network diagram to look as in Figure 2-11.

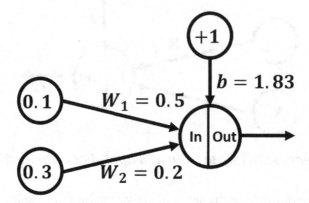

Figure 2-11. *The network of the first backpropagation example with inputs and parameters added*

Now, let us train the network and see whether the desired output will be returned based on the current weights and bias. The input of the activation function will be the SOP between each input and its weight. Then, the bias will be added to the total as follows:

$$s = X_1 * W_1 + X_2 * W_2 + b$$

$$s = 0.1 * 0.5 + 0.3 * 0.2 + 1.83$$

$$s = 1.94$$

The output of the activation function will be calculated by applying the previously calculated SOP to the used function (sigmoid) as follows:

$$f(s) = \frac{1}{1 + e^{-s}}$$

$$f(s) = \frac{1}{1 + e^{-1.94}}$$

$$f(s) = \frac{1}{1 + 0.143703949}$$

$$f(s) = \frac{1}{1.143703949}$$

$$f(s) = 0.874352143$$

The output of the activation function reflects the predicted output for the current inputs. It is obvious that there is a difference between the desired and the expected output. But what are the sources for that difference? How should the predicted output be changed to get closer to the desired result? These questions will be answered later. But at least, let us see the error of our neural network based on an error function.

The error functions tell how close the predicted outputs are to the desired outputs. The optimal value for the error is zero, meaning that there is no error at all and that the desired and predicted results are identical. One of the error functions is the squared error function, as in Equation 2-10.

$$E = \frac{1}{2}(desired - predicted)^2 \qquad \text{(Equation 2-10)}$$

Note that the $\frac{1}{2}$ added to the equation is for simplifying derivatives later. We can measure the error of our network as follows:

$$E = \frac{1}{2}(0.03 - 0.874352143)^2$$

$$E = \frac{1}{2}(-0.844352143)^2$$

$$E = \frac{1}{2}(0.712930542)$$

$$E = 0.356465271$$

The result ensures the existence of a large error (~**0.357**). This is what the error tells. It just gives us an indication of how far the predicted results are from the desired results. Now that we know how to measure the error, we need to find a way to minimize it. The only playable parameter we have is the weight. We can try different weights and then test our network.

Weights Update Equation

The weights can be changed according to Equation 2-7 (used in the previous section) where

- **n**: training step (0, 1, 2, ...).

- **$W(n)$**: weights in the current training step.

  $W(n) = [b(n),\ W_1(n),\ W_2(n),\ W_3(n),...,\ W_m(n)]$

- **η**: network learning rate.

- $d(n)$: desired output.

- $Y(n)$: predicted output.

- $X(n)$: current input at which the network made the false prediction.

For our network, these parameters have the following values:

- n: 0

- $W(n)$: [1.83, 0.5, 0.2]

- η: hyperparameter. We can choose 0.01, for example.

- $d(n)$: [0.03].

- $Y(n)$: [0.874352143].

- $X(n)$: [+1, 0.1, 0.3]. First value (+1) is for the bias.

We can update our neural network weights based on the previous equation:

$$W(n+1) = W(n) + \eta \big[d(n) - Y(n) \big] X(n)$$

$$= \big[1.83, 0.5, 0.2 \big] + 0.01 \big[0.03 - 0.874352143 \big] \big[+1, 0.1, 0.3 \big]$$

$$= \big[1.83, 0.5, 0.2 \big] + 0.01 \big[-0.844352143 \big] \big[+1, 0.1, 0.3 \big]$$

$$= \big[1.83, 0.5, 0.2 \big] + -0.00844352143 \big[+1, 0.1, 0.3 \big]$$

$$= \big[1.83, 0.5, 0.2 \big] + \big[-0.008443521, -0.000844352, -0.002533056 \big]$$

$$= \big[1.821556479, 0.499155648, 0.197466943 \big]$$

The new weights are given in Table 2-10.

Table 2-10. *Updated Weights for the Network of the First Backpropagation Example*

W_{1new}	W_{2new}	b_{new}
0.197466943	0.499155648	1.821556479

Based on the new weights, we will recalculate the predicted output and continue updating weights and calculating the predicted output until reaching an acceptable value for the error for the problem at hand.

Here we successfully updated the weights without using the backpropagation algorithm. Are we still in need of that algorithm? Yes. The reasons will be explained next.

Why Is the Backpropagation Algorithm Important?

Suppose, for the optimal case, that the weight update equation generated the best weights; it is still unclear what this function actually did. It is like a black box in that we don't understand its internal operations. All we know is that we should apply this equation in case there is a classification error. Then the function will generate new weights to be used in the next training steps. But why are new weights better at prediction? What is the effect of each weight on the prediction error? How does increasing or decreasing one or more weights affect the prediction error?

It is required to have a better understanding of how the best weights are calculated. To do that, we should use the backpropagation algorithm. It helps us to understand how each weight affects the NN total error and tells us how to minimize the error to a value very close to zero.

Forward vs. Backward Passes

When training a neural network, there are two passes, namely, forward and backward, as in Figure 2-12. The first pass is always the forward pass, in which the inputs are applied to the input layer and move toward the output layer, calculating the SOP between inputs and weights, applying activation functions to generate outputs, and finally calculating the prediction error to know how accurate the current network is.

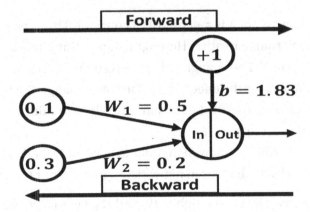

Figure 2-12. *Forward and backward passes of training an ANN*

But what if there is a prediction error? We should modify the network to reduce that error. This is done in the backward pass. In the forward pass, we start from the inputs, until calculating the prediction errors. But in the backward pass, we start from the errors until reaching the inputs. The goal of this pass is to learn how each weight affects the total error. Knowing the relationship between the weight and the error allows us to modify network weights to decrease the error. For example, in the backward pass, we can get useful information, such as that increasing the current value of W_1 by 1.0 will increase the prediction error by 0.07. This helps us understand how to select the new value of W_1 in order to minimize the error (W_1 should not be increased).

Partial Derivative

One important operation used in the backward pass is to calculate derivatives. Before getting into the calculations of derivatives in the backward pass, we can start with a simple example to make things easier.

For a multivariate function such as $Y = X^2 Z + H$, what is the effect on the output Y given a change in variable X? This question is answered using the partial derivative. It is written as follows:

$$\frac{\partial Y}{\partial X} = \frac{\partial}{\partial X}\left(X^2 Z + H\right)$$

$$\frac{\partial Y}{\partial X} = 2XZ + 0$$

$$\frac{\partial Y}{\partial X} = 2XZ$$

Note that everything except X is regarded as a constant. This is why H is replaced by 0 after calculating the partial derivative. Here, ∂X means a tiny change of variable X and ∂Y means a tiny change of Y. The change of Y is the result of changing X. By making a very small change in X, what is the effect on Y? The small change can be an increase or decrease by a tiny value such as 0.01. By substituting different values of X, we can find how Y changes with respect to X.

The same procedure will be followed in order to learn how the NN prediction error changes with respect to (wrt) changes in network weights. So, our target is to calculate $\frac{\partial E}{\partial W_1}$ and $\frac{\partial E}{\partial W_2}$, as we have just two weights: W_1 and W_2. Let's calculate them.

Change in Prediction Error wrt Weights

Looking at this equation, $Y = X^2 Z + H$, it seems straightforward to calculate the partial derivate $\dfrac{\partial Y}{\partial X}$ because there is an equation relating both Y and X. But there is no direct equation between the prediction error and the weights. This is why we are going to use the multivariate chain rule to find the partial derivative of Y wrt X.

Prediction Error to Weights Chain

Let us try to find the chain relating the prediction error to the weights. The prediction error is calculated based on Equation 2-10.

But this equation doesn't have any weights. No problem: we can follow the calculations for each input of the previous equation until we reach the weights. The desired output is a constant, and thus there is no chance of reaching the weights through it. The predicted output is calculated based on the sigmoid function, as in Equation 2-8.

Again, the equation for calculating the predicted output doesn't have any weight. But there is still variable s (SOP), which already depends on weights for its calculation according to Equation 2-11.

$$s = X_1 * W_1 + X_2 * W_2 + b \qquad \text{(Equation 2-11)}$$

Figure 2-13 presents the chain of calculations to be followed to reach the weights.

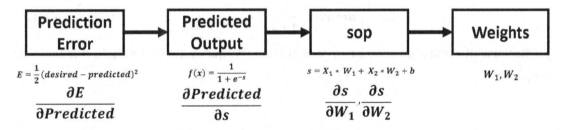

Figure 2-13. *Chain of calculations to reach the weights starting from the error of prediction*

As a result, to know how the prediction error changes wrt changes in the weights, we should do some intermediate operations, including finding how the prediction error changes wrt changes in the predicted output. Then, we need to find the relation between the predicted output and the SOP. Finally, we will find how the SOP change by changing the weights. There are four intermediate partial derivatives as follows:

$$\frac{\partial E}{\partial Predicted}, \frac{\partial Predicted}{\partial s}, \frac{\partial s}{\partial W_1}, \text{ and } \frac{\partial s}{\partial W_2}$$

This chain will finally tell how the prediction error changes wrt changes in each weight, which is our goal, by multiplying all individual partial derivatives as follows:

$$\frac{\partial E}{\partial W_1} = \frac{\partial E}{\partial Predicted} * \frac{\partial Predicted}{\partial s} * \frac{\partial s}{\partial W_1}$$

$$\frac{\partial E}{\partial W_2} = \frac{\partial E}{\partial Predicted} * \frac{\partial Predicted}{\partial s} * \frac{\partial s}{\partial W_2}$$

Important note   Currently, there is no equation directly relating prediction error to network weights, but we can create one relating them and apply a partial derivative directly to it. Here it is in Equation 2-12.

$$E = \frac{1}{2}\left(desired - \frac{1}{1 + e^{-(X_1 * W_1 + X_2 * W_2 + b)}} \right)^2 \qquad \text{(Equation 2-12)}$$

Because this equation seems complex, we can use the multivariate chain rule for simplicity.

Calculating Chain Partial Derivatives

Let us calculate the partial derivatives of each part of the chain previously created.

Error - Predicted Output Partial Derivative:

$$\frac{\partial E}{\partial Predicted} = \frac{\partial}{\partial Predicted}\left(\frac{1}{2}(desired - predicted)^2\right)$$

$$= 2*\frac{1}{2}(desired - predicted)^{2-1}*(0-1)$$

$$= (desired - predicted)*(-1)$$

$$= predicted - desired$$

By value substitution,

$$\frac{\partial E}{\partial Predicted} = predicted - desired = 0.874352143 - 0.03$$

$$\frac{\partial E}{\partial Predicted} = 0.844352143$$

Predicted Output - SOP Partial Derivative:

$$\frac{\partial Predicted}{\partial s} = \frac{\partial}{\partial s}\left(\frac{1}{1+e^{-s}}\right)$$

Remember that the quotient rule can be used to find the derivative of the sigmoid function as follows:

$$\frac{\partial Predicted}{\partial s} = \frac{1}{1+e^{-s}}\left(1 - \frac{1}{1+e^{-s}}\right)$$

By value substitution,

$$\frac{\partial\, Predicted}{\partial s} = \frac{1}{1+e^{-s}}\left(1-\frac{1}{1+e^{-s}}\right) = \frac{1}{1+e^{-1.94}}\left(1-\frac{1}{1+e^{-1.94}}\right)$$

$$= \frac{1}{1+0.143703949}\left(1-\frac{1}{1+0.143703949}\right)$$

$$= \frac{1}{1.143703949}\left(1-\frac{1}{1.143703949}\right)$$

$$= 0.874352143(1-0.874352143)$$

$$= 0.874352143(0.125647857)$$

$$\frac{\partial\, Predicted}{\partial s} = 0.109860473$$

SOP - W_1 Partial Derivative:

$$\frac{\partial s}{\partial W_1} = \frac{\partial}{\partial W_1}\left(X_1 * W_1 + X_2 * W_2 + b\right)$$

$$= 1 * X_1 * \left(W_1\right)^{(1-1)} + 0 + 0$$

$$= X_1 * \left(W_1\right)^{(0)}$$

$$= X_1(1)$$

$$\frac{\partial s}{\partial W_1} = X_1$$

By value substitution,

$$\frac{\partial s}{\partial W_1} = X_1 = 0.1$$

SOP - W_2 Partial Derivative:

$$\frac{\partial s}{\partial W_2} = \frac{\partial}{\partial W_2}\left(X_1 * W_1 + X_2 * W_2 + b\right)$$

$$= 0 + 1 * X_2 * \left(W_2\right)^{(1-1)} + 0$$

$$= X_2 * \left(W_2\right)^{(0)}$$

$$= X_2\left(1\right)$$

$$\frac{\partial s}{\partial W_2} = X_2$$

By value substitution,

$$\frac{\partial s}{\partial W_2} = X_2 = 0.3$$

After calculating each individual derivative, we can multiply all of them to get the desired relationship between the prediction error and each weight.

Prediction Error - W_1 Partial Derivative:

$$\frac{\partial E}{\partial W_1} = 0.844352143 * 0.109860473 * 0.1$$

$$\frac{\partial E}{\partial W_1} = 0.009276093$$

Prediction Error - W_2 Partial Derivative:

$$\frac{\partial E}{\partial W_2} = 0.844352143 * 0.109860473 * 0.3$$

$$\frac{\partial E}{\partial W_2} = 0.027828278$$

Finally, there are two values reflecting how the prediction error changes with respect to the weights (0.009276093 for W_1 and 0.027828278 for W_2). But what does that mean? The results need interpretation.

Interpreting Results of Backpropagation

There are two useful conclusions from each of the last two derivatives obtained from the following:

- Derivative sign

- Derivative magnitude (DM)

If the derivative is positive, that means increasing the weight will increase the error, and likewise, decreasing the weight will decrease the error. If the derivative is negative, then increasing the weight will decrease the error, and correspondingly, decreasing the weight will increase the error.

But by how much will the error increase or decrease? The DM can tell us. For a positive derivative, increasing the weight by p will increase the error by $DM * p$. For a negative derivative, increasing the weight by p will decrease the error by $DM * p$.

Because the result of the $\dfrac{\partial E}{\partial W_1}$ derivative is positive, this means that if W_1 increased by 1 then the total error will increase by 0.009276093. Also, because the result of the $\dfrac{\partial E}{\partial W_2}$ derivative is positive, this means that if W_2 increases by 1 then the total error will increase by 0.027828278.

Updating Weights

After successfully calculating the derivatives of the error with respect to each individual weight, we can update the weights in order to enhance the prediction. Each weight will be updated based on its derivative as follows:

$$W_{1new} = W_1 - \eta * \frac{\partial E}{\partial W_1}$$

$$= 0.5 - \mathit{0.01} * 0.009276093$$

$$W_{1new} = 0.49990723907$$

For the second weight,

$$W_{2new} = W_2 - \eta * \frac{\partial E}{\partial W_2}$$

$$= 0.2 - 0.01 * 0.027828278$$

$$W_{2new} = 0.1997217172$$

Note that the derivative is subtracted rather than added to the weight because it is positive.

Then, continue the process of prediction and updating the weights until the desired outputs are generated with an acceptable error.

Backpropagation for NN with Hidden Layer

To make the ideas more clear, we can apply the backpropagation algorithm over the following NN after adding one hidden layer with two neurons. The new network is shown in Figure 2-14.

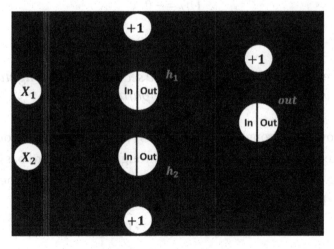

Figure 2-14. *The network architecture of the second backpropagation example*

The same inputs, output, activation function, and learning rate used previously will also be applied in this example. Here are the complete weights of the network:

W_1	W_2	W_3	W_4	W_5	W_6	b_1	b_2	b_3
0.5	0.1	0.62	0.2	–0.2	0.3	0.4	–0.1	1.83

Figure 2-15 shows the previous network with all inputs and weights added.

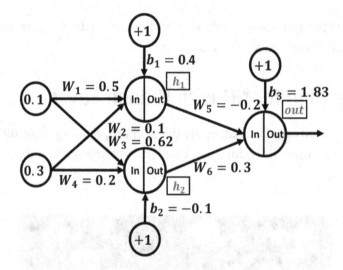

Figure 2-15. *The network architecture of the second backpropagation example after adding the values of the inputs and the parameters*

At first, we should go through the forward pass to get the predicted output. If there was an error in prediction, then we should go through the backward pass to update the weights according to the backpropagation algorithm. Let us calculate the inputs to the first neuron in the hidden layer (h_1):

$$h_{1in} = X_1 * W_1 + X_2 * W_2 + b_1$$

$$= 0.1 * 0.5 + 0.3 * 0.1 + 0.4$$

$$h_{1in} = 0.48$$

The input to the second neuron in the hidden layer (h_2):

$$h_{2in} = X_1 * W_3 + X_2 * W_4 + b_2$$

$$= 0.1 * 0.62 + 0.3 * 0.2 - 0.1$$

$$= 0.022$$

The output of the first neuron of the hidden layer:

$$h_{1ou} = \frac{1}{1 + e^{-h_{1in}}}$$

$$= \frac{1}{1 + e^{-0.48}}$$

$$= \frac{1}{1 + 0.619}$$

$$= \frac{1}{1.619}$$

$$h_{1out} = 0.618$$

And the output of the second neuron of the hidden layer:

$$h_{2out} = \frac{1}{1 + e^{-h_{2in}}}$$

$$= \frac{1}{1 + e^{-0.022}}$$

$$= \frac{1}{1 + 0.978}$$

$$= \frac{1}{1.978}$$

$$h_{2out} = 0.506$$

The next step is to calculate the input of the output neuron:

$$out_{in} = h_{1out} * W_5 + h_{2out} * W_6 + b_3$$

$$= 0.618 * -0.2 + 0.506 * 0.3 + 1.83$$

$$out_{in} = 1.858$$

And the output of the output neuron:

$$out_{out} = \frac{1}{1+e^{-out_{in}}}$$

$$= \frac{1}{1+e^{-1.858}}$$

$$= \frac{1}{1+0.156}$$

$$= \frac{1}{1.156}$$

$$out_{out} = 0.865$$

Thus, the expected output of our NN based on the current weights is 0.865. We can then calculate the prediction error according to the following equation:

$$E = \frac{1}{2}\left(desired - out_{out}\right)^2$$

$$= \frac{1}{2}\left(0.03 - 0.865\right)^2$$

$$= \frac{1}{2}\left(-0.835\right)^2$$

$$= \frac{1}{2}\left(0.697\right)$$

$$E = 0.349$$

The error seems very high, and thus we should update the network weights using the backpropagation algorithm.

Partial Derivatives

Our goal is to get how the total error E changes wrt each of the six weights ($W_1 : W_6$):

$$\frac{\partial E}{\partial W_1}, \frac{\partial E}{\partial W_2}, \frac{\partial E}{\partial W_3}, \frac{\partial E}{\partial W_4}, \frac{\partial E}{\partial W_5}, \frac{\partial E}{\partial W_6}$$

Let us start by calculating the partial derivative of the output wrt the hidden-output layers weights (W_5 and W_6).

E–W_5 Partial Derivative:

Starting with W_5, we will follow that chain:

$$\frac{\partial E}{\partial W_5} = \frac{\partial E}{\partial out_{out}} * \frac{\partial out_{out}}{\partial out_{in}} * \frac{\partial out_{in}}{\partial W_5}$$

We can calculate each individual part at first and then combine them to get the desired derivative.

For the first derivative $\dfrac{\partial E}{\partial out_{out}}$:

$$\frac{\partial E}{\partial out_{out}} = \frac{\partial}{\partial out_{out}}\left(\frac{1}{2}\left(desired - out_{out}\right)^2\right)$$

$$= 2 * \frac{1}{2}\left(desired - out_{out}\right)^{2-1} * \left(0 - 1\right)$$

$$= desired - out_{out} * \left(-1\right)$$

$$= out_{out} - desired$$

By substituting with the values of these variables,

$$= out_{out} - desired = 0.865 - 0.03$$

$$\frac{\partial E}{\partial out_{out}} = 0.835$$

For the second derivative $\dfrac{\partial out_{out}}{\partial out_{in}}$:

$$\frac{\partial out_{out}}{\partial out_{in}} = \frac{\partial}{\partial out_{in}}\left(\frac{1}{1 + e^{-out_{in}}}\right)$$

$$= \left(\frac{1}{1 + e^{-out_{in}}}\right)\left(1 - \frac{1}{1 + e^{-out_{in}}}\right)$$

$$= \left(\frac{1}{1 + e^{-1.858}}\right)\left(1 - \frac{1}{1 + e^{-1.858}}\right)$$

$$= \left(\frac{1}{1.56} \right) \left(1 - \frac{1}{1.56} \right)$$

$$= \left(0.865 \right) \left(1 - 0.865 \right) = \left(0.865 \right) \left(0.135 \right)$$

$$\frac{\partial out_{out}}{\partial out_{in}} = 0.117$$

For the last derivative $\dfrac{\partial out_{in}}{\partial W_5}$:

$$\frac{\partial out_{in}}{\partial W_5} = \frac{\partial}{\partial W_5} \left(h_{1out} * W_5 + h_{2out} * W_6 + b_3 \right)$$

$$= 1 * h_{1out} * \left(W_5 \right)^{1-1} + 0 + 0$$

$$= h_{1out}$$

$$\frac{\partial out_{in}}{\partial W_5} = 0.618$$

After calculating all three required derivatives, we can calculate the target derivative as follows:

$$\frac{\partial E}{\partial W_5} = \frac{\partial E}{\partial out_{out}} * \frac{\partial out_{out}}{\partial out_{in}} * \frac{\partial out_{in}}{\partial W_5}$$

$$\frac{\partial E}{\partial W_5} = 0.835 * 0.23 * 0.618$$

$$\frac{\partial E}{\partial W_5} = 0.119$$

$E - W_6$ Partial Derivative:

For calculating $\dfrac{\partial E}{\partial W_6}$, we will use the following chain:

$$\frac{\partial E}{\partial W_6} = \frac{\partial E}{\partial out_{out}} * \frac{\partial out_{out}}{\partial out_{in}} * \frac{\partial out_{in}}{\partial W_6}$$

The same calculations will be repeated with just a change in the last derivative $\dfrac{\partial out_{in}}{\partial W_6}$. It can be calculated as follows:

$$\frac{\partial out_{in}}{\partial W_6} = \frac{\partial}{\partial W_6}\left(h_{1out} * W_5 + h_{2out} * W_6 + b_3\right)$$

$$= 0 + 1 * h_{2out} * \left(W_6\right)^{1-1} + 0$$

$$= h_{2out}$$

$$\frac{\partial out_{in}}{\partial W_6} = 0.506$$

Finally, the derivative $\dfrac{\partial E}{\partial W_6}$ can be calculated:

$$\frac{\partial E}{\partial W_6} = \frac{\partial E}{\partial out_{out}} * \frac{\partial out_{out}}{\partial out_{in}} * \frac{\partial out_{in}}{\partial W_6}$$

$$= 0.835 * 0.23 * 0.506$$

$$\frac{\partial E}{\partial W_6} = 0.097$$

This is for W_5 and W_6. Let's calculate the derivative wrt to W_1 to W_4.

E–W_1 Partial Derivative:

Starting with W_1, we will follow that chain:

$$\frac{\partial E}{\partial W_1} = \frac{\partial E}{\partial out_{out}} * \frac{\partial out_{out}}{\partial out_{in}} * \frac{\partial out_{in}}{\partial h1_{out}} * \frac{\partial h1_{out}}{\partial h1_{in}} * \frac{\partial h1_{in}}{\partial W_1}$$

We will follow the previous procedure by calculating each individual derivative and finally combining all of them. The first two derivatives $\dfrac{\partial E}{\partial out_{out}}$ and $\dfrac{\partial out_{out}}{\partial out_{in}}$ have already been calculated previously, and their results are as follows:

$$\frac{\partial E}{\partial out_{out}} = 0.835$$

$$\frac{\partial out_{out}}{\partial out_{in}} = 0.23$$

For the next derivative $\dfrac{\partial out_{in}}{\partial h1_{out}}$:

$$\frac{\partial out_{in}}{\partial h1_{out}} = \frac{\partial}{\partial h1_{out}}\left(h_{1out} * W_5 + h_{2out} * W_6 + b_3\right)$$

$$= \left(h_{1out}\right)^{1-1} * W_5 + 0 + 0$$

$$= W_5$$

$$\frac{\partial out_{in}}{\partial h1_{out}} = -0.2$$

For $\dfrac{\partial h1_{out}}{\partial h1_{in}}$:

$$\frac{\partial h1_{out}}{\partial h1_{in}} = \frac{\partial}{\partial h1_{in}}\left(\frac{1}{1+e^{-h_{1in}}}\right)$$

$$= \left(\frac{1}{1+e^{-h_{1in}}}\right)\left(1-\frac{1}{1+e^{-h_{1in}}}\right)$$

$$= \left(\frac{1}{1+e^{-0.48}}\right)\left(1-\frac{1}{1+e^{-0.48}}\right)$$

$$= \left(\frac{1}{1.619}\right)\left(1-\frac{1}{1.619}\right)$$

$$= \left(0.618\right)\left(1-0.618\right) = 0.618 * 0.382$$

$$\frac{\partial h_{2out}}{\partial h_{2in}} = 0.236$$

For $\dfrac{\partial h1_{in}}{\partial W_1}$:

$$\frac{\partial h1_{in}}{\partial W_1} = \frac{\partial}{\partial W_1}\left(X_1 * W_1 + X_2 * W_2 + b_1\right)$$

$$= X_1 * \left(W_1\right)^{1-1} + 0 + 0$$

$$= X_1$$

$$\frac{\partial h1_{in}}{\partial W_1} = 0.1$$

Finally, the target derivative can be calculated:

$$\frac{\partial E}{\partial W_1} = 0.835 * 0.23 * -0.2 * 0.236 * 0.1$$

$$\frac{\partial E}{\partial W_1} = -0.001$$

E−W_2 Partial Derivative:

Similar to the method of calculating $\frac{\partial E}{\partial W_1}$, we can calculate $\frac{\partial E}{\partial W_2}$. The only change will be in the last derivative $\frac{\partial h1_{in}}{\partial W_2}$.

$$\frac{\partial E}{\partial W_2} = \frac{\partial E}{\partial out_{out}} * \frac{\partial out_{out}}{\partial out_{in}} * \frac{\partial out_{in}}{\partial h1_{out}} * \frac{\partial h1_{out}}{\partial h1_{in}} * \frac{\partial h1_{in}}{\partial W_2}$$

$$\frac{\partial h1_{in}}{\partial W_2} = \frac{\partial}{\partial W_2}\left(X_1 * W_1 + X_2 * W_2 + b_1\right)$$

$$= 0 + X_2 * \left(W_2\right)^{1-1} + 0$$

$$= X_2$$

$$\frac{\partial h1_{in}}{\partial W_2} = 0.3$$

Then:

$$\frac{\partial E}{\partial W_2} = 0.835 * 0.23 * -0.2 * 0.236 * 0.3$$

$$\frac{\partial E}{\partial W_2} = -.003$$

The last two weights (W_3 and W_4) can be calculated similarly to W_1 and W_2.

E–W_3 Partial Derivative:

Starting with W_3, we should follow this chain:

$$\frac{\partial E}{\partial W_3} = \frac{\partial E}{\partial out_{out}} * \frac{\partial out_{out}}{\partial out_{in}} * \frac{\partial out_{in}}{\partial h2_{out}} * \frac{\partial h2_{out}}{\partial h2_{in}} * \frac{\partial h2_{in}}{\partial W_3}$$

The missing derivatives to be calculated are $\dfrac{\partial out_{in}}{\partial h2_{out}}, \dfrac{\partial h2_{out}}{\partial h2_{in}}$ and $\dfrac{\partial h2_{in}}{\partial W_3}$.

$$\frac{\partial out_{in}}{\partial h2_{out}} = \frac{\partial}{\partial h2_{out}} \left(h_{1out} * W_5 + h_{2out} * W_6 + b_3 \right)$$

$$= 0 + \left(h_{2out} \right)^{1-1} * W_6 + 0$$

$$= W_6$$

$$\frac{\partial out_{in}}{\partial h2_{out}} = 0.3$$

For $\dfrac{\partial h2_{out}}{\partial h2_{in}}$:

$$\frac{\partial h2_{out}}{\partial h2_{in}} = \frac{\partial}{\partial h_{2in}} \left(\frac{1}{1 + e^{-h_{2in}}} \right)$$

$$= \left(\frac{1}{1 + e^{-h_{2in}}} \right) \left(1 - \frac{1}{1 + e^{-h_{2in}}} \right)$$

$$= \left(\frac{1}{1 + e^{-0.022}} \right) \left(1 - \frac{1}{1 + e^{-0.022}} \right)$$

$$= \left(\frac{1}{1.978} \right) \left(1 - \frac{1}{1.978} \right)$$

$$= \left(0.506 \right) \left(1 - 0.506 \right)$$

$$\frac{\partial h_{2out}}{\partial h_{2in}} = 0.25$$

For $\dfrac{\partial h2_{in}}{\partial W_3}$:

$$\frac{\partial h2_{in}}{\partial W_3} = \frac{\partial}{\partial W_3}\left(X_1 * W_3 + X_2 * W_4 + b_2 \right)$$

$$= X_1 * W_3 + X_2 * W_4 + b_2$$

$$= \left(X_1 \right)^{1-1} * X_1 + 0 + 0$$

$$= X_1$$

$$= 0.1$$

Finally, we can calculate the desired derivative as follows:

$$\frac{\partial E}{\partial W_3} = \frac{\partial E}{\partial out_{out}} * \frac{\partial out_{out}}{\partial out_{in}} * \frac{\partial out_{in}}{\partial h2_{out}} * \frac{\partial h2_{out}}{\partial h2_{in}} * \frac{\partial h2_{in}}{\partial W_3}$$

$$\frac{\partial E}{\partial W_3} = 0.835 * 0.23 * 0.3 * 0.25 * 0.1$$

$$\frac{\partial E}{\partial W_3} = 0.00014$$

E–W_4 Partial Derivative:

We can now calculate $\dfrac{\partial E}{\partial W_4}$ similarly:

$$\frac{\partial E}{\partial W_4} = \frac{\partial E}{\partial out_{out}} * \frac{\partial out_{out}}{\partial out_{in}} * \frac{\partial out_{in}}{\partial h2_{out}} * \frac{\partial h2_{out}}{\partial h2_{in}} * \frac{\partial h2_{in}}{\partial W_4}$$

We should calculate the missing derivative $\dfrac{\partial h2_{in}}{\partial W_4}$:

$$\frac{\partial h2_{in}}{\partial W_4} = \frac{\partial}{\partial W_4}\left(X_1 * W_3 + X_2 * W_4 + b_2 \right)$$

$$= X_1 * W_3 + X_2 * W_4 + b_2$$

$$= 0 + \left(X_2 \right)^{1-1} * W_4 + 0$$

$$= W_4$$

$$= 0.2$$

Then calculate $\dfrac{\partial E}{\partial W_4}$:

$$\frac{\partial E}{\partial W_4} = \frac{\partial E}{\partial out_{out}} * \frac{\partial out_{out}}{\partial out_{in}} * \frac{\partial out_{in}}{\partial h2_{out}} * \frac{\partial h2_{out}}{\partial h2_{in}} * \frac{\partial h2_{in}}{\partial W_4}$$

$$\frac{\partial E}{\partial W_4} = 0.835 * 0.23 * 0.3 * 0.25 * 0.2$$

$$\frac{\partial E}{\partial W_4} = .003$$

Updating Weights

At this point, we have successfully calculated the derivative of the total error according to each weight in the network. Next is to update the weights according to the derivatives and retrain the network. The updated weights will be calculated as follows:

$$W_{1new} = W_1 - \eta * \frac{\partial E}{\partial W_1} = 0.5 - .01 * -0.001 = 0.50001$$

$$W_{2new} = W_2 - \eta * \frac{\partial E}{\partial W_2} = 0.1 - .01 * -0.003 = 0.10003$$

$$W_{3new} = W_3 - \eta * \frac{\partial E}{\partial W_3} = 0.62 - .01 * 0.00014 = 0.6199$$

$$W_{4new} = W_4 - \eta * \frac{\partial E}{\partial W_4} = 0.2 - .01 * 0.003 = 0.1997$$

$$W_{5new} = W_5 - \eta * \frac{\partial E}{\partial W_5} = -0.2 - .01 * 0.618 = -0.20618$$

$$W_{6new} = W_6 - \eta * \frac{\partial E}{\partial W_6} = 0.3 - .01 * 0.097 = 0.29903$$

Overfitting

Have you ever created a ML model that is perfect for the training samples but gives very bad predictions with unseen samples? Did you ever wonder why this happens? The reason might be due to overfitting. A model with the problem of overfitting makes great predictions for training samples but poor ones for validation data. This is because the model adapted itself to every piece of information in the training data until collecting some properties that could be found only within the training data. Let's try to understand this problem.

The focus of ML is to train an algorithm with training data in order to create a model that is able to make the correct predictions for unseen data (test data). To create a classifier, for example, a human expert will start by collecting the data required to train the ML algorithm. The human is responsible for finding the best types of features which are the things capable of discriminating between the different classes in order to represent each class. These features will be used to train the ML algorithm. Suppose we are to build a ML model that classifies the images in Figure 2-16 as containing cats or not.

Figure 2-16. *Images of cats to train a model*

The first question we have to answer is "what are the best features to use?" This is a critical question in ML, as the better the features used, the better the predictions the trained ML model makes, and vice versa. Let us try to visualize these images and extract some features that are representative of cats. Some of the representative features may be the existence of two dark eye pupils and two ears with a diagonal direction. Let's assume that we have extracted the features somehow from the preceding training images and that a trained ML model has been created. This model can work with a wide range of cat images because the features used exist in most cats. We can test the model using some unseen data as in Figure 2-17. Assume that the classification accuracy of the test data is **x%**.

Figure 2-17. *Test images of cats*

One may want to increase the classification accuracy. The first thing to think of is using more features than the two used previously. This is because the more discriminative features used, the better the accuracy. By inspecting the training data again, we can find more features, such as the overall image color, as all training cat samples are white, and the iris color in the training data is yellow. The feature vector will have these four features:

1. Dark Eye Pupils

2. Diagonal Ears

3. White Fur

4. Yellow Irises

They will be used to retrain the ML model.

After creating the trained model, the next step is to test it. The expected result after using the new feature vector is that the classification accuracy will decrease to be less than **x%**. But why? The cause of the drop in accuracy is the use of some features that already exist in the training data but not generally in all cat images. The features are not general across all cat images. In the testing data, some cats have black or yellow fur, not the white fur used in training.

Our case, in which the features used are powerful for the training samples but very poor for the testing samples, can be described as overfitting. The model is trained with some features that are exclusive to the training data but do not exist in the testing data.

The goal of the previous discussion is to make the idea of overfitting simple by use of a high-level example. To get into the details, it is preferable to work with a simpler example. That is why the rest of the discussion will be based on a regression example.

Understand Regularization Based on a Regression Example

Assume we want to create a regression model that fits the data shown in Figure 2-18. We can use polynomial regression.

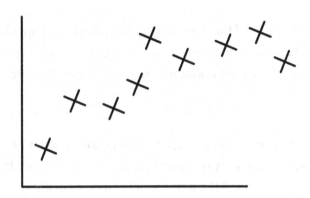

Figure 2-18. *Data to fit a regression model*

The simplest model that we can start with is the linear model with a first-degree polynomial equation, as in Equation 2-13.

$$y_1 = f_1(x) = \Theta_1 x + \Theta_0 \qquad \text{(Equation 2-13)}$$

Where Θ_0 and Θ_1 are the model parameters and x is the only feature used.
The plot of the previous model is shown in Figure 2-19.

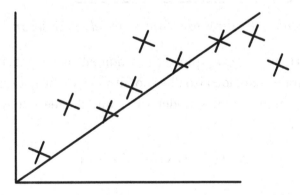

Figure 2-19. *An initial model to fit the data using a model of the first degree*

Based on a loss function such as the one in Equation 2-14, we can conclude that the model is not fitting the data well.

$$L = \frac{\sum_{i=0}^{N} \left| f_1(x_i) - d_i \right|}{N}$$

(Equation 2-14)

Where $f_i(x_i)$ is the expected output for sample i and d_i is the desired output for the same sample.

The model is too simple and there are many predictions that are not accurate. For this reason, we should create a more complex model that can fit the data well, and we can increase the degree of the equation from one to two, as in Equation 2-15.

$$y_2 = f_1(x) = \Theta_2 x^2 + \Theta_1 x + \Theta_0$$

(Equation 2-15)

By using the same feature x after being raised to power 2 (x^2), we created a new feature and we will capture not only the linear properties of the data, but also some nonlinear properties. The graph of the new model will be as in Figure 2-20.

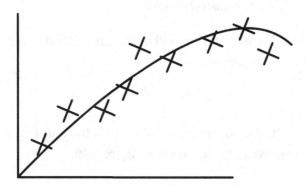

Figure 2-20. *Using more features to create a model of the second degree*

The graph shows that the second-degree polynomial fits the data better than the first degree. But the quadratic equation also does not fit some of the data samples well. This is why we can create a more complex model of the third degree with Equation 2-16. The graph is in Figure 2-21.

$$y_3 = f_3(x) = \Theta_3 x^3 + \Theta_2 x^2 + \Theta_1 x + \Theta_0$$

(Equation 2-16)

Figure 2-21. *Model of the third degree*

It may be noted that the model fits the data better after a new feature that captures the data properties of the third degree is added. To fit the data better than before, we can increase the degree of the equation to be of the fourth degree, as in Equation 2-17. The graph is in Figure 2-22.

$$y_4 = f_4(x) = \Theta_4 x^4 + \Theta_3 x^3 + \Theta_2 x^2 + \Theta_1 x + \Theta_0 \qquad \text{(Equation 2-17)}$$

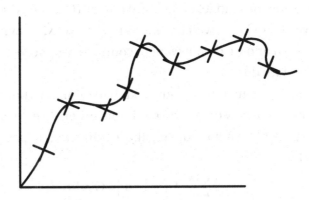

Figure 2-22. *Model of the fourth degree*

It seems that the higher the degree of the polynomial equation, the better it fits the data. But there are some important questions to be answered. If increasing the degree of the polynomial equation by adding new features enhances the results, why shouldn't a very high degree, such as 100th degree, be used? What is the best degree to use for a problem?

Model Capacity/Complexity

The term "model capacity/complexity" refers to the level of variation that the model can work with. The higher the capacity, the more variation the model can cope with. The first model y_1 is said to be of a small capacity compared to y_4. In our case, the capacity increases by increasing the polynomial degree.

For sure, the higher the degree of the polynomial equation, the better fit it will be for the data. But remember that increasing the polynomial degree increases the complexity of the model. Using a model with a capacity higher than required may lead to overfitting. The model becomes very complex and fits the training data very well but unfortunately is very weak for unseen data. The goal of ML is creating a model that is robust not only with the training data but also with unseen data samples.

The model of the fourth degree (y_4) is very complex. Yes, it fits the seen data well but it will not do so for unseen data. For this case, the newly used feature in y_4, namely x^4, captures more details than required. Because that new feature makes the model too complex, we should get rid of it.

In this example, we actually know which features to remove. So, we can remove them and return back to the previous model of the third degree ($\Theta_4 x^4 + \Theta_3 x^3 + \Theta_2 x^2 + \Theta_1 x + \Theta_0$). But in actual work, we do not know which features to remove. Moreover, assume that the new feature is not too bad and we do not want to completely remove it and just want to penalize it. What should we do?

Looking back at the loss function, the only goal is to minimize/penalize the prediction error. We can set a new objective to minimize/penalize the effect of the new feature x^4 as much as possible. After modifying the loss function to penalize x^3, the new one is in Equation 2-18.

$$L_{new} = \frac{\left[\sum_{i=0}^{N} \left| f_4(x_i) - d_i \right| + \Theta_4 x^4 \right]}{N}$$

(Equation 2-18)

Our objective now is to minimize the loss function. We are now just interested in minimizing this term $\Theta_4 x^4$. It is obvious that to minimize $\Theta_4 x^4$ we should minimize Θ_4, as it is the only free parameter we can change. We can set its value to a value equal to zero if we want to remove that feature completely in case it is a very bad one, as in Equation 2-19.

$$L_{new} = \frac{\left[\sum_{i=0}^{N} \left| f_4(x_i) - d_i \right| + 0 * x^4 \right]}{N}$$

(Equation 2-19)

By removing it, we go back to the third-degree polynomial equation (y_3). y_3 does not fit the seen data perfectly as in y_4, but generally, it will give better performance for unseen data than y_4 would.

But in case x^4 is a relatively good feature and we just want to penalize it rather than removing it completely, we can set it to a value close to but not zero (say 0.1), as in Equation 2-20. By doing that, we limit the effect of x^4. As a result, the new model will not be as complex as before.

$$L_{new} = \frac{\left[\sum_{i=0}^{N} \left| f_4(x_i) - d_i \right| + 0.1 * x^4 \right]}{N} \qquad \text{(Equation 2-20)}$$

Going back to y_2, it seems that it is simpler than y_3. It can work well with both seen and unseen data samples. So, we should remove the new feature used in y_3, which is x^3, or just penalize it if it does relatively well. We can modify the loss function to do that, as in Equation 2-21.

$$L_{new} = \frac{\left[\sum_{i=0}^{N} \left| f_4(x_i) - d_i \right| + 0.1 * x^4 + \Theta_3 x^3 \right]}{N}$$

$$L_{new} = \frac{\left[\sum_{i=0}^{N} \left| f_4(x_i) - d_i \right| + 0.1 * x^4 + 0.04 * x^3 \right]}{N} \qquad \text{(Equation 2-21)}$$

L1 Regularization

Note that we actually knew that y_2 is the best model to fit the data because the data graph is available for us. It is a very simple task that we can solve manually. But if such information is not available to us and as the number of samples and data complexity increase, we will not be able to reach such conclusions easily. There must be something automatic to tell us which degree will fit the data and tell us which features to penalize to get the best predictions for unseen data. This is regularization.

Regularization helps us to select the model complexity to fit the data. It is useful to automatically penalize features that make the model too complex. Remember that regularization is useful if the features are not bad and will help us to get good predictions in a relative sense; we just need to penalize but not remove them completely. Regularization penalizes all used features, not a selected subset. Previously, we penalized just two features, x^4 and x^3, not all features. But this is not the case with regularization.

Using regularization, a new term is added to the loss function to penalize the features, so the loss function will be as in Equation 2-22.

$$L_{new} = \frac{\left[\sum_{i=0}^{N} \left| f_4(x_i) - d_i \right| + \sum_{j=1}^{N} \lambda \Theta_j \right]}{N}$$

(Equation 2-22)

It can also be written as in Equation 2-23 after moving Λ outside the summation.

$$L_{new} = \frac{\left[\sum_{i=0}^{N} \left| f_4(x_i) - d_i \right| + \lambda \sum_{j=1}^{N} \Theta_j \right]}{N}$$

(Equation 2-23)

The newly added term $\lambda \sum_{j=1}^{N} \Theta_j$ is used to penalize the features to control the level of model complexity. Our previous goal before adding the regularization term is to minimize the prediction error as much as possible. Now our goal is to minimize the error but to be careful of making the model too complex and to avoid overfitting.

There is a regularization parameter called lambda (λ) that controls how to penalize the features. It is a hyperparameter with no fixed value. Its value is variable based on the task at hand. As its value increases, there will be higher penalization for the features. As a result, the model becomes simpler. When its value decreases, there will be lower penalization of the features and thus the model complexity increases. A value of zero means no removal of features at all.

When λ is zero, then the values of Θ_j will not be penalized at all, as shown in the next equation. This is because setting λ to zero means the removal of the regularization term and just leaving the error term. So, our objective will return back to just minimize the error to be close to zero. When error minimization is the objective, the model may overfit.

$$L_{new} = \frac{\left[\sum_{i=0}^{N} \left| f_4(x_i) - d_i \right| + 0 * \sum_{j=1}^{N} \Theta_j \right]}{N}$$

$$L_{new} = \frac{\left[\sum_{i=0}^{N} \left| f_4(x_i) - d_i \right| + 0 \right]}{N}$$

$$L_{new} = \frac{\sum_{i=0}^{N} \left| f_4(x_i) - d_i \right|}{N}$$

But when the value of the penalization parameter λ is very high (say 10^9), then there must be a very high penalization for the parameters Θ_j in order to keep the loss at its minimum value. As a result, the parameters Θ_j will be zeros. As a result, the model (y_4) will have its Θ_i pruned as shown in the following.

$$y_4 = f_4(x) = \Theta_4 x^4 + \Theta_3 x^3 + \Theta_2 x^2 + \Theta_1 x + \Theta_0$$

$$y_4 = 0 * x^4 + 0 * x^3 + 0 * x^2 + 0 * x + \Theta_0$$

$$y_4 = \Theta_0$$

Please note that the regularization term starts its index j from 1 not zero. Actually, we use the regularization term to penalize features (x_i). Because Θ_0 has no associated feature, there is no reason to penalize it. In this case, the model will be $y_4 = \Theta_0$ with the graph shown in Figure 2-23.

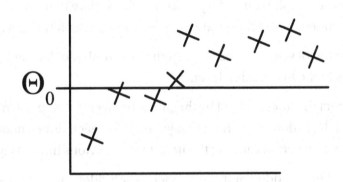

Figure 2-23. *Model parallel to the x axis after penalizing all features*

Designing ANN

Beginners in ANNs are likely to ask some questions, including the following: What is the correct number of hidden layers to use? How many hidden neurons are in each hidden layer? What is the purpose of using hidden layers/neurons? Does increasing the number of hidden layers/neurons always give better results? I am pleased to say that we can answer these questions. To be clear, answering such questions might be too complex if the problem being solved is complicated. By the end of this section, you might at least get an idea of how these questions can be answered and be able to test yourself based on simple examples. Let's start.

ANN is inspired by the biological neural network. For simplicity, in computer science, it is represented as a set of layers. These layers are categorized into three classes: input, hidden, and output.

Knowing the number of input and output layers and the number of their neurons is the easiest part. Every network has single input and output layers. The number of neurons in the input layer equals the number of input variables in the data being processed. The number of neurons in the output layer equals the number of outputs associated with each input. But the challenge is knowing the number of hidden layers and their neurons.

Here are some guidelines to learning the number of hidden layers and neurons in each hidden layer in a classification problem:

- Based on the data, draw an expected decision boundary to separate the classes.

- Express the decision boundary as a set of lines. Note that the combination of these lines must yield to the decision boundary.

- The number of selected lines represents the number of hidden neurons in the first hidden layer.

- To connect the lines created by the previous layer, a new hidden layer is added. Note that a new hidden layer is added each time you need to create connections among the lines in the previous hidden layer.

- The number of hidden neurons in each new hidden layer equals the number of connections to be made.

To make things clearer, let's apply the previous guidelines to a couple of examples.

Example 1: ANN Without Hidden Layer

Let's start with a simple example of a classification problem with two classes, as shown in Figure 2-24. Each sample has two inputs and one output that represents the class label. It is quite similar to the XOR problem.

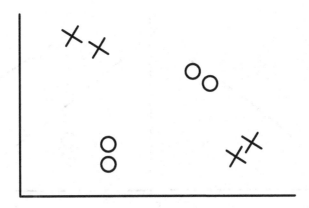

Figure 2-24. *Two-class classification problem*

The first question to answer is whether hidden layers are required or not. A rule to follow in order to determine this is as follows:

> **In ANNs, hidden layers are required if and only if the data must be separated nonlinearly.**

Looking at Figure 2-25, it seems that the classes must be nonlinearly separated. A single line will not work. As a result, we must use hidden layers in order to get the best decision boundary. In this case, we may still not use hidden layers, but this will affect the classification accuracy. So, it is better to use hidden layers.

Knowing that we need hidden layers then requires us to answer two important questions. These questions are as follows:

1. What is the required number of hidden layers?

2. What is the number of the hidden neurons across each hidden layer?

Following the previous procedure, the first step is to draw a decision boundary that splits the two classes. There is more than one possible decision boundary that splits the data correctly, as shown in Figure 2-25. The one we will use for further discussion is in Figure 2-25(a).

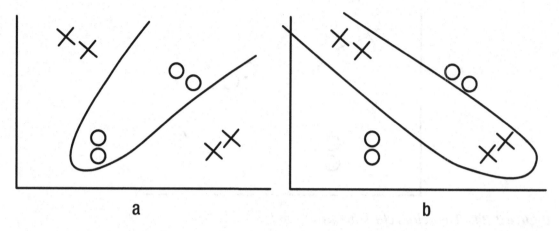

Figure 2-25. *Nonlinear classification problem cannot be solved using a single line*

Following the guidelines, the next step is to express the decision boundary by a set of lines.

The idea of representing the decision boundary using a set of lines comes from the fact that any ANN is built using the single layer perceptron as a building block. The single layer perceptron is a linear classifier that separates the classes using a line created according to Equation 2-24.

$$y = w_1x_1 + w_2x_2 + \dots + w_ix_i + b \qquad \text{(Equation 2-24)}$$

Where x_i is the ith input, w_i is its weight, b is the bias, and y is the output. Because each hidden neuron added will increase the number of weights, it is recommended to use the lowest number of hidden neurons that accomplishes the task. Using more hidden neurons than required will add more complexity.

Returning back to our example, saying that the ANN is built using multiple perceptron networks is identical to saying that the network is built using multiple lines.

In this example, the decision boundary is replaced by a set of lines. The lines start from the points at which the boundary curve changes direction. At this point, two lines are placed, each in a different direction.

Because there is just one point at which the boundary curve changes direction, as shown in Figure 2-26 by a gray circle, then there will be just two lines required. In other words, there are two single layer perceptron networks. Each perceptron produces a line.

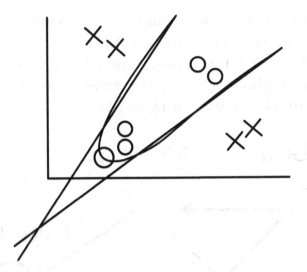

Figure 2-26. *Two lines required to classify the problem*

Knowing that there are just two lines required to represent the decision boundary tells us that the first hidden layer will have two hidden neurons.

Up to this point, we have a single hidden layer with two hidden neurons. Each hidden neuron could be regarded as a linear classifier that is represented as a line, as in Figure 2-26. There will be two outputs, one from each classifier (i.e., hidden neuron). But we are to build a single classifier with one output representing the class label, not two classifiers. As a result, the outputs of the two hidden neurons are to be merged into a single output. In other words, the two lines are to be connected by another neuron. The result is shown in Figure 2-27.

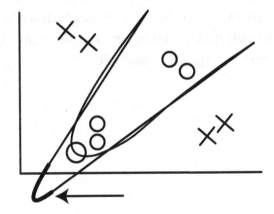

Figure 2-27. *Two lines connected to each other using a hidden neuron*

Fortunately, we do not need to add another hidden layer with a single neuron to do that job. The output layer neuron will do the task. This neuron will merge the two lines generated previously so that there is only one output from the network.

After learning the number of hidden layers and their neurons, the network architecture is now complete, as shown in Figure 2-28.

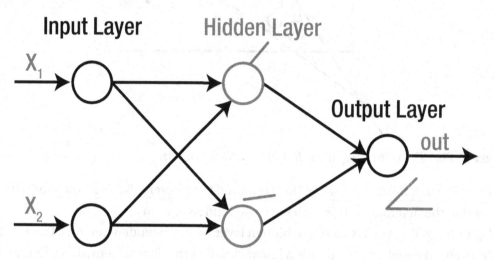

Figure 2-28. *Network structure for a classification problem with a curve created by connecting two lines, each one created using a hidden layer neuron*

Example 2: ANN with a Single Hidden Layer

Another classification example is shown in Figure 2-29. It is similar to the previous example, in which there are two classes where each sample has two inputs and one output. The difference is in the decision boundary. The boundary in this example is more complex than the one in the previous example.

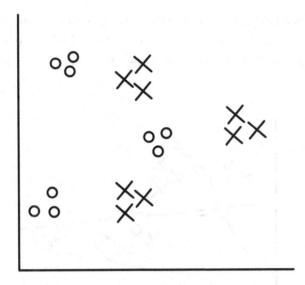

Figure 2-29. *A more complex classification problem to find the best network architecture*

According to the guidelines, the first step is to draw the decision boundary. The decision boundary to be used in our discussion is shown in Figure 2-30(a).

The next step is to split the decision boundary into a set of lines; each line will be modeled as a perceptron in the ANN. Before drawing lines, the points at which the boundary change direction should be marked as shown in Figure 2-30(b).

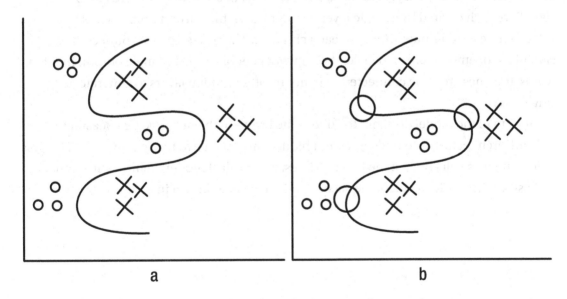

a   b

Figure 2-30. *Decision boundary to classify the second example*

The question is how many lines are required. Each of the top and bottom points will have two lines associated with them, for a total of four lines. The in-between point will have its two lines shared from the other points. The lines to be created are shown in Figure 2-31.

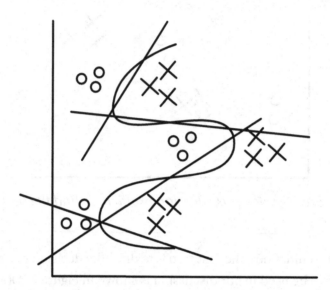

Figure 2-31. *Lines required to create the decision boundary of the second example*

Because the first hidden layer will have hidden layer neurons equal to the number of lines, the first hidden layer will have four neurons. In other words, there are four classifiers each created by a single layer perceptron. At the current time, the network will generate four outputs, one from each classifier. The next step is to connect these classifiers together in order to make the network generating just a single output. In other words, the lines are to be connected together by other hidden layers to generate just a single curve.

It is up to the model designer to choose the layout of the network. One feasible network architecture is to build a second hidden layer with two hidden neurons. The first hidden neuron will connect the first two lines, and the last hidden neuron will connect the last two lines. The result of the second hidden layer is shown in Figure 2-32.

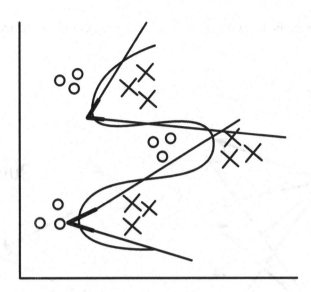

Figure 2-32. *Connecting lines to create a single decision boundary*

Up to this point, there have been two separated curves. Thus, there are two outputs from the network. The next step is to connect these curves together in order to have just a single output from the entire network. In this case, the output layer neuron could be used to do the final connection rather than adding a new hidden layer. The final result is shown in Figure 2-33.

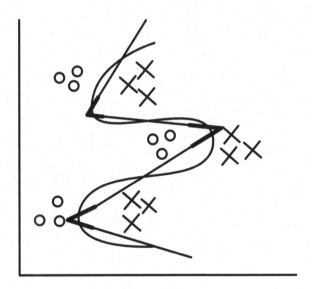

Figure 2-33. *Connecting the outputs of the hidden layer using the output layer*

The network design is now complete, and the complete network architecture is shown in Figure 2-34.

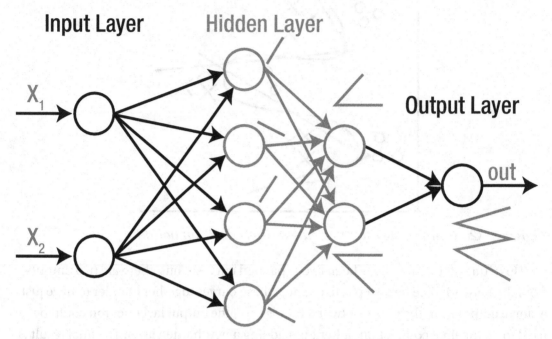

Figure 2-34. *The network architecture to classify the second example*

CHAPTER 3

Recognition Using ANN with Engineered Features

The three pillars for a successful ML application are the data, features, and model. They should cope with each other. The most relevant features that differentiate among the different cases existing in the data are used. Representative features are critical in building an accurate ML application. They should be accurate enough to work well under different conditions such as a change in scale and rotation. Such features should work well with the selected ML model. You shouldn't use more features than needed, because this adds more complexity to the model. Feature selection and reduction techniques are used to find the minimum set of features to build an accurate model.

This chapter explores the feature categories presented in Chapter 2 to find the suitable set of hand-engineered features for the Fruits 360 dataset. Feature reduction is applied to minimize the feature vector length and just use the most relevant features. ANN is implemented to map the image features to their output labels. By the end of the chapter, we will recognize how it is complex to manually find features for complex problems with multiple variations among samples even within the same class.

Fruits 360 Dataset Feature Mining

The Fruits 360 dataset is used to find a suitable set of features to train the ANN in order to achieve high classification performance. It is a high-quality dataset of images collected from 60 fruits including apple, guava, avocado, banana, cherry, date, kiwi, peach, and more. On average, each fruit has around 491 training and 162 test images for a total of 28,736 for training and 9,673 for testing. The size of each image is 100×100 pixels. Working with a dataset in which all images are of equal size saves one preprocessing step of resizing them.

© Ahmed Fawzy Gad 2018
A. F. Gad, *Practical Computer Vision Applications Using Deep Learning with CNNs*,
https://doi.org/10.1007/978-1-4842-4167-7_3

Feature Mining

For making things simple at the beginning, just four classes are selected: Braeburn apple, Meyer lemon, mango, and raspberry. Based on the feature categories presented in Chapter 2 (color, texture, and edge), we need to find the most suitable set of features to differentiate these classes.

Based on our knowledge about these four fruits, we know that they have different colors. Apple is red, lemon is orange, mango is green, and raspberry is magenta. As a result, the color category is the first one that comes to our minds.

We can start by using each pixel as input to the ANN. Each image size is 100×100 pixels. Because the image is color, then there are three existing channels based on the RGB color space: red, green, and blue. Thus, the total number of inputs to the ANN is 100×100×3=30,000. Based on these inputs, an ANN is to be created.

Also, these inputs will make the ANN huge, with a large number of parameters. The network will have 30,000 inputs and 4 outputs. Assuming there is a single hidden layer of 10,000 neurons, then the total number of parameters in the network is 30,000×10,000+10,000×4, which is more than 300 million parameters. Optimizing such a network is complex. We should find a way to reduce this number of input features in order to reduce the number of parameters.

One way is by using a single channel rather than using all three RGB channels. The selected channel should be able to capture the color changes among the used classes. The three channels for each image in addition to their histograms are available in Figure 3-1. A histogram helps us to visualize the intensity values easier than looking at the image would.

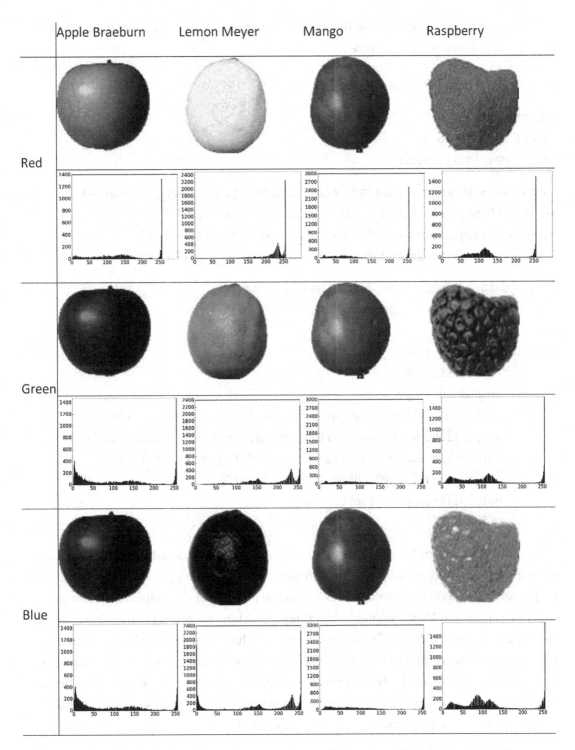

Figure 3-1. *Red, green, and blue channels in addition to their histograms for a single sample from the four classes of the Fruits 360 dataset used*

The Python code used to read the images, along with creating and visualizing their histogram, is available in Listing 3-1.

Listing 3-1. RGB Channel Histogram

```
import numpy
import skimage.io
import matplotlib.pyplot

raspberry = skimage.io.imread(fname="raspberry.jpg", as_grey=False)
apple = skimage.io.imread(fname="apple.jpg", as_grey=False)
mango = skimage.io.imread(fname="mango.jpg", as_grey=False)
lemon = skimage.io.imread(fname="lemon.jpg", as_grey=False)

fruits_data = [apple, raspberry, mango, lemon]
fruits = ["apple", "raspberry", "mango", "lemon"]
idx = 0
for fruit_data in fruits_data:
    fruit = fruits[idx]
    for ch_num in range(3):
        hist = numpy.histogram(a=fruit_data[:, :, ch_num], bins=256)
        matplotlib.pyplot.bar(left=numpy.arange(256), height=hist[0])
        matplotlib.pyplot.savefig(fruit+"-histogram-channel-"+
        str(ch_num)+".jpg", bbox_inches="tight")
        matplotlib.pyplot.close("all")
    idx = idx + 1
```

It seems that it is difficult to find the best channel to use. According to the histogram for any channel, there is overlap in some regions across the images. The only metric to differentiate the different images in such a case is the intensity values. For example, Braeburn apple and Meyer lemon have values for all bins according to the blue channel histogram, but their values differ. Apple has small values compared to lemon in the rightmost part. According to illumination changes, the intensity values will change and we might have a case in which both apple and lemon have close values to each other in the histogram. We should add a margin between the different classes. Even with little changes, there is no ambiguity in making the decision.

We can benefit from the fact that the four fruits used have different colors. A color space that decouples illumination channels from color channels is a good option. Figure 3-2 shows the hue channel from the HSV color space from the four samples used previously in addition to their histograms.

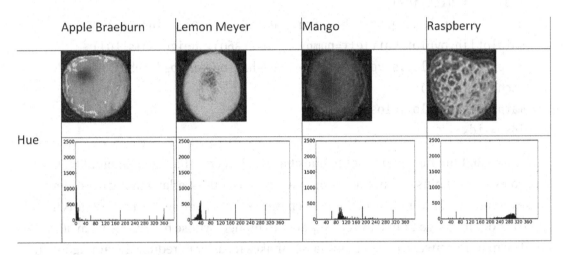

Figure 3-2. *Hue channel from the HSV color space with its histograms*

The Python code used to return the histogram of the hue channel of all samples is in Listing 3-2.

Listing 3-2. Hue Channel Histograms

```python
import numpy
import skimage.io, skimage.color
import matplotlib.pyplot

raspberry = skimage.io.imread(fname="raspberry.jpg", as_grey=False)
apple = skimage.io.imread(fname="apple.jpg", as_grey=False)
mango = skimage.io.imread(fname="mango.jpg", as_grey=False)
lemon = skimage.io.imread(fname="lemon.jpg", as_grey=False)

apple_hsv = skimage.color.rgb2hsv(rgb=apple)
mango_hsv = skimage.color.rgb2hsv(rgb=mango)
raspberry_hsv = skimage.color.rgb2hsv(rgb=raspberry)
lemon_hsv = skimage.color.rgb2hsv(rgb=lemon)
```

```
fruits = ["apple", "raspberry", "mango", "lemon"]
hsv_fruits_data = [apple_hsv, raspberry_hsv, mango_hsv, lemon_hsv]
idx = 0
for hsv_fruit_data in hsv_fruits_data:
    fruit = fruits[idx]
    hist = numpy.histogram(a=hsv_fruit_data[:, :, 0], bins=360)
    matplotlib.pyplot.bar(left=numpy.arange(360), height=hist[0])
    matplotlib.pyplot.savefig(fruit+"-hue-histogram.jpg", bbox_
    inches="tight")
    matplotlib.pyplot.close("all")
    idx = idx + 1
```

Using a 360-bin histogram for the hue channel, it seems that each different type of fruit votes specific bins within the histogram. There is little overlap among the different classes compared to using any of the RGB channels. For example, the highest bins in the apple histogram range from 0 to 10 compared to mango, whose bins range from 90 to 110. The margin between each of the classes makes it easier to reduce the ambiguity in classification and thus increases the prediction accuracy.

Based on the previous simple experiments on the four classes selected, the hue channel histogram can classify the data correctly. The umber of features, in this case, is just 360 rather than 30,000. This helps very much to reduce the number of ANN parameters.

A feature vector of 360 elements is small compared to the previous one, but we can also minimize it. However, some elements in the feature vector might not be representative enough to separate between the different classes. They might reduce the accuracy of the classification model. Thus, it is better to remove them to keep the best set of features.

This is not the end. If we are to add more classes, is the hue channel histogram enough for accurate classification? Let's see how things work after using an additional two fruits (strawberry and mandarin).

Based on our knowledge about these two fruits, strawberry is red, which is similar to apple, while mandarin is orange, which is similar to Meyer lemon. Figure 3-3 shows the hue channel of the selected samples from these classes in addition to their histogram.

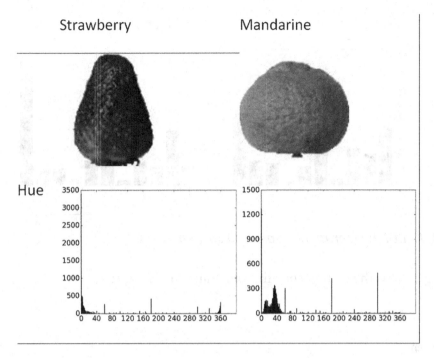

Figure 3-3. *Samples from new two classes that share some similarities among the previously used samples*

The histograms of both strawberry and apple are similar as they share the same bins ranging from 1 to 10. Also, both mandarin and lemon histograms are similar. How to differentiate among the different classes that share the same color? The answer is to search for another type of feature.

Fruits that are similar in color likely have different textures. Using a texture descriptor such as GLCM or LBP, we can capture these differences. The previous process is repeated until the best set of features that can increase the classification accuracy as much as possible is selected.

LBP produces a matrix with a size equal to that of the input image. To avoid increasing the feature vector length, a 10-bin histogram is created based on the LBP matrix as in Figure 3-4. It seems that there is a difference in the bin values.

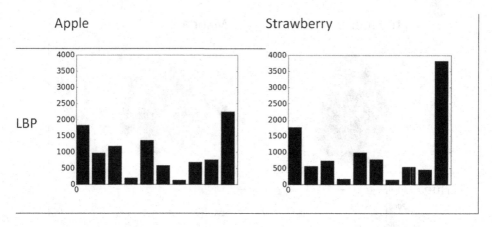

Figure 3-4. *LBP histogram of apple and strawberry*

Listing 3-3 lists the Python code that generates the LBP histogram.

Listing 3-3. LBP Histogram

```
import numpy
import skimage.io, skimage.color, skimage.feature
import matplotlib.pyplot

apple = skimage.io.imread(fname="apple.jpg", as_grey=True)
strawberry = skimage.io.imread(fname="strawberry.jpg", as_grey=True)

fig, ax = matplotlib.pyplot.subplots(nrows=1, ncols=2)
apple_lbp = skimage.feature.local_binary_pattern(image=apple, P=7, R=1)
hist1 = numpy.histogram(a=apple_lbp, bins=10)
ax[0].bar(left=numpy.arange(10), height=hist1[0])

strawberry_lbp = skimage.feature.local_binary_pattern(image=strawberry,
P=7, R=1)
hist = numpy.histogram(a=strawberry_lbp, bins=10)
ax[1].bar(left=numpy.arange(10), height=hist[0])
```

The data scientist has to search for the best type of discriminating feature, which is not easily accomplished when the complexity increases due to the number of overlapping classes. Even with the simple high-quality Fruits 360 dataset, there is the challenge of discriminating between different classes. Working with a dataset such as ImageNet, with thousands of classes with a difference between samples within the same class, finding the best features is a complex task to be done manually. Automatic approaches are preferred for cases in which there is plenty of data.

Feature Reduction

This subsection will work on the feature vector consisting of the hue channel histogram based on the first four fruits. Looking at the histograms in Figure 3-2, it is obvious that there are too many bins with almost zero value. This means they are not used by any class. It is better to remove such elements, as this helps to reduce the feature vector length.

According to the feature reduction techniques presented in Chapter 2, wrapper and embedded categories are used when it is difficult to know what element to remove. For example, some elements might be doing well with some classes but very badly with others. Thus, we have to remove them. Wrapper and embedded approaches depend on a model to train with multiple feature sets in order to know what elements help to increase the classification accuracy. In our case, we do not have to use them. The reason is that some elements are bad across all classes, and thus it is obvious what we should remove. Thus, the filter approach is a good option.

In turn, STD is a good option for filtering elements. The good elements are those that have high values for STD. A sigh STD value means that the element is discriminative for the different classes. An element with a low STD value has almost identical values across all different classes. This means it is unable to differentiate between the different classes.

STD is calculated for a given element according to Equation 3-1.

$$STD = \sqrt{\frac{X - \hat{X}}{n - 1}} \qquad \text{(Equation 3-1)}$$

Where X is the element value for a given sample, $\hat{X}$ is the mean of the element across all samples in the dataset, and n is the number of samples.

Before deciding which element to remove, we have to extract the feature vector from all samples within the dataset. Listing 3-4 extracts the feature vector from each sample across the four fruits used.

Listing 3-4. Feature Vector Extraction from All Samples

```python
import numpy
import skimage.io, skimage.color, skimage.feature
import os
import pickle

fruits = ["apple", "raspberry", "mango", "lemon"]
#492+490+490+490=1,962
dataset_features = numpy.zeros(shape=(1962, 360))
outputs = numpy.zeros(shape=(1962))

idx = 0
class_label = 0
for fruit_dir in fruits:
    curr_dir = os.path.join(os.path.sep,'train', fruit_dir)
    all_imgs = os.listdir(os.getcwd()+curr_dir)
    for img_file in all_imgs:
        fruit_data = skimage.io.imread(fname=os.getcwd()+curr_dir+img_file,
        as_grey=False)
        fruit_data_hsv = skimage.color.rgb2hsv(rgb=fruit_data)
        hist = numpy.histogram(a=fruit_data_hsv[:, :, 0], bins=360)
        dataset_features[idx, :] = hist[0]
        outputs[idx] = class_label
        idx = idx + 1
    class_label = class_label + 1

with open("dataset_features.pkl", "wb") as f:
    pickle.dump("dataset_features.pkl", f)

with open("outputs.pkl", "wb") as f:
    pickle.dump(outputs, f)
```

The array named "dataset_features" holds all features. It is given a size of 1,962×360, where 360 is the number of histogram bins and 1,962 refers to the number of samples (492 apple + 490 for the other three fruits). The class labels are saved into the "outputs" array, where apple is given label 0, 1 for raspberry, 2 for mango, and 3 for lemon. At the end of the code, the features and the output labels are saved in order to reuse them later.

This code assumes that there are four folders named according to each fruit. It loops through these folders, reads all of their images, calculates the histogram, and returns it into the "dataset_features" variable. After that, we are ready to calculate the STD. The STD for all features is calculated according to this line:

```
features_STDs = numpy.std(a=dataset_features, axis=0)
```

This returns a vector of length 360, where an element in a given position refers to the STD of the element of the feature vector at that position. The distribution of the 360 STDs is in Figure 3-5.

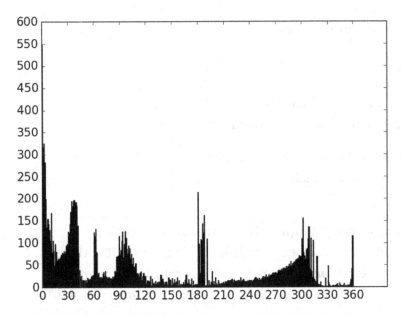

Figure 3-5. *Distribution of the STDs for all elements of the feature vector across all samples*

Based on this distribution, the minimum, maximum, and mean values for the STD are 0.53, 549.13, and 44.22, respectively. Features with small STD values should be removed because they cannot differentiate between the different classes. We have to select a threshold that splits the features into bad (below-threshold) and good (above-threshold) ones.

Filtering Using ANN

One way to select the threshold is trial and error. Try different values for the threshold. By the reduced feature vector returned by each threshold, train a classification model and notice the accuracy. Use the reduced feature vector that maximizes the accuracy.

Listing 3-5 gives the Python code to create and train an ANN using the scikit-learn library with a set of features generated by using a threshold.

Listing 3-5. Building ANN Using scikit-learn Trained with STD Thresholded Features

```
import sklearn.neural_network
import numpy
import pickle

with open("dataset_features.pkl", "rb") as f:
    dataset_features = pickle.load(f)

with open("outputs.pkl", "rb") as f:
    outputs = pickle.load(f)

threshold = 50
features_STDs = numpy.std(a=dataset_features, axis=0)
dataset_features2 = dataset_features[:, features_STDs>threshold]
ANN = sklearn.neural_network.MLPClassifier(hidden_layer_sizes=[150, 60],
                                           activation="relu",
                                           solver="sgd",
                                           learning_rate="adaptive",
                                           max_iter=300,
                                           shuffle=True)

ANN.fit(X=dataset_features2, y=outputs)
predictions = ANN.predict(X=dataset_features2)
num_flase_predictions = numpy.where(predictions != outputs)[0]
```

The features and the outputs are loaded in order to calculate their STDs and filter the features based on a predefined threshold. A multilayer perceptron classifier is created with two hidden layers, where the first hidden layer has 150 neurons and the second one has 60 neurons. Some properties of this classifier are specified: the activation function is set to the rectified linear unit (ReLU) function, the stochastic gradient descent (GD) is the learning algorithm, the learning rate is selected automatically by the learner, there are 300 maximum iterations to train the network, and finally the network is set to True in order to select different training samples in each iteration.

With a threshold of 50, the remaining features have the distribution in Figure 3-6. All low-quality elements are removed and thus the best set of elements is used. This reduces the amount of data used to train the network; thus, faster training. It also prevents bad feature elements from reducing the accuracy. When using all the elements in the feature vector, there are 490 false predictions. After thresholding, with the feature elements using an STD threshold of 50, the number of false predictions dropped to zero.

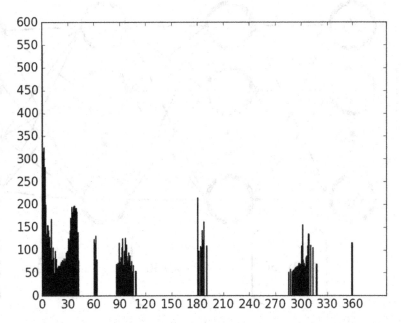

Figure 3-6. *Distribution of STDs after removing elements with STD lower than 50*

Reduction of the classification errors is not the only benefit; the ANN parameters are also reduced. After using only the feature elements with an STD of greater than 50, the number of remaining elements is just 102. According to the ANN structure in Listing 3-5, the number of parameters in the input layer and the first hidden layer will be 102×150= 15,300 compared to 54,000 parameters when the complete feature vector of length 360 is used. There is a reduction of 38,700 parameters.

119

ANN Implementation

This section implements an ANN in Python. The ANN is made to accept the network structure in terms of the number of neurons in each layer (input, hidden, and output), and then it trains the network in a number of iterations. For getting familiar with the steps of implementation, Figure 3-7 visualizes the ANN structure. There is an input layer with 102 inputs, two hidden layers with 150 and 60 neurons, and an output layer with 4 outputs (one for each fruit class).

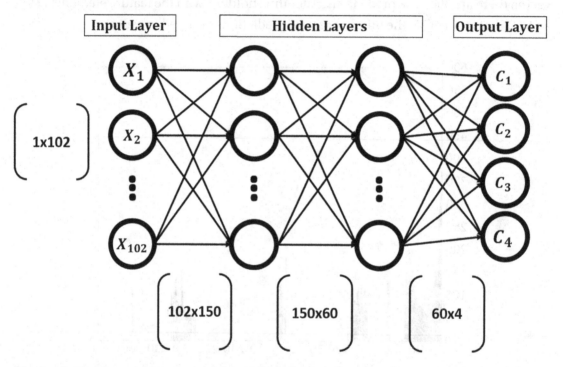

Figure 3-7. *The architecture of the ANN to be implemented*

The input vector at any layer is multiplied (matrix multiplication) by the weights matrix connecting it to the next layer to produce an output vector. The output vector is again multiplied by the weights matrix connecting its layer to the next layer. The process continues until reaching the output layer. A summary of the matrix multiplications is in Figure 3-8.

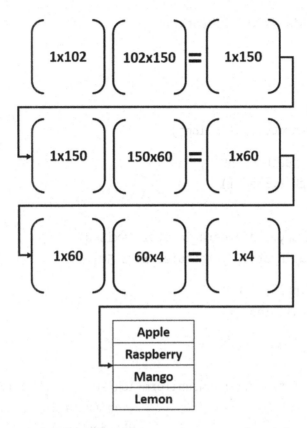

Figure 3-8. *Matrix multiplications between inputs and weights*

The input vector of size 1×102 is to be multiplied by the weights matrix of the first hidden layer of size 102×150. This is matrix multiplication. Thus, the output size is 1×150. The output is then used as the input to the second hidden layer, where it is multiplied by a weights matrix of size 150×60. The result size is 1×60. Finally, the output is multiplied by the weights between the second hidden layer and the output layer of size 60×4. The result has a final size of 1×4. Every element in the resulting vector refers to an output class. The input sample is labeled according to the class with the highest score.

The Python code for implementing such multiplications is in Listing 3-6.

Listing 3-6. ANN Matrix Multiplications

```
import numpy
import pickle

def sigmoid(inpt):
    return 1.0/(1+numpy.exp(-1*inpt))

f = open("dataset_features.pkl", "rb")
data_inputs2 = pickle.load(f)
f.close()

features_STDs = numpy.std(a=data_inputs2, axis=0)
data_inputs = data_inputs2[:, features_STDs>50]

f = open("outputs.pkl", "rb")
data_outputs = pickle.load(f)
f.close()

HL1_neurons = 150
input_HL1_weights = numpy.random.uniform(low=-0.1, high=0.1,
                                         size=(data_inputs.shape[1],
                                         HL1_neurons))
HL2_neurons = 60
HL1_HL2_weights = numpy.random.uniform(low=-0.1, high=0.1,
                                      size=(HL1_neurons, HL2_neurons))
output_neurons = 4
HL2_output_weights = numpy.random.uniform(low=-0.1, high=0.1,
                                         size=(HL2_neurons,
                                         output_neurons))

H1_outputs = numpy.matmul(a=data_inputs[0, :], b=input_HL1_weights)
H1_outputs = sigmoid(H1_outputs)
H2_outputs = numpy.matmul(a=H1_outputs, b=HL1_HL2_weights)
H2_outputs = sigmoid(H2_outputs)
out_outputs = numpy.matmul(a=H2_outputs, b=HL2_output_weights)

predicted_label = numpy.where(out_outputs == numpy.max(out_outputs))[0][0]
print("Predicted class : ", predicted_label)
```

After reading the previously saved features and their output labels and filtering the features with an STD threshold equal to 50, the weights matrices of the layers are defined. They are randomly given values from –0.1 to 0.1. For example, the variable "input_HL1_weights" holds the weights matrix between the input layer and the first hidden layer. The size of this matrix is defined according to the number of feature elements and the number of neurons in the hidden layer.

After creating the weights matrices, the next step is to apply matrix multiplications. For example, the variable "H1_outputs" holds the output of multiplying the feature vector of a given sample to the weights matrix between the input layer and the first hidden layer.

Usually, an activation function is applied to the outputs of each hidden layer to create a nonlinear relationship between the inputs and the outputs. For example, outputs of the matrix multiplications are applied to the sigmoid activation function as in Equation 3-2.

$$sigmoid(x) = \frac{1}{1 + e^{(-x)}} \qquad \text{(Equation 3-2)}$$

After generating the output layer outputs, prediction takes place. The predicted class label is saved into the "predicted_label" variable.

These steps are repeated for each input sample. The complete code that works across all samples is in Listing 3-7.

Listing 3-7. Complete Code for ANN

```
import numpy
import pickle

def sigmoid(inpt):
    return 1.0/(1+numpy.exp(-1*inpt))

def relu(inpt):
    result = inpt
    result[inpt<0] = 0
    return result

def update_weights(weights, learning_rate):
    new_weights = weights - learning_rate*weights
    return new_weights
```

```python
def train_network(num_iterations, weights, data_inputs, data_outputs,
learning_rate, activation="relu"):
    for iteration in range(num_iterations):
        print("Itreation ", iteration)
        for sample_idx in range(data_inputs.shape[0]):
            r1 = data_inputs[sample_idx, :]
            for idx in range(len(weights)-1):
                curr_weights = weights[idx]
                r1 = numpy.matmul(a=r1, b=curr_weights)
                if activation == "relu":
                    r1 = relu(r1)
                elif activation == "sigmoid":
                    r1 = sigmoid(r1)
            curr_weights = weights[-1]
            r1 = numpy.matmul(a=r1, b=curr_weights)
            predicted_label = numpy.where(r1 == numpy.max(r1))[0][0]
            desired_label = data_outputs[sample_idx]
            if predicted_label != desired_label:
                weights = update_weights(weights,
                                    learning_rate=0.001)
    return weights

def predict_outputs(weights, data_inputs, activation="relu"):
    predictions = numpy.zeros(shape=(data_inputs.shape[0]))
    for sample_idx in range(data_inputs.shape[0]):
        r1 = data_inputs[sample_idx, :]
        for curr_weights in weights:
            r1 = numpy.matmul(a=r1, b=curr_weights)
            if activation == "relu":
                r1 = relu(r1)
            elif activation == "sigmoid":
                r1 = sigmoid(r1)
        predicted_label = numpy.where(r1 == numpy.max(r1))[0][0]
        predictions[sample_idx] = predicted_label
    return predictions
```

```
f = open("dataset_features.pkl", "rb")
data_inputs2 = pickle.load(f)
f.close()
features_STDs = numpy.std(a=data_inputs2, axis=0)
data_inputs = data_inputs2[:, features_STDs>50]

f = open("outputs.pkl", "rb")
data_outputs = pickle.load(f)
f.close()

HL1_neurons = 150
input_HL1_weights = numpy.random.uniform(low=-0.1, high=0.1,
                                         size=(data_inputs.shape[1],
                                         HL1_neurons))
HL2_neurons = 60
HL1_HL2_weights = numpy.random.uniform(low=-0.1, high=0.1,
                                       size=(HL1_neurons, HL2_neurons))
output_neurons = 4
HL2_output_weights = numpy.random.uniform(low=-0.1, high=0.1,
                                          size=(HL2_neurons,
                                          output_neurons))

weights = numpy.array([input_HL1_weights,
                       HL1_HL2_weights,
                       HL2_output_weights])

weights = train_network(num_iterations=2,
                        weights=weights,
                        data_inputs=data_inputs,
                        data_outputs=data_outputs,
                        learning_rate=0.01,
                        activation="relu")

predictions = predict_outputs(weights, data_inputs)
num_flase = numpy.where(predictions != data_outputs)[0]
print("num_flase ", num_flase.size)
```

The "weights" variables hold all weights across the entire network. Based on the size of each weight matrix, the network structure is dynamically specified. For example, if the size of the "input_HL1_weights" variable is 102×80, then we can deduce that the first hidden layer has 80 neurons.

The "train_network" is the core function, as it trains the network by looping through all samples. For each sample, the steps discussed in Listing 3-6 are applied. It accepts the number of training iterations, features, output labels, weights, the learning rate, and the activation function. There are two options for the activation functions: either ReLU or sigmoid. ReLU is a thresholding function that returns the same input as long as it is greater than zero. Otherwise, it returns zero.

If the network made a false prediction for a given sample, then weights are updated using the "update_weights" function. No optimization algorithm is used to update the weights; they are simply updated according to the learning rate. The accuracy does not exceed 45%. The next chapter discusses using the GA optimization technique for this task, which increases the classification accuracy.

After the specified number of training iterations, the network is tested according to the training data to see if the network is working well on the training samples. If the accuracy is acceptable based on the training data, then we can test the model based on new unseen data.

Engineered Feature Limitations

Fruits 360 dataset images are captured in a restricted environment with many details available about each fruit. This makes mining the data for finding the best features much easier. Unfortunately, real-world applications are not easy that way. There are many variations among the samples within the same class, such as different viewing angles, perspective distortion, illumination changes, occlusion, and more. Creating a feature vector for such data is a complex task.

Figure 3-9 gives some samples from the MNIST (Modified National Institute of Standards and Technology) dataset for handwritten number recognition. It consists of 70,000 samples. The images are binary and thus color feature category is not applicable. Looking for another feature, it seems that there is no single feature able to work across the entire dataset. Thus, we have to use multiple features to cover all variations existing in the dataset. This will definitely create a huge feature vector.

Figure 3-9. *Samples from the CIFAR10 (Canadian Institute for Advanced Research) dataset*

Assuming that we are able to find a good feature, there is also another problem. A single-layer ANN resulted in a 12.0% error rate. Thus, we could increase the depth of the ANN. Unfortunately, large feature vectors used with deep ANN architectures are very tiresome to compute, but this is the way to work with complex problems.

The alternative approach is to avoid manual feature mining approaches. Start looking for an automatic feature mining that searches for the best set of features in terms of maximizing accuracy.

Not the End of Engineered Features

Engineered features are not legacy and can still do great with some problems. It is not a good option when working with some complex datasets.

Every data scientist would have used a calculator for doing mathematical calculations. After the invention and evolution of the mobile phone, smartphones with different applications for operations previously done on the calculator came out. Here is the question: does the appearance of a new technology (smartphones) mean that the previous technology (calculator) gets destroyed and will not be used anymore?

Calculators were dedicated just to mathematical operations, but smartphones are not. Smartphones have many features not existing in the calculator. Is the availability of many features rather than limited ones a disadvantage? In some cases, the fewer features in the tool, the better its performance; also, the more features, the more overhead. It is simple to do an operation using a calculator but there is overhead when doing the same operation with a smartphone.

The phone might ring for an incoming call, which breaks into whatever you were doing. It might be connected to the Internet and thus may also beep for an e-mail. This might take you away from doing the operations. As a result, one using a smartphone should care about all such effects in order to do the math operations nicely. Using calculators with limited features compared to smartphones has the advantage of being simple and focused on the task, even if it is an old technology. Indeed, the newest is not always the best. According to your needs, the old technology may be better or worse than a newer technology. The same holds from a data science perspective.

There are different types of learning algorithms and features to be used for different tasks, such as classification and regression. Some of them may go back to 1950 while others are recent. But we can't say that the old models are always worse than the recent ones. We can't absolutely conclude that DL models such as CNN are better than previous models. This depends on your needs.

Many researchers tend to use DL blindly just because it is the state-of-the-art method. Some problems are simple, and using DL may add more complexity. For example, using DL with just 100 images divided across 10 classes is not a good option. Shallow learning is sufficient in this case. If a classifier is to be created to discriminate among the four types of fruits used previously, DL is not mandatory and previous handcrafted/engineered features are sufficient.

If CNN is to be used in this case, some overhead is added that makes the task complex. There are different parameters to be specified, such as the types of layers, the number of layers, activation function, learning rate, and others. In comparison, using a hue channel histogram is sufficient for achieving a very high accuracy. It is like getting to the top of a wall using a ladder. If you reached the top of the wall after climbing five stairs, you do not need to go up another stair in the ladder. Similarly, if you can get the best results using hand-engineered features, you do not have to use automatic feature learning.

CHAPTER 4

ANN Optimization

Before the innovation of automatic feature learning approaches, a data scientist was asked to know what features to use, which model to use, how to optimize the result, and more. With the existence of huge amounts of data and high-speed devices, DL is available to automatically deduce the best features. Two of the core tasks of a data scientist are model design and optimization.

Model optimization is as important as building the model itself if not more. The previously created DL models that proved their accuracy could be reused and thus model design is solved. The remaining task is optimization. We are in the era of optimization, in which operation research (OR) scientists play a critical role. The field of optimization is closely related to artificial intelligence.

Selection of the optimal parameters for ML tasks is challenging. Some results may be bad not because the data is noisy or the used learning algorithm is weak, but due to the bad selection of the parameter values. Ideally, optimization guarantees returning the best solution by looking at different solutions and selecting the best. The more metrics defining the solution goodness, the harder it is to find the best solution. This chapter gives an introduction to optimization and discusses a simple optimization technique called GA. Based on the examples given, it will become clear how to use it in both single- and multiobjective optimization problems (MOOPs) based on the concept of dominance. This algorithm is used with ANN to produce better weights, helping to increase the classification accuracy.

© Ahmed Fawzy Gad 2018
A. F. Gad, *Practical Computer Vision Applications Using Deep Learning with CNNs*,
https://doi.org/10.1007/978-1-4842-4167-7_4

Introduction to Optimization

Suppose that a data scientist has an image dataset divided into a number of classes and an image classifier is to be created. After the data scientist investigated the dataset, the K-nearest neighbor (KNN) seems to be a good option. To use the KNN algorithm, there is an important parameter to use, which is K, referring to the number of neighbors. Suppose that an initial value of 3 is selected.

The scientist starts the learning process of the KNN algorithm with the selected K=3. The trained model reached a classification accuracy of 85%. Is that percentage acceptable? In another way, can we get a better classification accuracy than what we currently reached? We cannot say that 85% is the best possible accuracy before conducting different experiments. But to do another experiment, we definitely must change something in the experiment, such as changing the K value used in the KNN algorithm. We cannot definitely say 3 is the best value to use in this experiment unless we try different values for K and notice how the classification accuracy varies. The question is how to find the best value for K that maximizes the classification performance. This is called hyperparameter optimization.

In optimization, we start with some kind of initial values for the variables used in the experiment. Because these values may not be the best ones, we have to change them until getting the best ones. In some cases, these values are generated by complex functions that we cannot solve manually easily. But it is very important to do optimization because a classifier may produce a bad classification accuracy. The reason might not be that the data is noisy or the used learning algorithm is weak, but that the selection of the parameters is bad. As a result, there are different optimization techniques suggested by OR researchers to do such work.

Single- vs. Multiobjective Optimization

One way to categorize optimization problems is based on whether it is a single- or multiobjective problem. Let's differentiate between them in this subsection.

Assume there is a book publisher that would like to maximize its profit from selling books. They are using Equation 4-1 to calculate their profit per day, where X represents the number of books and Y represents the profit. The question to ask yourself when optimizing something is what to change in order to make the results better.

$$Y = -(X-2)^3 + 3 \qquad \text{(Equation 4-1)}$$

We could backtrack to the preceding problem. In order to optimize the preceding problem, we want to reach the best values for the output variables. Here, we have just a single output variable, which is Y.

To get the best value for the output variable Y, what could we change in the problem in order to change the variable Y? In other words, what are the variables that Y depends on? Looking at Equation 4-1, there is only a single variable that Y depends on, which is the input variable X. By changing X we could change Y to a better value. As a result, the previous question could be adapted to this specific problem to be as follows: what is the best value for the input variable X that returns the best value for the output variable Y?

Assume that the range of the input variable X is 1 to 3, inclusive. Which value gives the highest profit? If there is no information to direct us toward the best solution, we have to try all possible solutions (i.e., all possible values of the input variable X) and select the one that maximizes the profit (i.e., the solution corresponding to the largest value for the output variable Y). Table 4-1 shows all possible X values and their corresponding Y values. Based on it, the best solution is Y=4, which corresponds to X=1.

Table 4-1. *All Possible Solutions to a Single-Variable Problem*

X	Y
1	4
2	3
3	2

Let us make the problem a bit complex. Assume that the problem has another factor to use in profit calculation, which is the number of visitors to its online site. It is represented as the variable Z, with a range of values from 1 to 2. The modification is in Equation 4-2. Following the previous procedure, we need to try all possible combinations of the inputs X and Z as in Table 4-2. The best solution corresponds to X=2 and Z=2.

$$Y = Z^3 - (X - 2)^3 + 3 \qquad \text{(Equation 4-2)}$$

Table 4-2. *All Possible Solutions*
to the Problem with Two Input
Variables

X	Z	Y
1	1	5
1	2	6
2	1	4
2	2	11
3	1	3
3	2	10

Sometimes the range of the input variable is unbounded and we cannot try all of its values. For example, the range of the inputs X and Z might be all real numbers. Following the previous procedure of trying all possible values, we will fail in that case. There must be something to guide us toward the best solution without trying all possible values for the inputs.

The previous optimization problem has only one objective, which is maximizing the profit. Another objective might be minimizing the wastepaper represented by Equation 4-3, where W represents the amount of wastepaper, with a range from 2 to 4 tons. As a result, the problem becomes a MOOP, as shown in Equation 4-4.

$$K = (X - 2)^2 + 1 \qquad \text{(Equation 4-3)}$$

$$\left. \begin{array}{l} Max\ Y \\ Min\ K \end{array} \right\}$$

Where

$$Y = Z^3 - (X - 2)^2 + 3 \qquad \text{(Equation 4-4)}$$
$$K = (X - 2)^2 + 1$$

Subject to

$$1 \le X \le 3 \quad \& \quad 1 \le Z \le 2$$

Our goal is not only maximizing the profit but also minimizing the amounts of wastepaper. This makes the problem more complex, because we have to keep in mind that the selected value for X should meet two objectives rather than one, especially when the two objectives are conflicting. This is because a value reducing the amounts of wastepaper might decrease the profit. There must be a trade-off between the objectives, as one solution might be better in one objective while worse in another. Note that for simplicity, maximization objectives are translated into minimization ones.

As the number of objectives and variables increases, the complexity also increases, and the problem becomes difficult to solve manually. That is why we are in need of automatic optimization techniques to solve such problems for us.

This chapter discusses the GA, which is a simple technique for solving single- and multiobjective optimization problems. Nondominated sorting GA-II (NSGA-II) is a multiobjective EA (MOEA) based on GA that finds feasible solutions satisfying multiple objectives. Because MOOPs might have multiple solutions, NSGA-II could return the possible feasible solutions for all objectives. Based on user preference, the best single solution could then be filtered.

Looking at various natural species, we can note how they evolve and adapt to their environments. We can benefit from these already existing natural systems and their natural evolution to create our artificial systems doing the same job. This is called bionics. For example, the plane is based on how birds fly, radar comes from bats, the submarine was invented based on fish, and so on. As a result, the principles of some optimization algorithms come from nature. For example, GA has its core idea from Charles Darwin's theory of natural evolution: "survival of the fittest."

We can say that optimization is performed using EAs. The difference between traditional algorithms and EAs is that EAs are not static but dynamic, as they can evolve over time.

EAs have three main characteristics:

1. Population-Based: EAs are to optimize a process in which current solutions are bad to generate new and better solutions. The set of current solutions from which new solutions are to be generated is called the population.

2. Fitness-Oriented: If there are several solutions, how can we say that one solution is better than another? There is a fitness value associated with each individual solution calculated from a fitness function. Such a fitness value reflects how good the solution is.

133

3. Variation-Driven: If there is no acceptable solution in the current population according to the fitness function calculated from each individual, we should make something to generate new better solutions. As a result, individual solutions will undergo a number of variations to generate new solutions.

We will now start discussing GA to apply these concepts.

GA

GA is a randomly based optimization technique. By "random," it is meant that in order to find a solution using GA, random changes are applied to the current solutions to generate new ones. GA is based on Darwin's theory of evolution. It is a slow, gradual process that works by making slight changes to its solutions until better ones are found. By evolving the solutions across a number of generations, it is expected that the new solutions will be better than the old ones.

GA works on a population consisting of multiple solutions. The population size is the number of solutions. Each solution is called individual. Each individual is represented as a chromosome. The chromosome is represented as a set of genes that defines the features or parameters of the individual. There are different ways to represent the genes, such as binary or decimal. Figure 4-1 gives an example of a population with four individuals (chromosomes) where each chromosome has four genes and each gene is represented as a binary digit.

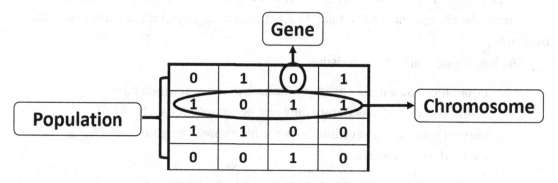

Figure 4-1. *Population, chromosome, and gene for the GA*

After building the population of the first generation (generation 0), next is to select the best solutions for mating and producing new better solutions. To select the best solutions, a fitness function is used. The result of the fitness function is the fitness value representing the quality of the solution. The higher the fitness value, the higher the quality of the solution. Solutions with the highest fitness values are selected within the mating pool. Such solutions will mate to produce new solutions.

Solutions inside the mating pool are called parents. Parents mate together for generating offspring (children). Just by mating high-quality individuals, it is expected to get offspring of better quality than its parents. This stops bad individuals from generating more bad individuals. Keeping selecting and mating high-quality individuals, there is a higher chance to enhance the quality of the solutions by just keeping the good properties and removing the bad ones. Finally, this will end up with the desired optimal or acceptable solution.

When the parents are simply mated, the offspring have only the characteristics of the parents; no new property is added. Assuming that all parents suffer from a limitation, mating them together will definitely produce offspring with the same limitation. To overcome this problem, some changes are applied to each offspring to create new individuals with new properties. The new offspring will be the solutions in the population of the next generation.

Because changes applied to the offspring are random, we are not sure that the new offspring will be better than the parents. There is a chance that the solutions within the current generation are worse than those of their parents. For this reason, the new population will consist of both the parents and the offspring. Half of it is the parents and the other half is the new offspring. If the population size is eight, then the new population will consist of the previous four parents and four offspring. In the worst case, when all offspring are worse than the parents, the quality will not decrease, as we have kept the parents. Figure 4-1 summarizes the steps of GA.

There are two questions to be answered to get the full idea about GA:

1. How are the two offspring generated from the two parents?

2. How does each offspring get slightly changed?

We will answer these questions later.

There are different representations available for the chromosome, and the selection of the proper representation is problem specific. A good representation is one that makes the search space smaller and thus easier to search.

The representations available for the chromosome include the following:

- Binary: Each chromosome is represented as a string of zeros and ones.

- Permutation: Useful for ordering problems such as the traveling salesman problem.

- Value: The actual value is encoded as it is.

For example, if we are to encode the number 5 in binary, it might look like the first chromosome in Figure 4-2.

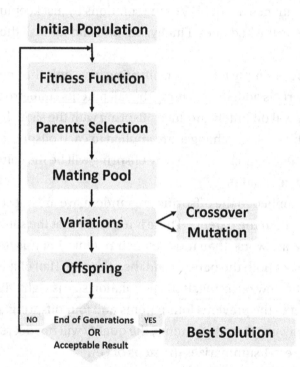

Figure 4-2. *GA steps*

Each part of the preceding chromosome is called a gene. Each gene has two properties. The first one is its value (allele) and the second one is the location (locus) within the chromosome. The rightmost location of each chromosome in Figure 4-1 represents location 0 and the leftmost location represents location 3.

Each chromosome has two representations:

1. Genotype: The set of genes representing the chromosome.

2. Phenotype: The actual physical representation of the chromosome.

The binary number 0101_2 is the genotype and 5_{10} is the phenotype representation. Binary representation might not be the best way to represent solutions for a given problem, especially when the number of bits to represent the genes is not fixed.

After representing each chromosome the right way, next is to calculate the fitness value of each individual.

Best-Parents Selection

Assume that Equation 4-5 is the fitness function used in our example in Figure 4-1, where x is the chromosome decimal value.

$$f(x) = 2x - 2 \qquad \text{(Equation 4-5)}$$

The fitness value of the first solution is with decimal value 5 and is calculated as follows:

$$f(5) = 2(5) - 2 = 8$$

The process of calculating the fitness value of a chromosome is called evaluation. The fitness values of all solutions are given in Table 4-3.

Table 4-3. *Fitness Value of Each Solution*

Solution Number	Decimal Value	Fitness Value
1	5	8
2	11	20
3	12	22
4	2	2

The best individuals from the current population are selected in the mating pool. After that step, we will end up selecting a subset of the population in the mating pool. But what is the number of parents to choose? It depends on the problem being solved.

In our example, we can select just two parents. These two parents will mate to produce two offspring. The combination of the parents and the offspring will create a new population of four parents. According to Table 4-3, the best two solutions are solutions with numbers 2 and 3.

Variation Operators

The two parents selected are applied to variation operators to produce the offspring. The operators are crossover and mutation.

Crossover

Using the crossover operation, genes from both parents are selected to create the new child. As a result, the child will carry properties from both parents. The amount of genes carried by each parent is not fixed. Sometimes the offspring takes half of its genes from one parent and the other half from the other parent, and sometimes these percentages change.

For every two parents, crossover takes place by selecting a random point in the chromosome and exchanging genes before and after this point from the two parents. The resulting chromosomes are offspring. Because we used a single point to split the chromosome, this operator is called single-point crossover. There are different types of operators, such as blend, two points, and uniform. Figure 4-3 shows how crossover is applied between the two parents to produce the two offspring.

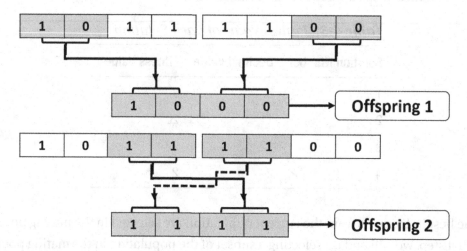

Figure 4-3. *Single-point crossover between two parents to produce two offspring*

Mutation

Based on the crossover operation, there is no new property added to the gene other than ones existing in the parents. This is because all genes are taken from the parents. Mutation is applied by selecting a percentage of genes from each chromosome and changing their values randomly. Mutation varies based on the chromosome representation. If binary encoding is used (i.e., the value spaces of each gene are just 0 and 1), then flip the bit value of each gene participating in the mutation operation. Other types of mutation include swap, inverse, uniform, nonuniform, Gaussian, and shrink.

The percentage of genes to which mutation is applied should be small because changes are random. We shouldn't take the risk of losing much of the existing information due to random changes that do not guarantee better results. For our problem, we can just select one gene for random flipping of its value. Figure 4-4 shows the result when the leftmost gene at location 0 is selected for mutation. Note that mutation is applied over the crossover result.

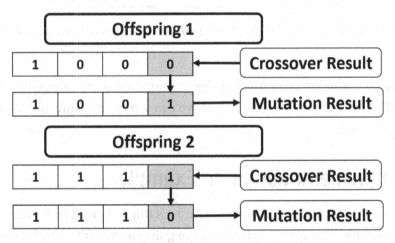

Figure 4-4. *Bit-flip mutation over the crossover result*

By applying crossover and mutation, the new offspring are completely prepared. We can measure whether they are better or worse than the parents based on the fitness value. The fitness values for the two offspring are 16 for the first offspring and 26 for the second one. Compared to the fitness values of the parents (20 and 22), one of the second offspring is better than all parents, and GA is able to evolve the solutions to produce a better one. But the first offspring with fitness value 16 is worse than all parents. Keeping the parents selected within the new populations ensures that such a bad solution will not be selected as a parent in the next generation. Thus, we are sure that the quality of solutions in the next generations will not be worse than the quality in the previous generations.

In some problems, the gene is not represented in binary, and thus mutation differs. If the gene value comes from a space of more than two values such as (1, 2, 3, 4, 5), then the bit-flip mutation is not applicable. One way is by randomly selecting a value from this set. Figure 4-5 gives an example of a solution represented by limited values for its genes (more than two values). The gene selected for mutation has its value changed to one of the other values randomly.

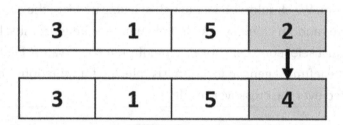

Figure 4-5. *Uniform mutation for a solution with more than two values for its genes*

Sometimes the solution is represented by an unlimited set of values. For example, if the range of values is between –1.0 and 1.0, we can select any value in that range to replace the old value.

Python Implementation of an Example

Now that we've looked at the concepts of GA, let's implement it in Python in order to optimize a simple example, in which we are going to maximize the output of Equation 4-6. This is the fitness function. Decimal representation, one-point crossover, and uniform mutation are used in the implementation.

$$Y = w_1x_1 + w_2x_2 + w_3x_3 + w_4x_4 + w_5x_5 + w_6x_6 \qquad \text{(Equation 4-6)}$$

The equation has six inputs (x_1 to x_6) and six weights (w_1 to w_6) as shown, and input values are (x_1,x_2,x_3,x_4,x_5,x_6)=(4,–2,7,5,11,1). We are looking to find the parameters (weights) that maximize this equation. The idea of maximizing this equation seems simple. The positive input is to be multiplied by the largest possible positive number and the negative number is to be multiplied by the smallest possible negative number. But the idea we are looking to implement is how to make GA do that on its own. GA should know itself that it is better to use positive weights with positive inputs and negative weights with negative inputs. Let's start implementing GA.

According to Listing 4-1, a list is created that holds the six inputs in addition to a variable that holds the number of weights.

Listing 4-1. Inputs of the Function to Optimize

```
# Inputs of the equation.
equation_inputs = [4,-2,3.5,5,-11,-4.7]
# Number of the weights we are looking to optimize.
num_weights = 6
```

The next step is to define the initial population. Based on the number of weights, each chromosome (solution or individual) in the population will definitely have six genes, one gene for each weight. But the question is, how many solutions are there per population? There is no fixed value for that, and we can select the value that fits well with our problem. But we could leave it generic so that it can be changed in the code. In Listing 4-2, a variable is created to hold the number of solutions per population, another to hold the size of the population, and finally, a variable to hold the actual initial population.

Listing 4-2. Creating the Initial Population

```
import numpy
sol_per_pop = 8
# Defining the population size.
pop_size = (sol_per_pop,num_weights) # The population will have sol_per_pop
chromosome where each chromosome has num_weights genes.
#Creating the initial population.
new_population = numpy.random.uniform(low=-4.0, high=4.0, size=pop_size)
```

After importing the numpy library, we are able to create the initial population randomly using the numpy.random.uniform function. According to the selected parameters, its shape is (8, 6). That is, there are eight chromosomes and each one has six genes, one for each weight. Table 4-4 presents the solutions of the population after running the previous code. Note that it is generated randomly by the code and thus it will definitely change when you run it.

Table 4-4. *Initial Population*

	W_1	W_2	W_3	W_4	W_5	W_6
Solution 1	−2.19	−2.89	2.02	−3.97	3.45	2.06
Solution 2	2.13	2.97	3.6	3.79	0.29	3.52
Solution 3	1.81	0.35	1.03	−0.33	3.53	2.54
Solution 4	−0.64	−2.86	2.93	−1.4	−1.2	0.31
Solution 5	−1.49	−1.54	1.12	−3.68	1.33	2.86
Solution 6	1.14	2.88	1.75	−3.46	0.96	2.99
Solution 7	1.97	0.51	0.53	−1.57	−2.36	2.3
Solution 8	3.01	−2.75	3.27	−0.72	0.75	0.01

After preparing the population, next is to follow the steps of GA as in Figure 4-2. Based on the fitness function, we are going to select the best individuals within the current population as parents for mating. Next is to apply the GA variants (crossover and mutation) to produce the offspring of the next generation, creating the new population by appending both parents and offspring, and repeating these steps for a number of iterations/generations. Listing 4-3 applies these steps.

Listing 4-3. Iterating Through GA Steps

```
import GA
num_generations = 10,000
num_parents_mating = 4
for generation in range(num_generations):
    # Measuring the fitness of each chromosome in the population.
    fitness = GA.cal_pop_fitness(equation_inputs, new_population)

    # Selecting the best parents in the population for mating.
    parents = GA.select_mating_pool(new_population, fitness,
                                    num_parents_mating)

    # Generating next generation using crossover.
    offspring_crossover = GA.crossover(parents,
                                offspring_size=(pop_size[0]-parents.
                                shape[0], num_weights))
```

```
# Adding some variations to the offspring using mutation.
offspring_mutation = GA.mutation(offspring_crossover)

# Creating the new population based on the parents and offspring.
new_population[0:parents.shape[0], :] = parents
new_population[parents.shape[0]:, :] = offspring_mutation
```

A module named "GA" holds the implementation of the functions used in Listing 4-3. The first function called, GA.cal_pop_fitness, finds the fitness value of each solution within the population. This function is defined inside the GA module according to Listing 4-4.

Listing 4-4. GA Fitness Function

```
def cal_pop_fitness(equation_inputs, pop):
    # Calculating the fitness value of each solution in the current
    population.
    # The fitness function calculates the SOP between each input and its
    corresponding weight.
    fitness = numpy.sum(pop*equation_inputs, axis=1)
    return fitness
```

The fitness function accepts the equation input values (x_1 to x_6) in addition to the population. The fitness value is calculated as the SOP between each input and its corresponding gene (weight) according to Equation 4-6. Based on the number of solutions per population, there will be an equal number of SOPs as in Table 4-5. Note that the higher the fitness value, the better the solution.

Table 4-5. *Fitness Values of the Initial Population Solutions*

	Solution1	Solution2	Solution3	Solution4	Solution5	Solution6	Solution7	Solution8
Fitness	63.41	14.40	−42.23	18.24	−45.44	−37.0	16.0	17.07

After calculating the fitness values for all solutions, the next step is to select the best of them as parents in the mating pool according to the GA.select_mating_pool function. This function accepts the population, fitness values, and the number of parents needed, and it returns the parents selected. Its implementation inside the GA module is in Listing 4-5.

Listing 4-5. Selecting the Best Parents According to Fitness Values

```
def select_mating_pool(pop, fitness, num_parents):
# Selecting the best individuals in the current generation as parents for
producing the offspring of the next generation.
    parents = numpy.empty((num_parents, pop.shape[1]))
    for parent_num in range(num_parents):
        max_fitness_idx = numpy.where(fitness == numpy.max(fitness))
        max_fitness_idx = max_fitness_idx[0][0]
        parents[parent_num, :] = pop[max_fitness_idx, :]
        fitness[max_fitness_idx] = -99999999999
    return parents
```

Based on the number of parents required as defined in the variable num_parents_ mating, the "parents" empty array is created to hold them. Inside the loop, the function iterates through the solutions in the current population to get the index of the solution with highest fitness value because it is the best solution to be selected. The index is stored into the "max_fitness_idx" variable. Based on this index, the solution that corresponds to it is returned to the "parents" array. To avoid selecting this solution again, its fitness value is set to –99999999999, which is a very small value. This value makes the solution unlikely to be selected again. After selecting the number of parents needed, the parents array is returned as in Table 4-6. Note that these three parents are the best individuals within the current population based on their fitness values, which are 63.41, 18.24, 17.07, and 16.0, respectively.

Table 4-6. *Selected Parents from the First Population*

	W_1	W_2	W_3	W_4	W_5	W_6
Parent 1	−0.64	−2.86	2.93	−1.4	−1.2	0.31
Parent 2	3.01	−2.75	3.27	−0.72	0.75	0.01
Parent 3	1.97	0.51	0.53	−1.57	−2.36	2.3
Parent 4	2.13	2.97	3.6	3.79	0.29	3.52

The next step is to use the selected parents for mating in order to generate the offspring. The mating starts with the crossover operation according to the GA.crossover function. This function accepts the parents and the offspring size. It uses the offspring size to learn the number of offspring to produce from the parents. This function is implemented according to Listing 4-6 inside the GA module.

Listing 4-6. Crossover

```
def crossover(parents, offspring_size):
    offspring = numpy.empty(offspring_size)
    # The point at which crossover takes place between two parents.
    Usually, it is at the center.
    crossover_point = numpy.uint8(offspring_size[1]/2)

    for k in range(offspring_size[0]):
        # Index of the first parent to mate.
        parent1_idx = k%parents.shape[0]
        # Index of the second parent to mate.
        parent2_idx = (k+1)%parents.shape[0]
        # The new offspring will have its first half of its genes taken
        from the first parent.
        offspring[k, 0:crossover_point] = parents[parent1_idx, 0:crossover_
        point]
        # The new offspring will have its second half of its genes taken
        from the second parent.
        offspring[k, crossover_point:] = parents[parent2_idx, crossover_
        point:]
    return offspring
```

Because we are using single-point crossover, we need to specify the point at which crossover takes place. The point is selected to divide the solution into two equal halves. Then we need to select the two parents to cross over. The indices of these parents are stored into parent1_idx and parent2_idx. The parents are selected in a way similar to a ring. Indices 0 and 1 are selected at first to produce two offspring. If there still remaining offspring to produce, then we select parents 1 and 2 to produce the other two offspring. If we are in need of more offspring, then we select the next two parents with indices 2 and 3. By index 3, we reach the last parent. If we need to produce more offspring, then we select the parent with index 3 and go back to the parent with index 0, and so on. The offspring after applying crossover are stored into the offspring variable. Table 4-7 shows the contents of this variable.

Table 4-7. *Offspring After Crossover*

	W_1	W_2	W_3	W_4	W_5	W_6
Offspring 1	−0.64	−2.86	2.93	−0.72	0.75	0.01
Offspring 2	3.01	−2.75	3.27	−1.57	−2.36	2.3
Offspring 3	1.97	0.51	0.53	3.79	0.29	3.52
Offspring 4	2.13	2.97	3.6	−1.4	−1.2	0.31

Next is to apply the second GA variant, mutation, to the results of the crossover using the mutation function inside the GA module implemented in Listing 4-7. This function accepts the crossover offspring and returns them after applying uniform mutation.

Listing 4-7. Mutation

```
def mutation(offspring_crossover):
# Mutation changes a single gene in each offspring randomly.
    for idx in range(offspring_crossover.shape[0]):
        # The random value to be added to the gene.
        random_value = numpy.random.uniform(-1.0, 1.0, 1)
        offspring_crossover[idx, 4] = offspring_crossover[idx, 4] + random_
        value
    return offspring_crossover
```

It loops through each offspring and adds a uniformly generated random number, say in the range from −1.0 to 1.0. This random number is then added to the gene with one randomly chosen index (e.g., index 4) of the offspring. Note that the index could be changed to any other index. Results are stored into the variable "offspring_crossover" and get returned by the function as in Table 4-8. At this point, we have successfully produced four offspring from the four selected parents and are ready to create the new population of the next generation.

Table 4-8. *The Results of Mutation*

	W_1	W_2	W_3	W_4	W_5	W_6
Offspring 1	−0.64	−2.86	2.93	−0.72	1.66	0.01
Offspring 2	3.01	−2.75	3.27	−1.57	−1.95	2.3
Offspring 3	1.97	0.51	0.53	3.79	0.45	3.52
Offspring 4	2.13	2.97	3.6	−1.4	−1.58	0.31

Note that GA is a randomly based optimization technique. It tries to enhance the current solutions by applying some random changes to them. Because these changes are random, we are not sure that they will produce better solutions. For this reason, it is preferred to keep the previous best solutions (parents) in the new population. In the worst case, when all the new offspring are worse than the parents, we will continue using these parents. As a result, we guarantee that the new generation will at least preserve the previous good results and will not get worse. The new population will have its first four solutions from the previous parents. The last four solutions come from the offspring created after applying crossover and mutation.

Table 4-9 presents the fitness of all solutions (parents and offspring) of the first generation. The highest fitness previously was 18.24112489 but now it is 31.7328971158. That means that the random changes moved toward a better solution. This is great. But these results could be enhanced by going through more generations. After going through 10,000 iterations, the result reached a value of more than 40,000 as in Figure 4-6.

Table 4-9. *Fitness Values of All Solutions in the New Population*

	Solution 1	Solution 2	Solution 3	Solution 4	Solution 5	Solution 6	Solution 7	Solution 8
Fitness	18.24	17.07	16.0	14.4	−8.46	31.73	6.1	24.09

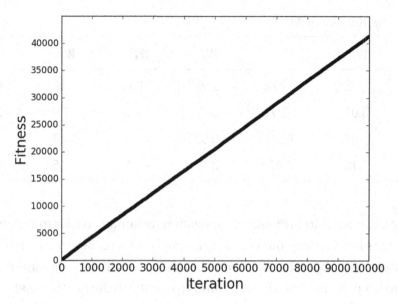

Figure 4-6. *Fitness values vs. 10,000 iterations*

Complete Implementation

The complete code that implements the GA is given in Listing 4-8.

Listing 4-8. The Complete Code for Optimizing a Linear Equation with Six Parameters

```
import numpy
import GA

#The y=target is to maximize this equation ASAP:
#    y = w1x1+w2x2+w3x3+w4x4+w5x5+6wx6
#    where (x1,x2,x3,x4,x5,x6)=(4,-2,3.5,5,-11,-4.7)
#    What are the best values for the 6 weights w1 to w6?
#    We are going to use the GA for the best possible values #after a
#    number of generations.

# Inputs of the equation.
equation_inputs = [4,-2,3.5,5,-11,-4.7]

# Number of the weights we are looking to optimize.
num_weights = 6
```

```
#GA parameters:
#    Mating pool size
#    Population size

sol_per_pop = 8
num_parents_mating = 4

# Defining the population size.
pop_size = (sol_per_pop,num_weights) # The population will have sol_per_pop
chromosome where each chromosome has num_weights genes.
#Creating the initial population.
new_population = numpy.random.uniform(low=-4.0, high=4.0, size=pop_size)
print(new_population)

num_generations = 10,000
for generation in range(num_generations):
    print("Generation : ", generation)
    # Measuring the fitness of each chromosome in the population.
    fitness = GA.cal_pop_fitness(equation_inputs, new_population)

# Selecting the best parents in the population for mating.
    parents = GA.select_mating_pool(new_population, fitness,
                                    num_parents_mating)

    # Generating next generation using crossover.
    offspring_crossover = GA.crossover(parents,
                                    offspring_size=(pop_size[0]-parents.
                                    shape[0], num_weights))

    # Adding some variations to the offspring using mutation.
    offspring_mutation = GA.mutation(offspring_crossover)

    # Creating the new population based on the parents and offspring.
    new_population[0:parents.shape[0], :] = parents
    new_population[parents.shape[0]:, :] = offspring_mutation

    # The best result in the current iteration.
    print("Best result : ", numpy.max(numpy.sum(new_population*equation_
    inputs, axis=1)))
```

```
# Getting the best solution after iterating finishing all generations.
#At first, the fitness is calculated for each solution in the final
generation.
fitness = GA.cal_pop_fitness(equation_inputs, new_population)
# Then return the index of that solution corresponding to the best fitness.
best_match_idx = numpy.where(fitness == numpy.max(fitness))

print("Best solution : ", new_population[best_match_idx, :])
print("Best solution fitness : ", fitness[best_match_idx])
```

The GA module implementation is in Listing 4-9.

Listing 4-9. GA Module

```
import numpy

def cal_pop_fitness(equation_inputs, pop):
# Calculating the fitness value of each solution in the current population.
    # The fitness function calcuates the SOP between each input and its
    corresponding weight.
    fitness = numpy.sum(pop*equation_inputs, axis=1)
    return fitness

def select_mating_pool(pop, fitness, num_parents):
    # Selecting the best individuals in the current generation as parents
    for producing the offspring of the next generation.
    parents = numpy.empty((num_parents, pop.shape[1]))
    for parent_num in range(num_parents):
        max_fitness_idx = numpy.where(fitness == numpy.max(fitness))
        max_fitness_idx = max_fitness_idx[0][0]
        parents[parent_num, :] = pop[max_fitness_idx, :]
        fitness[max_fitness_idx] = -99999999999
    return parents

def crossover(parents, offspring_size):
    offspring = numpy.empty(offspring_size)
    # The point at which crossover takes place between two parents. Usually
    it is at the center.
    crossover_point = numpy.uint8(offspring_size[1]/2)
```

```
for k in range(offspring_size[0]):
    # Index of the first parent to mate.
    parent1_idx = k%parents.shape[0]
    # Index of the second parent to mate.
    parent2_idx = (k+1)%parents.shape[0]
    # The new offspring will have its first half of its genes taken
    from the first parent.
    offspring[k, 0:crossover_point] = parents[parent1_idx, 0:
    crossover_point]
    # The new offspring will have its second half of its genes taken
    from the second parent.
    offspring[k, crossover_point:] = parents[parent2_idx, crossover_point:]
return offspring

def mutation(offspring_crossover):
    # Mutation changes a single gene in each offspring randomly.
    for idx in range(offspring_crossover.shape[0]):
        # The random value to be added to the gene.
        random_value = numpy.random.uniform(-1.0, 1.0, 1)
        offspring_crossover[idx, 4] = offspring_crossover[idx, 4] +
        random_value
    return offspring_crossover
```

NSGA-II

The main difference between GA and NSGA-II is the way of selecting the best individuals within a given population (i.e., parents of the new generation). In GA, a single value is used for selecting the best individuals. This is the fitness value generated from a fitness function. The higher the fitness value is, the better the solution/individual. For NSGA-II, there is no single value but multiple values generated from multiple objective functions. How do we make the selection based on these multiple values, keeping in mind that all of these objectives have equal importance? There must be a different way than the one used in regular GA for selecting the best individuals. NSGA-II selects its parents or best individuals based on two metrics:

1. Dominance.

2. Crowding Distance.

The example we will use in the discussion is about a person that would like to buy a shirt. That person has two objectives that are to be satisfied in the shirt:

1. Low cost (between $0 and $85).

2. Bad feedback from previous buyers (between 0 and 5).

Cost is measured in USD and feedback is measured as a real number between 0 and 5 inclusive, where 0 is the best feedback and 5 is the worst feedback. This means that the two objective functions are minimization. Assume that there are just eight samples of data as in Table 4-10; we will use them to start.

Table 4-10. *Data Samples*

ID	Cost $	Bad Feedback
A	20	2.2
B	60	4.4
C	65	3.5
D	15	4.4
E	55	4.5
F	50	1.8
G	80	4.0
H	25	4.6

NSGA-II Steps

NSGA-II follows the general steps in the traditional GA. The change is not using a fitness value to select the best solutions (parents) for the next generation; rather, it uses dominance and crowding distance. Here are the general stops of NSGA-II:

1. Select the initial population solutions of generation 0 from the data.

2. Split the solutions into levels using nondominant sorting.

3. Select the best solutions at the level 1 nondominated front as parents for mating and producing offspring for the next generation. (If all solutions inside the last-used level are selected completely without remainders, then go directly to step 5.)

4. If a subset of solutions is selected as parents from the last-used level, then you have to calculate the crowding distance for solutions in this level, sort these solutions in worse order according to the crowding distance, and select the number of remaining solutions from the top.

5. Use the selected parents to produce the offspring.

    a. Tournament selection on the selected parents.

    b. GA variants (i.e., crossover and mutation) on the results of the tournament. This will produce the new offspring of the next generation.

6. Repeat steps 2 to 5 until reaching a maximum number of iterations.

Note that you shouldn't expect to understand all of these steps at the current time. But don't worry: when you go through the details of each step, things will become easier and clearer. These steps are summarized in Figure 4-7.

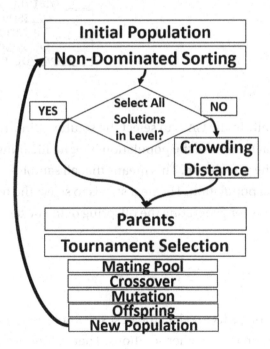

Figure 4-7. *NSGA-II steps*

NSGA is not different from GA but adds some operations to make it suitable for multiobjective problems. Figure 4-8 highlights the difference between GA and NSGA. The step of calculating the fitness values in GA is extended to multiple steps in NSGA starting from nondominated sorting until tournament selection. After determining what solutions will be used in the mating pool, the two algorithms are similar.

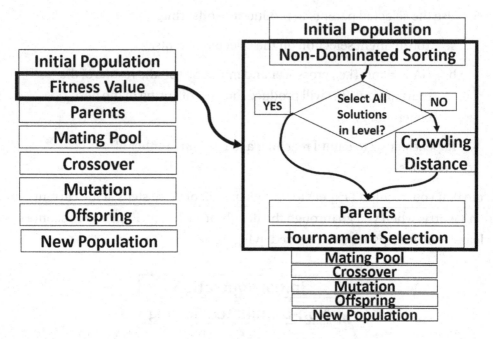

Figure 4-8. *GA vs. NSGA*

The first step generally in the GA is to select the solutions/individuals of the initial population. Assume that the size of the population is eight, meaning there are eight samples to be used in the population. This means that all samples in Table 4-10 will be used inside the initial population. The next step is to select the best solutions in this population as parents for generating the offspring of the next generation using the concept of dominance.

Dominance

Dominance in NSGA-II helps us to select the best set of solutions as parents. These solutions are said to dominate the other solutions. That is, they are better than all other solutions.

Realistically, the solutions are not always bad or worse than other solutions across all objectives. How do we find the best set of solutions in the data? Here is the rule to use in order to say that one solution dominates another solution:

Solution X is said to dominate solution Y if and only if

1. Solution X is no worse than solution Y in all objective functions and

2. Solution X is better than solution Y in at least one objective function.

Besides saying solution X dominates solution Y, we could say the following:

- Solution X is nondominated by solution Y.

- Solution Y is dominated by solution X.

- Solution Y nondominates solution X.

Note that if any of the preceding conditions are not met, then solution X does not dominate solution Y. That means no solution is better than another, and there is a trade-off between them. Note also that when solution X dominates solution Y, it means that solution X is better than solution Y.

The set of all solutions not satisfying at least one of the preceding two conditions is called the nondominant set. It is called so because no solution in that set dominates (i.e., is better than) another. The steps to find the nondominated set are as follows:

1. Select a solution with index i, where i starts from 1 corresponding to the first solution.

2. Check the dominance of that solution against all other solutions in the data.

3. If a solution is found to dominate that solution, then stop, as it is impossible to be in the nondominant set. Go to step 5 directly.

4. If no solution dominates that solution, then add it to the nondominant set.

5. Increment i by 1 and repeat steps 2 to 4.

Using nondominated sorting, the solutions are split into multiple sets. Each set is called a nondominated front. These fronts are sorted in levels, where the first nondominated front is at level 1, the second nondominated front is at level 2, and so on. Let us apply these steps in order to find the nondominant front at level 1 based on our example in Table 4-10.

1. Starting with solution A and comparing it to solution B, we find that A is better than B in the first objective (cost), as A's cost is $20, which is less (i.e., better) than B's cost of $60. Also, A is better than B in the second objective (feedback), as A's feedback is 2.2, which is less (i.e., better) than B's feedback of 4.4. As a result, A is better than B across all objectives. The conditions that make solution A dominate solution B are met. But we cannot conclude that A is a member of the nondominant set, and we still have to wait until checking A against all other solutions.

2. Comparing A to C, it is clear that A is better than C in all objectives, as A's cost and feedback are smaller than C's. As a result, C does not dominate A (i.e., A dominates C). We still have to explore the next solutions to decide whether A is a member of the nondominant set or not.

3. Comparing A to D, we find A's feedback of 2.2 is better than D's feedback of 4.4. But A's cost of $20 is worse than D's cost of $15. Thus, each solution is better than the other in just one objective. As a result, the two conditions of dominance are not met for solution D. As a result, we can conclude that D does not dominate A and also that A does not dominate D. We again have to check A against the remaining solutions to learn its decision.

4. Comparing A and E, it is obvious that A is better than E in all objectives. Thus, A dominates E. Let's compare A to the next solution, F.

5. Comparing A and F, neither solution is better than the other. This is identical to the case of comparing A to D. Thus, F does not dominate A and we have to compare A to the other solutions.

6. Comparing A to G, A is better than G in all objectives, as A's cost ($20) is less than G's cost ($80), and also A's feedback (2.2) is better than G's feedback (4.0). Let's move to the final solution.

7. Comparing A to H, A is better than H across all solutions. As a result, H does not dominate A. After checking the dominance of A across all solutions, it seems that no solution dominates A. So, A is regarded as a member of the nondominant set. The current nondominant set is P={A}. Let us move to the next solution.

8. Regarding solutions B and C, it is clear that solution A dominates them. As a result, we can go directly into checking dominance for solution D.

9. Comparing D by A, we find that D is better than D in the first objective (cost) because D's cost is $15, which is smaller than A's cost, which is $20. Regarding the second objective, D is worse than A because D's feedback of 4.4 is larger than A's feedback of 2.2. Because solution A does not dominate solution D, we have to compare D to the next solution.

10. Comparing D to B, we find that D is better than B in the first objective and they are equal in the second objective. As a result, B does not dominate D and we have to check D against the remaining solutions to learn its decision.

11. Comparing D to C, D is better than C in the first objective but D is worse than C in the second objective. Conditions that make C dominate D are not met. As a result, C does not dominate D and we have to check D against the next solution.

12. Comparing D to E, we find that D is better than E across all objectives. We can conclude that E does not dominate D. Continue comparing D to the next solution.

13. Comparing D to F, D's cost of $15 is smaller (better) than F's cost of $50. Because solution F is worse than D in at least one objective, we can stop and conclude that F does not dominate D. Let us compare D to the next solution.

14. Comparing D to G, the same scenario with F repeats itself. D's cost of 15$ is smaller (better) than G's cost of 80$. Because solution G is worse than D in at least one objective, we can conclude that G does not dominate D. Let us compare D to the next solution.

15. Comparing D to H, H is worse than D across all objectives and thus H does not dominate D. At this point, we can conclude that no solution dominates solution D and it is included in the nondominant set. The current nondominant set is P={A, D}. Let us move to the next solution.

16. Working with E, comparing it to A we find that A is better than E across all objectives because A's cost of $20 is smaller than E's cost of $55, and also A's feedback of 2.2 is better than E's feedback of 4.5. Thus, we can stop and conclude that A dominates E; E cannot be included in the nondominant set.

17. Working with F, comparing it to A we find that A is better than F in just the first objective and F is better than A in the second objective. Thus, no solution dominates the other. We still need to compare F with the remaining solutions to make the decision.

18. After comparing F with all solutions, there is no solution dominating solution F. Thus, F is included in the nondominant set. The current nondominant set is P={A, D, F}. Let us move to the next solution.

19. Working with G and comparing it to all solutions, we find that solutions A, C, and F dominate it. Thus, G cannot be included within the nondominant set. Let us move to the final solution.

20. Working with the final solution H, by comparing it to all solutions we find that solutions A and D dominate it. Thus, H cannot be included within the nondominant set. At this point, we have checked the dominance of all solutions.

After comparing each pair of solutions together, the final nondominant set is P={A, D, F}. This is the level 1 nondominated front. No solution in the same front is better than any other solution within the same front across all objectives. This is why it is called the nondominant set as no solution dominates another.

The Python code for checking dominance of a given solution is in Listing 4-10. Given an index of a solution, it returns the IDs of solutions dominating it. It uses pandas DataFrame (DF) for sorting the objective values for each solution in addition to their IDs. This helps to refer back to the solution ID. A simple way to create this DF is to insert the data into a Python dictionary and then convert it into a pandas DF.

Listing 4-10. Returning Dominating Solutions

```
import numpy
import pandas

d = {'A': [20, 2.2],
     'B': [60, 4.4],
     'C': [65, 3.5],
     'D': [15, 4.4],
     'E': [55, 4.5],
     'F': [50, 1.8],
     'G': [80, 4.0],
     'H': [25, 4.6]}

df = pandas.DataFrame(data=d).T
data_labels = list(df.index)

data_array = numpy.array(df).T

# ****Specify the index of the solution here****
sol_idx = 1
sol = data_array[:, sol_idx]

obj1_not_worse = numpy.where(sol[0] >= data_array[0, :])[0]
obj2_not_worse = numpy.where(sol[1] >= data_array[1, :])[0]
not_worse_candidates = set.intersection(set(obj1_not_worse),
set(obj2_not_worse))

obj1_better = numpy.where(sol[0] > data_array[0, :])[0]
obj2_better = numpy.where(sol[1] > data_array[1, :])[0]
better_candidates = set.union(set(obj1_better), set(obj2_better))

dominating_solutions = list(set.intersection(not_worse_candidates,
                                             better_candidates))
```

```
if len(dominating_solutions) == 0:
    print("No solution dominates solution", data_labels[sol_idx], ".")
else:
    print("Labels of one or more solutions dominating this solution : ",
    end="")
    for k in dominating_solutions:
        print(data_labels[k], end=",")
```

For a given solution, the conditions of dominance are checked. For the first condition, the indices of solutions not worse than the current solutions across all objectives are returned in the "not_worse_candidates" variable. The second condition searches for solutions that are better than the current solution in at least one objective. Solutions satisfying the second condition are returned in the "better_candidates" solutions. For a given solution to dominate another, both conditions must be met. For this reason, the "dominating_solutions" variable just returns solutions meeting both conditions.

The previous three solutions are better than all five remaining solutions. In other words, solutions at the level 1 nondominated front are better than any solution on all remaining fronts. What about the other five solutions that are not selected in the first nondominated front at level 1? We will continue using the remaining samples from the population to further find the next nondominance levels.

The steps to find the nondominant set will be repeated to find the nondominated front at level 2 but after removing the three solutions selected previously in level 1 of the population. The set of remaining solutions is {B, C, E, G, H}. Let's find the next nondominated front:

1. Starting with solution B and checking its dominance to C, B's feedback of 4.4 is worse than C's feedback of 3.5. According to the first objective, B's cost of $60 is better than C's cost of $65. As a result, solution C nondominates solution B. We still have to wait until we compare B to the remaining solutions.

2. Comparing B to E, B is better than E in the second objective, as B's feedback is 4.4 and E's feedback is 4.5. As a result, solution E nondominates solution B. Let us check the next solution.

3. Comparing B to G, we find that B is better than G in the first objective, as B's cost is $60 and G's cost is $80. As a result, solution G nondominates solution B. Let us check the next solution.

4. Comparing B to H, we find that B is better than H in the second objective, as B's feedback is 4.4 and H's feedback is 4.6. As a result, solution H nondominates solution B. After comparing B to all solutions and finding that no solution dominates it, we can conclude that B is included in the nondominated front at level 2. The level 2 set is now P'={B}. Let us move to check the dominance of the second solution in the remaining set of solutions.

5. Comparing the next solution C to B, C is better than B in the second objective, as C's feedback is 3.5 and B's feedback is 4.4. As a result, solution B nondominates solution C.

6. Comparing C with the remaining solutions, there is no solution dominating C and it will be included in the nondominated front at level 2, which will be P'={B, C}. Let us move to the next solution.

7. Comparing the next solution E to all the remaining solutions from the population, we find that no solution dominates solution E. Thus, E will be included in the nondominated front at level 2, which is P'={B, C, E}. Let us move to the next solution.

8. Comparing the next solution G to all the remaining solutions from the population, we find that solution C dominates solution G because C is better than G across all objectives. As a result, solution G is not included in the level 2 nondominated front. Let us move to the next solution.

9. Comparing the last solution H to all the remaining solutions from the population, we find that no solution dominates solution H. As a result, it will be included in the nondominated front at level 2, which will be P'={B, C, E, H}.

This is the end of the nondominated front at level 2. The set of remaining solutions is {G}. This set will be used to find the level 3 nondominated front. Because there is just one remaining solution, it will be added alone into the nondominated front at level 3 to be P"={G}. At this point, we successfully split the data into three nondominance levels, as shown in Table 4-11.

Table 4-11. *Results of Splitting the Data into Three Nondominance Levels*

Level	Solutions
1	{A, D, F}
2	{B, C, E, H}
3	{G}

Note that the solutions in level i are better than the solutions in level $i + 1$. That is, the solutions in level 1 are better than the solutions in level 2, the level 2 solutions are better than the level 3 solutions, and so on. As a result, when selecting the best solutions for being parents, we will start selection from the first level. If the number of available solutions in the first level is less than the number of required parents, then we select the remaining parents from the second level, and so on.

In our problem, the population size is eight. For producing a new generation of the same size, we need to select half of its population as parents; the remaining half is the offspring produced by mating the parents. At first, we need to select the best four parents.

The first nondominance level has just three solutions. Because we are in need of four parents, then we will select all of these three solutions. As a result, the current parents are {A, D, F}. There is a remaining parent that we should select from level 2.

Level 2 has four solutions, and we need to select just one. The important question is, which solution should we select from level 2? The metric used to evaluate solutions inside the same nondominated front is the crowding distance. Next, we will learn how to calculate the crowding distance to solutions inside the level 2 front.

Crowding Distance

Crowding distance is the metric used to prioritize solutions within the same nondominated front. Here are the steps for calculating and using the crowding distance:

1. For each objective function, sort the set of solutions within the level in worse order.

2. For the two solutions at outliers (i.e., rightmost and leftmost solutions), set their crowding distance to infinity.

3. For the in-between solutions, the crowding distance is calculated according to Equation 4-7.

4. For each solution, take the summation of the crowding distances across all objectives.

5. Sort solutions in descending order to select the solutions from highest to lowest crowding distance.

$$d_m^n = \frac{S_m^{n+1} - S_m^{n-1}}{O_m^{max} - O_m^{min}}$$

(Equation 4-7)

After sorting the solutions according to one objective function, n refers to its position. m refers to the number of the objective function being used for calculating the crowding distance. d_m^n is the crowding distance of solution n according to objective m, S_m^n refers to the value of the objective m for solution n, O_m^{max} is the maximum value for objective m, and O_m^{min} is the minimum value for objective m.

For a minimization objective, sorting solutions in worse order refers to sorting in descending order in which the smallest (i.e., best) solution, according to the objective, is in the leftmost position and the largest (i.e., worst) is on the rightmost.

Because the two solutions at outliers will be given crowding distance equal to infinity, then we can start calculating the crowding distance for in-between solutions.

The data of the problem in Table 4-10 is available in the following for making it easier to calculate the crowding distance.

ID	Cost $	Bad Feedback
A	20	2.2
B	60	4.4
C	65	3.5
D	15	4.4
E	55	4.5
F	50	1.8
G	80	4.0
H	25	4.6

Figure 4-9 summarizes the values of the parameters for calculating the crowding distance for solutions E and B according to the cost objective.

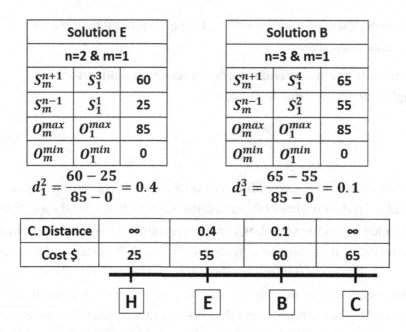

$$d_1^2 = \frac{60 - 25}{85 - 0} = 0.4 \qquad d_1^3 = \frac{65 - 55}{85 - 0} = 0.1$$

C. Distance	∞	0.4	0.1	∞
Cost $	25	55	60	65

Figure 4-9. *First objective crowding distance for level 2 solutions*

In the same way, Figure 4-10 shows how the crowding distance is calculated for solutions B and E according to the feedback objective.

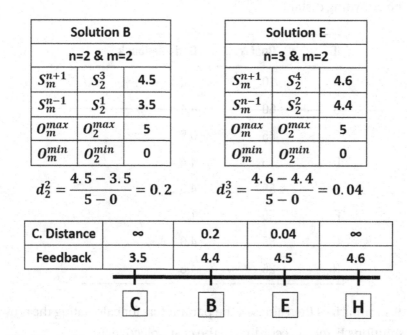

$$d_2^2 = \frac{4.5 - 3.5}{5 - 0} = 0.2 \qquad d_2^3 = \frac{4.6 - 4.4}{5 - 0} = 0.04$$

C. Distance	∞	0.2	0.04	∞
Feedback	3.5	4.4	4.5	4.6

Figure 4-10. *First objective crowding distance for level 2 solutions*

By summing the crowding distances of the two objectives and sorting the result in descending order, the result is shown in Table 4-12. If we are in need of just one solution from level 2 as a parent, then it will be the first solution in Table 4-12 after sorting the summation of the crowding distances in descending order. That solution is solution C. As a result, the set of selected solutions will be {A, D, F, C}. Note that not all of these solutions will be used for generating the new offspring because they might be filtered by tournament selection. But all of these solutions will be used to form the first half of the solutions in the new generation. The second half will come from mating the parents selected from the tournament.

Table 4-12. *Summation of the Crowding Distances of Level 2 Solutions from the Two Objective Functions*

ID	Summation
C	Infinity
H	Infinity
E	0.44
B	0.3

Tournament Selection

In the tournament selection, we create pairs of solutions from the selected parents. From each pair, a tournament made between them and the winner will be used further in crossover and mutation. All possible pairs are (A, D), (A, F), (A, C), (D, C), and (F, C).

Here is how the winners of the tournament are selected:

- If the two solutions are from different nondominance levels, then the solution coming from the high-priority level will be the winner.

- If the two solutions are from the same nondominance level, then the winner will be the one corresponding to higher crowding distance.

Let's consider the first pair (A, D). Because they are coming from the same level, we will use their crowding distance to learn the winner. Because we have not calculated the crowding distance of the first level, we need to first calculate it.

Figure 4-11 shows the final crowding distance for solutions in level 1 according to both objectives. Regarding the first pair (A, D), the winner is D because it has higher crowding distance than A. For the remaining tournaments, the winners are F, A, D, and F. These three unique solutions, A, D, and F, are used to generate four offspring.

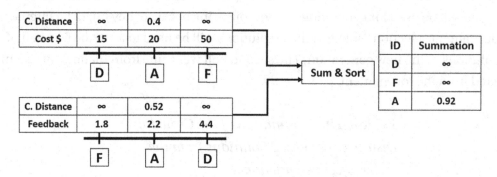

Figure 4-11. *Summation of the crowding distances of level 1 solutions from the two objective functions*

Crossover

Assume we choose four new solutions from the pairs (A, D), (A, F), (D, F), and (F, A), where the first and last half of the genes of the offspring are taken from the first and last solution in each pair, respectively. The result of the crossover is in Table 4-13.

Table 4-13. *Crossover Between Tournament Winners*

Offspring	Cost $	Feedback
(A, D)	20	4.4
(A, F)	20	1.8
(D, F)	15	1.8

Mutation

Mutation will be applied to the result of the crossover. Assume we applied mutation by randomly adding a number between –10 and 10 to the first half of each solution. The result of the mutation operation is as shown in Table 4-14.

Table 4-14. *Mutation on the Outputs of Crossover*

Offspring	Cost $	Feedback
(B, D)	27	4.4
(B, E)	25	1.8
(D, E)	10	1.8

After that, we have successfully produced the eight solutions of the next generation 1. The first four solutions are those produced by nondominated sorting and crowding distance. The remaining four solutions are what we just produced by tournament selection, crossover, and mutation as in Table 4-14. Solutions of the new population in generation 1 are in Table 4-15.

Table 4-15. *Solutions of Generation 1*

ID	Cost $	Feedback
A	20	2.2
D	15	4.4
F	50	1.8
C	65	3.5
K	27	4.4
L	25	1.8
M	10	1.8
N	45	2.2

At this point, we have completed all steps involved in the NSGA-II multiobjective EA. Next is to repeat steps 2 to 5 of NSGA-II until a number of predefined generations/ iterations. After the first generation, the algorithm found solution M, which is better than all solutions in the previous population. Going through multiple generations, the algorithm is likely to find a better solution.

Optimizing ANN Using GA

In Chapter 4, the ANN is trained using four classes of the Fruits 360 dataset without using a learning algorithm. Thus, the accuracy is low, not exceeding 45%. After understanding how GA works based on numerical examples in addition to implementation using Python, this section uses GA to optimize the ANN by updating its weights (parameters).

GA creates multiple solutions to a given problem and evolves them through a number of generations. Each solution holds all parameters that might help to enhance the results. For ANN, weights in all layers help achieve high accuracy. Thus, a single solution in GA will contain all weights in the ANN. According to Figure 4-7, the ANN has four layers (one input, two hidden, and one output). Any weight in any layer will be part of the same solution. A single solution to this network will contain a total number of weights equal to $102 \times 150 + 150 \times 60 + 60 \times 4 = 24,540$. If the population has eight solutions with 24,540 parameters per solution, then the total number of parameters in the entire population is $24,540 \times 8 = 196,320$.

Looking at Figure 4-8, the parameters of the network are in matrix form, because this makes calculations of ANN much easier. For each layer, there is an associated weights matrix. Just multiply the inputs matrix by the parameters matrix of a given layer to return the outputs in this layer. Chromosomes in GA are 1D vectors, and thus we have to convert the weights matrices into 1D vectors.

Because matrix multiplication is a good option to work with ANN, we will still represent the ANN parameters in the matrix form when using the ANN. Figure 4-12 summarizes the steps of using GA with ANN.

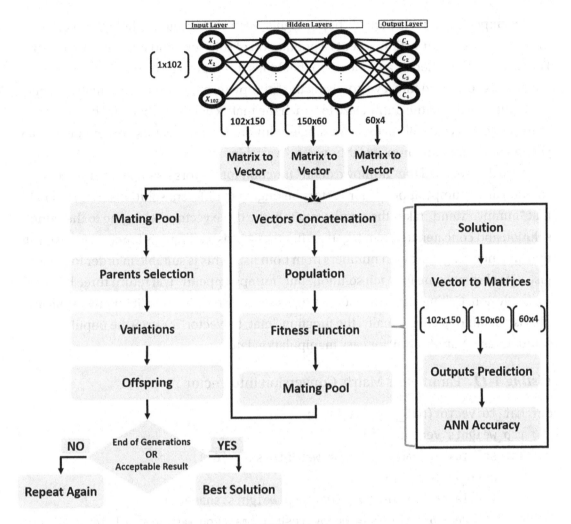

Figure 4-12. *Using GA to optimize ANN parameters*

Each solution in the population will have two representations. First is a 1D vector for working with GA and second is a matrix to work with ANN. Because there are three weights matrices for the three layers (two hidden + one output), there will be three vectors, one for each matrix. Because a solution in GA is represented as a single 1D vector, these three individual 1D vectors will be concatenated into a single 1D vector. Each solution will be represented as a vector of length 24,540. Listing 4-11 holds the Python code of the "mat_to_vector" function, which converts the parameters of all solutions within the population from matrix to vector.

An empty list variable named "pop_weights_vector" is created to hold the vectors of all solutions. The function accepts a population of solutions and loops through them. For each solution, there is an inner loop that loops through its three matrices. For each matrix, it is converted into a vector using the "numpy.reshape" function, which accepts the input matrix and the output size to which the matrix will be reshaped. The variable "curr_vector" accepts all vectors for a single solution. After all vectors are generated, they get appended into the "pop_weights_vector" variable.

Note that we used the "numpy.extend" function for vectors belonging to the same solution and "numpy.append" for vectors belonging to different solutions. The reason is that "numpy.extend" takes the numbers within the three vectors belonging to the same solution and concatenate them together. In other words, calling this function for two lists returns a new single list with numbers from both lists. This is suitable in order to create just a 1D chromosome for each solution. But "numpy.append" will return three lists for each solution. Calling it for two lists, it returns a new list, which is split into two sublists. This is not our objective. Finally, the function "mat_to_vector" returns the population solutions as a NumPy array for easy manipulation later.

Listing 4-11. Parameters Matrix Conversion into Vector

```python
def mat_to_vector(mat_pop_weights):
    pop_weights_vector = []
    for sol_idx in range(mat_pop_weights.shape[0]):
        curr_vector = []
        for layer_idx in range(mat_pop_weights.shape[1]):
            vector_weights = numpy.reshape(mat_pop_weights[sol_idx,
            layer_idx], newshape=(mat_pop_weights[sol_idx, layer_idx].
            size))
            curr_vector.extend(vector_weights)
        pop_weights_vector.append(curr_vector)
    return numpy.array(pop_weights_vector)
```

After converting all solutions from matrices to vectors and concatenating them together, we are ready to go through the GA steps according to Figure 4-2. All steps in Figure 4-2 except for the fitness values calculation are similar to the previously discussed GA implementation.

One of the common fitness functions for a classifier such as ANN is the accuracy. It is the ratio between the correctly classified samples and the total number of samples. It is calculated according to Equation 4-8. The classification accuracy of each solution is calculated according to the steps in Figure 4-12.

$$Accuracy = \frac{NumCorrectClassify}{TotalNumSamples} \qquad \text{(Equation 4-8)}$$

The single 1D vector of each solution is converted back into three matrices, one matrix for each layer (two hidden and one output). Conversion takes place using the "vector_to_mat" function defined in Listing 4-12. It reverses the work done previously. But there is an important question: if the vector of a given solution is just one piece, how we can split it into three different parts, each part representing a matrix? The size of the first parameters matrix between the input layer and the hidden layer is 102×150. When being converted into a vector, its length will be 15,300. Because it is the first vector to be inserted in the "curr_vector" variable according to Listing 4-11, then it will start from index 0 and end at index 15,299. The "mat_pop_weights" is used as an argument for the "vector_to_mat" function in order to learn the size of each matrix. It is not required to contain the recent weights; just the sizes of the matrices are used from it.

Listing 4-12. Solution Vector Conversion into Matrices

```python
def vector_to_mat(vector_pop_weights, mat_pop_weights):
    mat_weights = []
    for sol_idx in range(mat_pop_weights.shape[0]):
        start = 0
        end = 0
        for layer_idx in range(mat_pop_weights.shape[1]):
            end = end + mat_pop_weights[sol_idx, layer_idx].size
            curr_vector = vector_pop_weights[sol_idx, start:end]
            mat_layer_weights = numpy.reshape(curr_vector, newshape=
            (mat_pop_weights[sol_idx, layer_idx].shape))
            mat_weights.append(mat_layer_weights)
            start = end
    return numpy.reshape(mat_weights, newshape=mat_pop_weights.shape)
```

For the second vector in the same solution, it's the result of converting a matrix of size 150×60. Thus, the vector length is 9,000. This vector is inserted into the "curr_vector" variable just before the previous vector of length 15,300. As a result, it will start from index 15,300 and ends at index 15,300+9,000–1=24,299. The –1 is used because Python starts indexing at 0. For the last vector created from the parameters matrix of size 60×4, its length is 240. Because it is added into the "curr_vector" variable exactly after the previous vector of length 9,000, then its index will start after it. That is, its start index is 24,300 and its end index is 24,300+240–1=24,539. So, we can successfully restore the vector into the original three matrices.

The matrices returned for each solution are used to predict the class label for each of the 1,962 samples in the used dataset to calculate the accuracy. This is done using two functions ("predict_outputs" and "fitness") according to Listing 4-13.

Listing 4-13. Predicting Class Labels for Calculating Accuracy

```
def predict_outputs(weights_mat, data_inputs, data_outputs,
activation="relu"):
    predictions = numpy.zeros(shape=(data_inputs.shape[0]))
    for sample_idx in range(data_inputs.shape[0]):
        r1 = data_inputs[sample_idx, :]
        for curr_weights in weights_mat:
            r1 = numpy.matmul(a=r1, b=curr_weights)
            if activation == "relu":
                r1 = relu(r1)
            elif activation == "sigmoid":
                r1 = sigmoid(r1)
        predicted_label = numpy.where(r1 == numpy.max(r1))[0][0]
        predictions[sample_idx] = predicted_label
    correct_predictions = numpy.where(predictions == data_outputs)[0].size
    accuracy = (correct_predictions/data_outputs.size)*100
    return accuracy, predictions

def fitness(weights_mat, data_inputs, data_outputs, activation="relu"):
    accuracy = numpy.empty(shape=(weights_mat.shape[0]))
    for sol_idx in range(weights_mat.shape[0]):
        curr_sol_mat = weights_mat[sol_idx, :]
```

```
accuracy[sol_idx], _ = predict_outputs(curr_sol_mat, data_inputs,
    data_outputs, activation=activation)
return accuracy
```

The "predict_outputs" function accepts the weights of a single solution, inputs and outputs of the training data, and an optional parameter that specifies which activation function to use. It is similar to the previous function created in Listing 4-7, but the difference is being adapted to return the accuracy of the solution. But it returns the accuracy of just one solution, not all solutions within the population. This is the role of the "fitness" function to loop through each solution, pass it to the "predict_outputs" function, store the accuracy of all solutions into the "accuracy" array, and finally return the array.

After calculating the fitness value (i.e., accuracy) for each solution, the remaining steps of GA in Figure 4-12 are applied the same way as done previously. The best parents are selected, based on their accuracy, into the mating pool. Then mutation and crossover variants are applied in order to produce the offspring. The population of the new generation is created using both offspring and parents. These steps are repeated for a number of generations.

Complete Python Implementation

The Python implementation for this project has three Python files:

1. GA.py for implementing GA functions.

2. ANN.py for implementing ANN functions.

3. Third file for calling such functions through a number of generations.

The third file is the main file because it connects all functions. It reads the features and the class label files, filters features based on STD value 50, creates the ANN architecture, generates the initial solutions, loops through a number of generations by calculating the fitness values for all solutions, selects the best parents, applies crossover and mutation, and finally creates the new population. Its implementation is in Listing 4-14. This file defines the GA parameters, such as the number of solutions per population, number of selected parents, mutation percentage, and number of generations. You can try different values for them.

Listing 4-14. The Main File Connecting GA and ANN Together

```
import numpy
import GA
import pickle
import ANN
import matplotlib.pyplot

f = open("dataset_features.pkl", "rb")
data_inputs2 = pickle.load(f)
f.close()
features_STDs = numpy.std(a=data_inputs2, axis=0)
data_inputs = data_inputs2[:, features_STDs>50]

f = open("outputs.pkl", "rb")
data_outputs = pickle.load(f)
f.close()

#GA parameters:
#    Mating Pool Size (Number of Parents)
#    Population Size
#    Number of Generations
#    Mutation Percent

sol_per_pop = 8
num_parents_mating = 4
num_generations = 1000
mutation_percent = 10

#Creating the initial population.
initial_pop_weights = []
for curr_sol in numpy.arange(0, sol_per_pop):
    HL1_neurons = 150
    input_HL1_weights = numpy.random.uniform(low=-0.1, high=0.1,
                                             size=(data_inputs.shape[1],
                                             HL1_neurons))

    HL2_neurons = 60
```

```python
    HL1_HL2_weights = numpy.random.uniform(low=-0.1, high=0.1,
                                            size=(HL1_neurons, HL2_
                                            neurons))
    output_neurons = 4
    HL2_output_weights = numpy.random.uniform(low=-0.1, high=0.1,
                                              size=(HL2_neurons, output_
                                              neurons))

    initial_pop_weights.append(numpy.array([input_HL1_weights,
                                            HL1_HL2_weights,
                                            HL2_output_weights]))

pop_weights_mat = numpy.array(initial_pop_weights)
pop_weights_vector = GA.mat_to_vector(pop_weights_mat)

best_outputs = []
accuracies = numpy.empty(shape=(num_generations))

for generation in range(num_generations):
    print("Generation : ", generation)

    # converting the solutions from being vectors to matrices.
    pop_weights_mat = GA.vector_to_mat(pop_weights_vector,
                                       pop_weights_mat)

    # Measuring the fitness of each chromosome in the population.
    fitness = ANN.fitness(pop_weights_mat,
                          data_inputs,
                          data_outputs,
                          activation="sigmoid")
    accuracies[generation] = fitness[0]
    print("Fitness")
    print(fitness)

    # Selecting the best parents in the population for mating.
    parents = GA.select_mating_pool(pop_weights_vector,
                                    fitness.copy(),
                                    num_parents_mating)
    print("Parents")
    print(parents)
```

```python
    # Generating next generation using crossover.
    offspring_crossover = GA.crossover(parents,
                                       offspring_size=(pop_weights_vector.
                                       shape[0]-parents.shape[0],
                                       pop_weights_vector.shape[1]))
    print("Crossover")
    print(offspring_crossover)

    # Adding some variations to the offspring using mutation.
    offspring_mutation = GA.mutation(offspring_crossover,
                                     mutation_percent=mutation_percent)
    print("Mutation")
    print(offspring_mutation)

    # Creating the new population based on the parents and offspring.
    pop_weights_vector[0:parents.shape[0], :] = parents
    pop_weights_vector[parents.shape[0]:, :] = offspring_mutation

pop_weights_mat = GA.vector_to_mat(pop_weights_vector, pop_weights_mat)
best_weights = pop_weights_mat [0, :]
acc, predictions = ANN.predict_outputs(best_weights, data_inputs, data_
outputs, activation="sigmoid")
print("Accuracy of the best solution is : ", acc)

matplotlib.pyplot.plot(accuracies, linewidth=5, color="black")
matplotlib.pyplot.xlabel("Iteration", fontsize=20)
matplotlib.pyplot.ylabel("Fitness", fontsize=20)
matplotlib.pyplot.xticks(numpy.arange(0, num_generations+1, 100),
fontsize=15)
matplotlib.pyplot.yticks(numpy.arange(0, 101, 5), fontsize=15)

f = open("weights_"+str(num_generations)+"_iterations_"+str(mutation_
percent)+"%_mutation.pkl", "wb")
pickle.dump(pop_weights_mat, f)
f.close()
```

Based on 1,000 generations, a plot is created at the end of this file using Matplotlib visualization library, which shows how the accuracy changes across each generation. It is shown in Figure 4-13. After 1,000 iterations, the accuracy is more than 97%. This is compared to 45% without using an optimization technique. This is an evidence about why results might be bad, not because there is something wrong in the model or the data but because no optimization technique is used. Of course, using different values for the parameters such as 10,000 generations might increase the accuracy. At the end of this file, it saves the parameters in matrix form to the disk for use later.

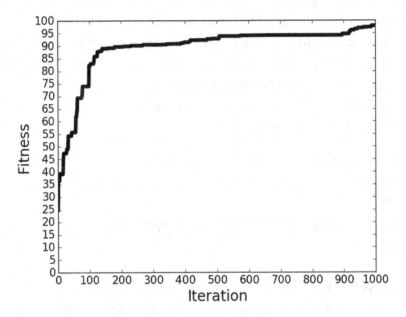

Figure 4-13. *Classification accuracy evolution according to 1,000 iterations*

The GA.py file implementation is in Listing 4-15. Note that the "mutation" function accepts the "mutation_percent" parameter, which defines the number of genes to change their values randomly. It is set to 10% in the main file in Listing 4-14. This file holds the two new functions "mat_to_vector" and "vector_to_mat".

Listing 4-15. GA.py File Holding the Functions of GA

```python
import numpy
import random

# Converting each solution from matrix to vector.
def mat_to_vector(mat_pop_weights):
    pop_weights_vector = []
    for sol_idx in range(mat_pop_weights.shape[0]):
        curr_vector = []
        for layer_idx in range(mat_pop_weights.shape[1]):
            vector_weights = numpy.reshape(mat_pop_weights[sol_idx,
            layer_idx], newshape=(mat_pop_weights[sol_idx, layer_idx].size))
            curr_vector.extend(vector_weights)
        pop_weights_vector.append(curr_vector)
    return numpy.array(pop_weights_vector)

# Converting each solution from vector to matrix.
def vector_to_mat(vector_pop_weights, mat_pop_weights):
    mat_weights = []
    for sol_idx in range(mat_pop_weights.shape[0]):
        start = 0
        end = 0
        for layer_idx in range(mat_pop_weights.shape[1]):
            end = end + mat_pop_weights[sol_idx, layer_idx].size
            curr_vector = vector_pop_weights[sol_idx, start:end]
            mat_layer_weights = numpy.reshape(curr_vector, newshape=(mat_
            pop_weights[sol_idx, layer_idx].shape))
            mat_weights.append(mat_layer_weights)
            start = end
    return numpy.reshape(mat_weights, newshape=mat_pop_weights.shape)

def select_mating_pool(pop, fitness, num_parents):
    # Selecting the best individuals in the current generation as parents
for producing the offspring of the next generation.
    parents = numpy.empty((num_parents, pop.shape[1]))
    for parent_num in range(num_parents):
```

```
        max_fitness_idx = numpy.where(fitness == numpy.max(fitness))
        max_fitness_idx = max_fitness_idx[0][0]
        parents[parent_num, :] = pop[max_fitness_idx, :]
        fitness[max_fitness_idx] = -99999999999
    return parents

def crossover(parents, offspring_size):
    offspring = numpy.empty(offspring_size)
    # The point at which crossover takes place between two parents.
    Usually, it is at the center.
    crossover_point = numpy.uint8(offspring_size[1]/2)

    for k in range(offspring_size[0]):
        # Index of the first parent to mate.
        parent1_idx = k%parents.shape[0]
        # Index of the second parent to mate.
        parent2_idx = (k+1)%parents.shape[0]
        # The new offspring will have its first half of its genes taken
        from the first parent.
        offspring[k, 0:crossover_point] = parents[parent1_idx, 0:crossover_
        point]
        # The new offspring will have its second half of its genes taken
        from the second parent.
        offspring[k, crossover_point:] = parents[parent2_idx, crossover_
        point:]
    return offspring

def mutation(offspring_crossover, mutation_percent):
    num_mutations = numpy.uint8((mutation_percent*offspring_crossover.
    shape[1])/100)
    mutation_indices = numpy.array(random.sample(range(0, offspring_
    crossover.shape[1]), num_mutations))
    # Mutation changes a single gene in each offspring randomly.
    for idx in range(offspring_crossover.shape[0]):
        # The random value to be added to the gene.
        random_value = numpy.random.uniform(-1.0, 1.0, 1)
```

```
        offspring_crossover[idx, mutation_indices] = offspring_
        crossover[idx, mutation_indices] + random_value
    return offspring_crossover
```

Finally, the ANN.py is implemented according to Listing 4-16. It contains the implementation of the activation functions (sigmoid and ReLU) in addition to the "fitness" and "predict_outputs" functions to calculate the accuracy.

Listing 4-16. ANN.py File Implementing the ANN

```python
import numpy

def sigmoid(inpt):
    return 1.0/(1.0+numpy.exp(-1*inpt))

def relu(inpt):
    result = inpt
    result[inpt<0] = 0
    return result

def predict_outputs(weights_mat, data_inputs, data_outputs,
activation="relu"):
    predictions = numpy.zeros(shape=(data_inputs.shape[0]))
    for sample_idx in range(data_inputs.shape[0]):
        r1 = data_inputs[sample_idx, :]
        for curr_weights in weights_mat:
            r1 = numpy.matmul(a=r1, b=curr_weights)
            if activation == "relu":
                r1 = relu(r1)
            elif activation == "sigmoid":
                r1 = sigmoid(r1)
        predicted_label = numpy.where(r1 == numpy.max(r1))[0][0]
        predictions[sample_idx] = predicted_label
    correct_predictions = numpy.where(predictions == data_outputs)[0].size
    accuracy = (correct_predictions/data_outputs.size)*100
    return accuracy, predictions
```

```python
def fitness(weights_mat, data_inputs, data_outputs, activation="relu"):
    accuracy = numpy.empty(shape=(weights_mat.shape[0]))
    for sol_idx in range(weights_mat.shape[0]):
        curr_sol_mat = weights_mat[sol_idx, :]
        accuracy[sol_idx], _ = predict_outputs(curr_sol_mat, data_inputs,
        data_outputs, activation=activation)
    return accuracy
```

CHAPTER 5

Convolutional Neural Networks

The previously discussed architecture of ANNs is called FC neural networks (FCNNs). The reason is that each neuron in a layer **i** is connected to all neurons in layers **i-1** and **i+1**. Each connection between two neurons has two parameters: the weight and the bias. Adding more layers and neurons increases the number of parameters. As a result, it is very time-consuming to train such networks even on devices on multiple graphics processing units (GPUs) and multiple central processing units (CPUs). It becomes impossible to train such networks on PCs with limited processing and memory capabilities.

In the analysis of multidimensional data such as images, CNNs (also known as ConvNets) are more time and memory efficient than FC networks. But why? What are the advantages of ConvNets over FC networks in image analysis? How is ConvNet derived from FC networks? Where does the term convolution in CNNs come from? These questions are to be answered in this chapter. To have a better understanding of how everything works, this chapter implements the CNN using the NumPy library by working through all steps required to build the different layers in these networks, including convolution, pooling, activation, and FC. Finally, a project called NumPyCNN will be created to help create a CNN easily and then learn how to deploy it in Appendix A.

From ANN to CNN

ANN is the base of the CNN, with some changes added to make it suitable for analyzing large amounts of data. Connecting all neurons together increases the number of parameters even when analyzing very small images (e.g., one of 150×150 pixels). The input layer in this case will have 22,500 neurons. Connecting it to another hidden

183

© Ahmed Fawzy Gad 2018
A. F. Gad, *Practical Computer Vision Applications Using Deep Learning with CNNs*,
https://doi.org/10.1007/978-1-4842-4167-7_5

layer with 500 neurons, the number of parameters required is 22,500×500=11,250,000. Real-world applications might work with high-dimensionality images where the least dimension might have 1,000 pixels and more. For an input image of size 1,000×1,000 and a hidden layer of 2,000 neurons, the number of parameters equals 2 billion. Note that the input image is gray.

The next subsections cover the following questions: What is the intuition behind using CNN over ANN? Do we really need all of the parameters used in traditional ANN? How is CNN different from ANN, and how is it derived from ANN? Finally, what is the source of the term convolution used in CNN? Let's start answering these questions.

The Intuition Behind DL

In Chapter 1, we handled the task of feature extraction. This is the traditional approach to perform image analysis tasks, which involve using a set of features that are representative for the problem being solved. This might require the help of experts in the field being studied, because one feature might be robust for a given problem but weak for another. Selecting the best features to a given problem is the challenge. Starting from a very large number of features, how can they be reduced to the best minimum set?

We might be able to find a set of features when working with a small amount of data in which there is a slight variation. The more variations existing in the data, the more difficult it is to find a set of features covering all of them.

In a traditional classification problem, the goal is to find the best set of features that separate the classes used. After calculating feature 1 based on the $f_1()$ function, the samples from each class are given in Figure 5-1. The function did well for the left part of the first class, but it is very bad for the part to the right of the same class. There is overlap between the two classes in this part, and thus classification accuracy is very bad. Even the most complex ML models cannot fit this data. This is because many samples almost have the same value as $f_1()$. The function $f_1()$ needs some changes in order to enhance the classification performance.

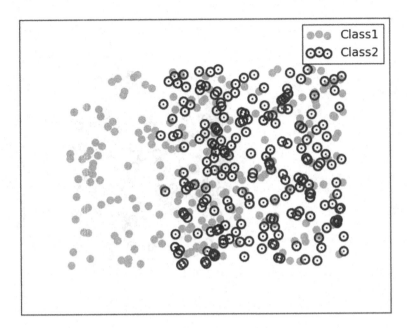

Figure 5-1. *Two-class data distribution using $f_1()$. Class 1 samples are represented as filled circles and class 2 samples as empty circles.*

To solve that problem, the result of $f_1()$ will be used as inputs for another function $f_2()$. As a result, for an input sample s_1, the final features for it will be the result of a chain of functions $f_2(f_1(s_1))$. The data distribution is as shown in Figure 5-2. It seems that the results enhanced more than the previous one. The percentage of overlap compared to the first case is reduced as some samples in the second class are clearly away from the first class. Still, there is overlap between the two classes. We aim to split the data so that each sample is near from the samples within its class and also far away from the samples in the other class.

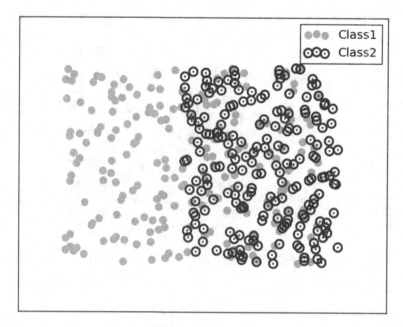

Figure 5-2. *Data distribution using $f_2(f_1())$*

To enhance the results of classification, we can use the outputs of the $f_2()$ as input to another function $f_3()$ so that the chain of functions is $f_3(f_2(f_1()))$. According to Figure 5-3, the results are better than the previous two cases.

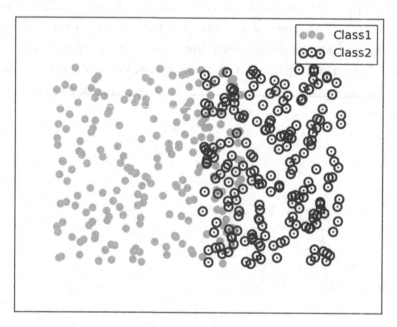

Figure 5-3. *Data distribution using $f_3(f_2(f_1()))$*

By working the same way and using a fourth function $\mathbf{f_4}()$, we can find an acceptable result as in Figure 5-4. At that point, we can build a very simple linear classifier that splits the data. We might note that after building a robust feature function, the classification becomes very easy. This is compared to a bad feature function, as in Figure 5-1, which requires the use of a very complex classifier.

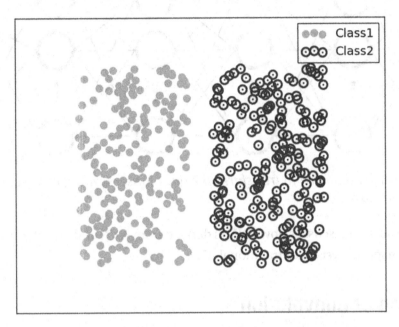

Figure 5-4. *Linear classification after separating the data correctly*

The previous discussion summarizes the target of DL models, which is automatic feature transformation. The goal is to create a feature transformation function that transforms the data samples from a bad state in which performing the ML task is complex to another state in which the task is simpler.

CNNs, which are the focus of this book, accept the pure image pixels and find by themselves the best set of features that classify the data correctly. Each layer within the CNN transforms the data from one state to another for enhancing the performance. The beauty of the ANN is that it is a universal function approximator that can approximate any type of function. Each function will have a set of parameters, which are the weights and bias. The output of one function (i.e., layer) is the input to another function (i.e., layer). The ANN architecture is extended until the classification performance is the best. For example, we can associate each step discussed previously with a hidden layer, and thus the network will have the architecture shown in Figure 5-5. This gives an understanding of the usefulness of hidden layers, which is a trouble for newbies in ANN.

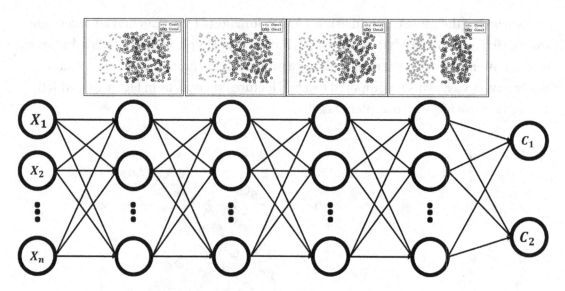

Figure 5-5. *ANN required to transform the data for separation of the class by using a linear classifier*

The next section discusses how CNN is derived from ANN and how it is more efficient in image analysis than traditional ANN.

Derivation of Convolution

Image analysis has a number of challenges, such as classification, object detection, recognition, description, and so forth. If an image classifier, for example, is to be created, it should be able to work with a high accuracy even with variations such as occlusion, illumination changes, viewing angles, and others. The traditional pipeline of image classification with its main step of feature engineering is not suitable for working in rich environments. Even experts in the field won't be able to give a single or a group of features that are able to reach high accuracy under different variations. From this problem, the idea of feature learning came out. The suitable features to work with images are learned automatically. This is why ANN is one of the most robust ways of performing image analysis. Based on a learning algorithm such as GD, ANN learns the image features automatically. The raw image is applied to the ANN and ANN is responsible for generating the features describing it.

Image Analysis Using FC Network

Let's see how ANN works with images and why CNN is efficient in its time and memory requirements with respect to the 3×3 gray image in Figure 5-6. The example given uses a small image size and a lower number of neurons for simplicity.

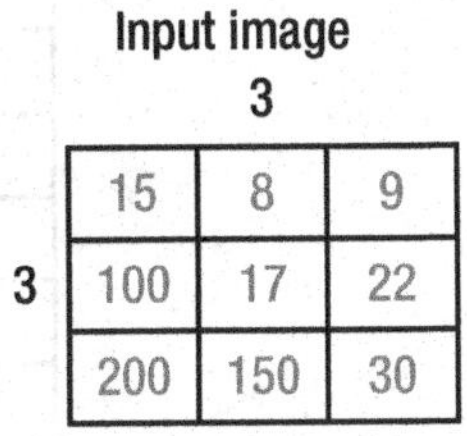

Figure 5-6. Tiny image as input to an FCNN

The inputs of the ANN input layer are the image pixels. Each pixel represents an input. Because the ANN works with 1D vectors, not 2D matrices, it is better to convert the preceding 2D image into a 1D vector, as in Figure 5-7.

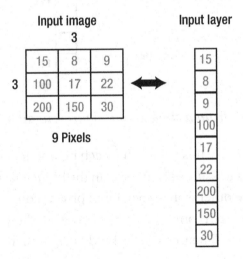

Figure 5-7. 2D image to 1D vector

Each pixel is mapped to an element in the vector. Each element in the vector represented a neuron in ANN. Because the image has **3×3=9** pixels, then there will be nine neurons in the input layer. Representing the vector as row or column doesn't matter, but ANN usually extends horizontally, and each of its layers is represented as a column vector.

After preparing the input of the ANN, next is to add the hidden layer(s) that learns how to convert the image pixels into representative features. Assume that there is a single hidden layer with 16 neurons, as in Figure 5-8.

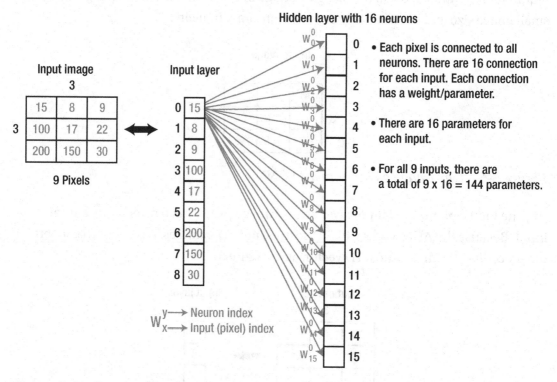

Figure 5-8.   Connections from a single input neuron to all hidden layer neurons

Because the network is FC, this means that each neuron in layer **i** is connected to all neurons in layer **i-1**. As a result, each neuron in the hidden layer is connected to all 9 pixels in the input layer. In other words, each input pixel is connected to the 16 neurons in the hidden layer, where each connection has a corresponding unique parameter. By connecting each pixel to all neurons in the hidden layer, there will be **9×16=144** parameters or weights for a tiny network such as that shown in Figure 5-9.

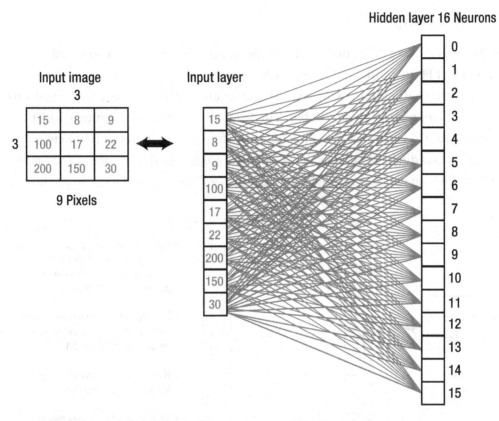

Figure 5-9. *Connecting all input neurons to all hidden layer neurons*

Large Number of Parameters

The number of parameters in this FC network seems acceptable. But this number greatly increases as the number of image pixels and hidden layers increases.

For example, if this network has two hidden layers with 90 and 50 neurons, respectively, then the number of parameters between the input layer and the first hidden layer is **9×90=810**. The number of parameters between the two hidden layers is **90×50=4,500**. The total number of parameters in this network is **810+4,500=5,310**. This is a large number for such a network. Another case of a very small image of size 32×32 (1,024 pixels). If the network operates with a single hidden layer of 500 neurons, there are a total of **1,024*500=512,000** parameters (weight). This is a huge number for a network with just a single hidden layer working with a small image. There must be a solution to decrease this number of parameters. This is where CNN has a critical role. It creates a very large network but with fewer parameters than FC networks.

Neuron Grouping

The problem that makes the number of parameters get very large even for small networks is that FC networks add a parameter between every two neurons in the successive layers. Rather than assigning a single parameter between every two neurons, a single parameter may be given to a block or group of neurons as in Figure 5-10. The pixel with index 0 in Figure 5-8 is connected to the first four neurons with indices (0, 1, 2, and 3) with four different weights. If the neurons are grouped in groups of four as in Figure 5-10, then all neurons inside the same group will be assigned a single parameter.

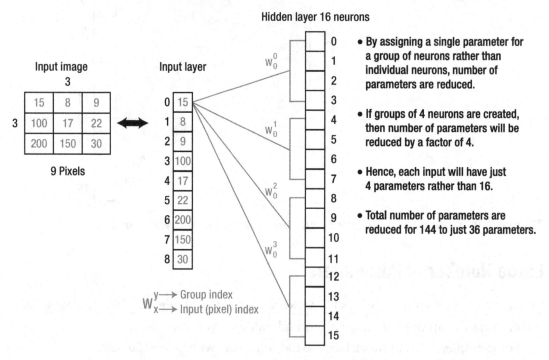

Figure 5-10. *Grouping every four hidden neurons to use the same weight*

As a result, the pixel with index 0 in Figure 5-10 will be connected to the first four neurons with the same weight as in Figure 5-11. The same parameter is assigned to every four successive neurons. As a result, the number of parameters is reduced by a factor of 4. Each input neuron will have **16/4=4** parameters. The entire network will have **144/4=36** parameters. It is a 75% reduction of the parameters. This is fine, but it is still possible to reduce more parameters.

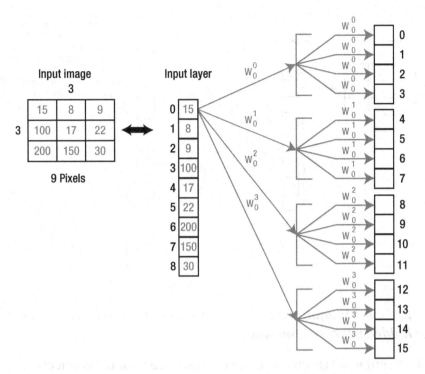

Figure 5-11. *All neurons in the same group are using the same weight*

Because there are four groups of neurons, that means there are four filters in this layer. As a result, the output of this layer will have its third dimension equal to 3, which means three filtered images will be returned. The goal of CNN is to find the best values for such filters that make each input image associated with its class label.

Figure 5-12 shows the unique connections from each pixel to the first neuron of each group. That is, all missing connections are just duplicates of the existing ones. Hypothetically, there is a connection from each pixel to each neuron in each group, as in Figure 5-9, because the network is still FC.

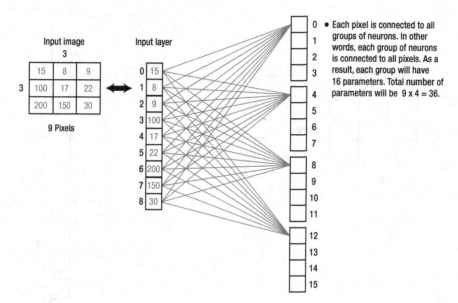

Figure 5-12. *Fewer unique connections between the input layer and the hidden layer after hidden neurons grouping*

To make it simple, all connections are omitted except for the connections between all pixels to just the first neuron in the first group, as shown in Figure 5-13. It seems that each group is still connected to all 9 pixels, and thus it will have 9 parameters. It is possible to reduce the number of pixels that this neuron is connected to.

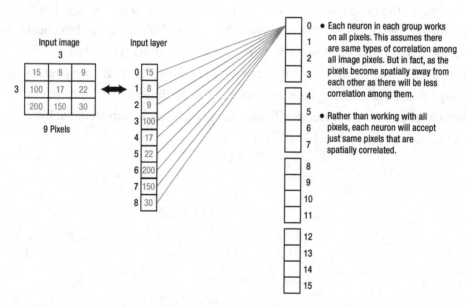

Figure 5-13. *Connections between all neurons in the input layer to the first group of neurons within the hidden layer*

Pixel Spatial Correlation

Current configuration makes each neuron accepts all pixels. If there is a function $f(x1, x2, x3, x4)$ that accepts four inputs, that means the decision is to be taken based on all four of these inputs. If the function with just two inputs gives the same results as using all four inputs, then we do not have to use all of these four inputs. The two inputs giving the required results are sufficient. This is similar to the preceding case. Each neuron accepts all 9 pixels as inputs. If the same or better results will be returned by using fewer pixels, then we should go through it.

Usually, in image analysis, each pixel is highly correlated to pixels surrounding it (i.e., neighbors). The higher the distance between two pixels, the more they will be uncorrelated. For example, in the cameraman image shown in Figure 5-14, a pixel inside the face is correlated to the surrounding face pixels around it. But it is less correlated to far pixels such as sky or ground.

Figure 5-14. *Cameraman image*

Based on this assumption, each neuron in the preceding example will accept just pixels that are spatially correlated to each other, because working on all of them is reasonable. Rather than applying all 9 pixels to each neuron as input, it is possible to just select 4 spatially correlated pixels as in Figure 5-15. The first pixel of index 0 in the column vector located at (0,0) in the image will be applied as an input to the first neuron with its 3 most spatially correlated pixels. Based on the input image, the 3 most spatially correlated pixels to that pixel are pixels with indices $(0,1)$, $(1,0)$, and $(1,1)$. As a result, the neuron will accept just 4 pixels rather than 9. Because all neurons in the same group share the same parameters, then the 4 neurons in each group will have just 4 parameters rather than 9. As a result, the total number of parameters will be 4×4=16. Compared to the FC network in Figure 5-9, there is a reduction of a 144–16=128 parameter (i.e., 88.89% reduction).

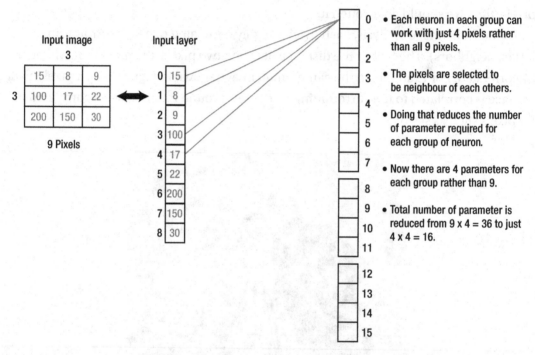

Figure 5-15. *Connecting the first group of correlated pixels to the first group*

Convolution in CNN

At this point, the question of why CNN is more time and memory efficient than the FC network is answered. Using fewer parameters allows the increase of a deep CNN with a huge number of layers and neurons, which is not possible in the FC network. Next is to get the idea of convolution in CNN.

Now there are just four weights assigned to all neurons in the same block. How will these four weights cover all 9 pixels? Let's see how this works.

Figure 5-16 shows the previous network in Figure 5-15 but after adding the weight labels to the connections. Inside the neuron, each of the 4 input pixels is multiplied by its corresponding weight. The equation is shown in Figure 5-16. The four pixels and weights would be better visualized as matrices as in Figure 5-16. The previous result will be achieved by multiplying the weights matrix to the current set of 4 pixels element by element. In practice, the size of the convolution mask should be odd, such as 3×3. For easier presentation, a 2×2 mask is used in this example.

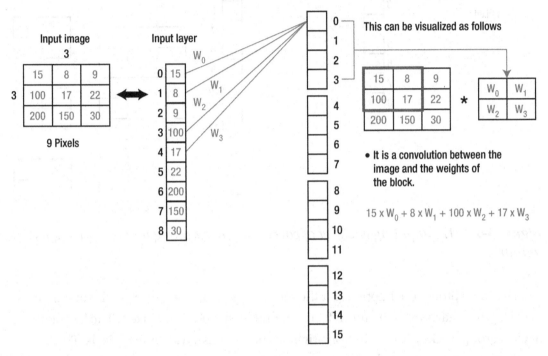

Figure 5-16. *Adding weights of each connection and visualizing them as a matrix*

Moving to the next neuron of index 1, it will work with another set of spatially correlated pixels with the same weights used by the neuron with index 0. Also, neurons with indices 2 and 3 will work with other two sets of spatially correlated pixels. This is shown in Figure 5-17. It seems that the first neuron in the group starts from the top-left pixel and chooses a number of pixels surrounding it. The last neuron in the group works on the bottom-right pixel and its surrounding pixels. The in-between neurons are adjusted to select in-between pixels. Such behavior is identical to convolution between the set of weights of the group and the image. This is why CNN has the term convolution.

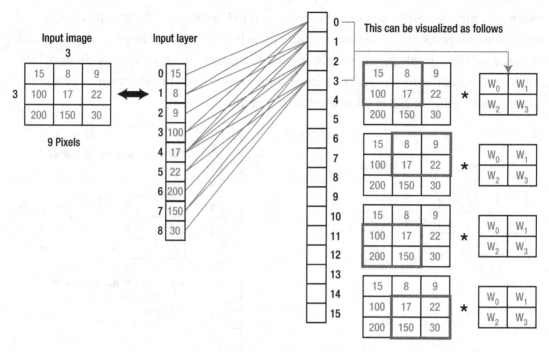

Figure 5-17. *Highlighting each set of correlated pixels along with their weights as a matrix*

The same procedure happens for the remaining groups of neurons. The first neuron of each group starts from the top-left corner and its surrounding pixels. The last neuron of each group works with the bottom-right corner and its surrounding pixels. The in-between neurons work on the in-between pixels.

After understanding how CNN is derived from ANN, we can take an example that performs convolution between an input image and a filter (i.e., a set of weights) and produces its result.

Designing a CNN

In the example we are going to design using CNN, there are three shapes: rectangle, triangle, and circle. Each one of them is represented by a 4×4 matrix as in Figure 5-18, where 1 represents white and 0 represents black. The goal is to build a CNN to return 1 when there is a rectangle and 0 otherwise. How can we do that?

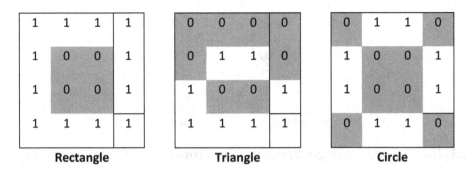

Figure 5-18. *Rectangle, triangle, and circle represented by 4×4 matrices. Pixel of 1 is white and pixel of 0 is black.*

When starting to design a CNN, the first step is to determine the number of layers and number of filters within each layer. Usually, CNN has more than just a convolution (conv for short) layer, but we will start only using this layer. You can test yourself to solve such a problem.

First, the convolution layer investigates the building blocks of the shape structure we are looking for. So, the first question to ask yourself is what is special about a rectangle compared to a triangle and a circle. The rectangular shape has four edges, two vertical and two horizontal. We can benefit from such information. But also note that properties existing in the rectangle should not exist in the other shapes. Other shapes already have different properties. Neither of the two other shapes have two horizontal edges and two vertical edges. This is great.

The next question is how to make the convolution layer recognize the existence of the edges. Remember that CNN starts by recognizing the individual elements of the shape and then connects these elements together. So, we are not looking to find the four edges nor looking to find two parallel vertical edges and two parallel horizontal edges, but instead to recognize any vertical or horizontal edge. So, the question becomes more specific. How can we to recognize vertical or horizontal edges? This can be simply done using gradients.

The first layer will have a filter that looks for horizontal edges and another filter for vertical edges. These filters are shown in Figure 5-19 as 3×3 matrices. So, we know how many filters to use in the first conv layer and also what these filters are. The size of 3×3 is chosen for the filters because it is a good size at which the structure of the horizontal and vertical edges is clear.

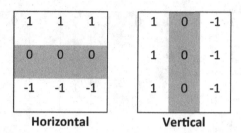

Horizontal   **Vertical**

Figure 5-19. *Filters for recognizing horizontal and vertical edges of size 3×3*

After applying these filters over the matrices in Figure 5-19, the conv layer will be able
to recognize the vertical edges in Figure 5-20 and the horizontal edges in Figure 5-21.
The layer is able to recognize the horizontal and vertical edges in the rectangle. It also
recognized the horizontal edge at the triangle base. But there is no edge in the circle. At the
current time, the CNN has two candidates to be a rectangle, which are the shapes having at
least one edge. Despite being sure that the third shape could not be a rectangle, the CNN
has to propagate it to the other layers until making its decision at the final layer. Because of
using two filters in the first conv layer, it results in two outputs, one for each filter.

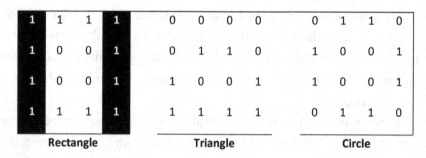

Rectangle   **Triangle**   **Circle**

Figure 5-20. *Recognized vertical edges in black*

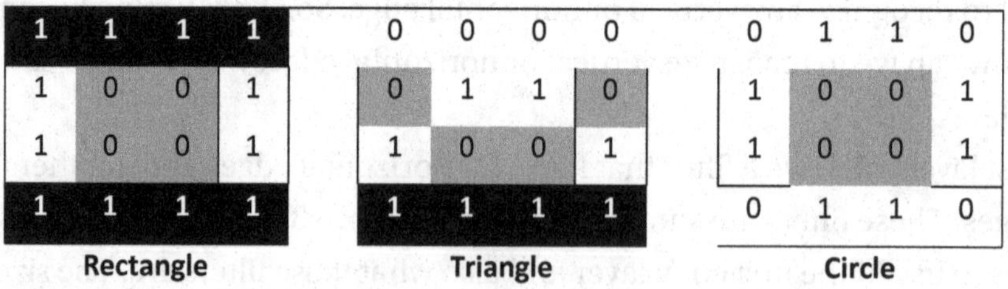

Rectangle   **Triangle**   **Circle**

Figure 5-21. *Recognized horizontal edges in black*

The next convolution layer will accept the results of the first convolution layer and continue based on it. Let's repeat the same questions asked in the first layer. What is the number of filters to use and what is their structure? Based on the rectangle structure, we find that each horizontal edge is connected to a vertical edge. Because there are two horizontal edges, this requires the use of the two filters in Figure 5-22 of size 3×3.

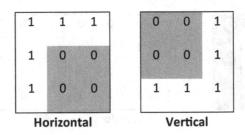

Horizontal   **Vertical**

Figure 5-22. *Filters for recognizing connected horizontal and vertical edges of size 3×3*

After applying those filters to the results of conv layer 1, the results of the filters used in the second conv layer are shown in Figure 5-23 and Figure 5-24, respectively. Regarding the rectangle, the filters are able to find the two required edges and connect them together. In the triangle, there is just a single horizontal edge with no vertical edge connected to it. As a result, there are no positive outputs for the triangle.

Rectangle				Triangle				Circle			
1	1	1	1	0	0	0	0	0	1	1	0
1	0	0	1	0	1	1	0	1	0	0	1
1	0	0	1	1	0	0	1	1	0	0	1
1	1	1	1	1	1	1	1	0	1	1	0

Figure 5-23. *Result of the first filter in the second layer in black*

Rectangle				Triangle				Circle			
1	1	1	1	0	0	0	0	0	1	1	0
1	0	0	1	0	1	1	0	1	0	0	1
1	0	0	1	1	0	0	1	1	0	0	1
1	1	1	1	1	1	1	1	0	1	1	0

Figure 5-24. *Result of the second filter in the second layer in black*

By the current result, we have not recognized that rectangle, but we have nevertheless done a nice job so far. We connected the individual edges to more meaningful structures. Now, there is just a single step toward recognizing the complete shape, which is connecting the recognized edges in Figures 5-23 and 5-24. The result is in Figure 5-25. This is great.

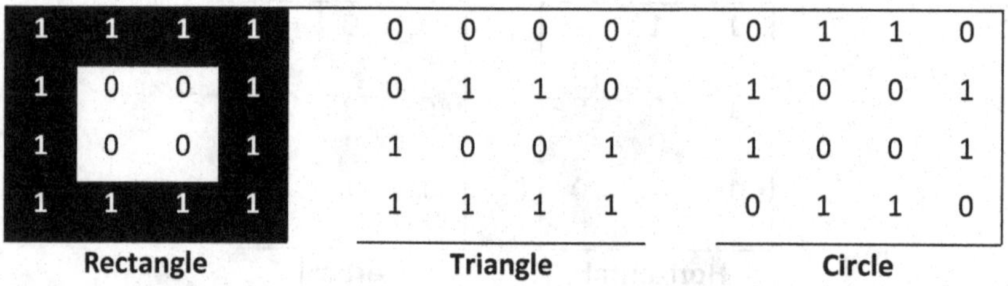

1	1	1	1		0	0	0	0		0	1	1	0
1	0	0	1		0	1	1	0		1	0	0	1
1	0	0	1		1	0	0	1		1	0	0	1
1	1	1	1		1	1	1	1		0	1	1	0
Rectangle					**Triangle**					**Circle**			

Figure 5-25. *Results of connecting recognized shapes by the second conv layer*

But we did the work manually, not automatically. We guided the CNN by telling it the filters to use. But this is not the case in regular problems. The CNN will find the filters itself. We just tried to simplify things by using the correct filters. Remember that these filters and the weights of connections between the different layers are automatically adjusted by the CNN. So, finding the correct filters means finding the correct weights. This links what we have learned now to what we got before.

Pooling Operation for Parameter Reduction

The convolution operation just finds the dot product between a mask and an image portion of the same size as the filter. If the filter matches a portion of the image, then the SOP will be high. Assume that the output of applying the convolution operation is as shown in Figure 5-26.

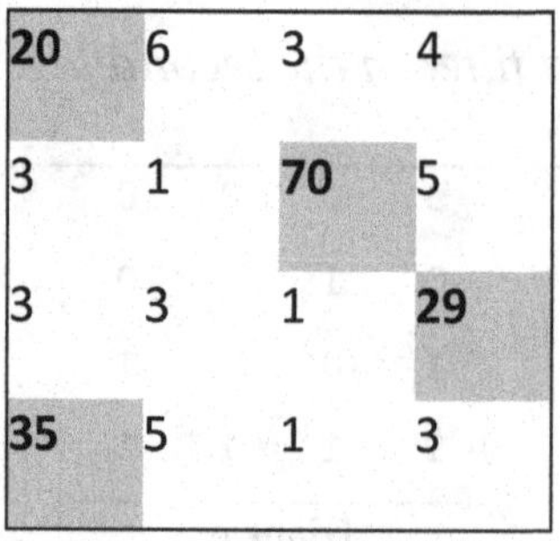

20	6	3	4
3	1	70	5
3	3	1	29
35	5	1	3

Figure 5-26. *Results of a convolution operation*

The shaded regions are the ones at which there is a high match between the image portions and the used filter. Note that there are two pieces of information here:

1. The existence of high scores means that the region of interest (ROI) exists in the image.

2. The location of the high scores tells the location in the image at which match occurs between the filter and the image portion.

But are we interested in both these pieces of information? The answer is no. We are just interested in the second piece. This is because the only goal of CNN is to tell whether the target object exists in the image or not. We are not interested in localizing it.

As a result, if the exact location is not of concern for us, we can avoid storing such spatial information. For example, we can say that the ROI exists in the image but avoid storing its exact location. The previous matrix size will be reduced if we do so, as shown in Figure 5-27.

Figure 5-27. *Results of a convolution operation*

We can get rid of the extra information that tells the exact location of the image portion with a match because it is not important for us. We just kept the information that tells that a match occurred. This is by keeping the maximum values of the convolution output matrix. Finding high scores tells us that there is a match.

But how did we reduce the matrix size? This is by just keeping the maximum value of each 2×2 region for example. This operation is called max pooling.

By applying the max pooling operation, there is a very important improvement over the computational time and memory requirements. Rather than keeping a matrix of size 4×4 in the memory, it is reduced to half size (2×2). This saves memory by just keeping 4 values compared to 16. Moreover, the time is reduced because the output of that max pooling operation will be the input of another convolution operation. This convolution operation will work on a matrix of size 2×2 rather than 4×4.

Finally, applying the max pooling operation helps us reduce the computational time and memory requirements by removing the spurious features that have no importance for us in CNN (this is the exact location at which match occurred). This operation makes the CNN translation invariance.

Convolution Operation Example

This subsection gives an example of how to apply the convolution operation over a sample of size 8×8 from a 2D image shown in Figure 5-28. A single filter will be used in the convolution, which is the horizontal gradient detector in Figure 5-19. Convolution is applied by centering the filter over each pixel, multiplying each element in the filter by its corresponding pixel in the image, returning the sum of these multiplications within a new image.

65	84	215	175	72	253	19	250
162	103	70	97	66	94	90	39
150	40	106	47	247	86	92	75
197	14	239	23	220	139	58	148
5	2	68	108	201	165	237	161
90	246	235	253	36	180	107	136
1	239	110	208	200	29	176	151
123	177	129	171	224	77	84	70

Figure 5-28. *Image sample of size 8×8 to apply the convolution operation*

Because the filter size is 3×3 and each of its elements is multiplied by an element within the image, then after centering the filter over any pixel there must be an element corresponding to each element in the filter. It is obvious that this does not work for the border of the image (i.e., leftmost and rightmost columns in addition to top and bottom rows), as marked by gray in Figure 5-28. There are two solutions in such a case. The first is to keep working with the pixels by padding extra rows and columns with zeros, or in other words, multiplying any element if the filter doesn't have a corresponding image pixel by zero. This will produce an output image of equal size to the original image.

In this case, the number of rows required for padding at the top and bottom borders is calculated according to Equation 5-1. The number of padded columns to the left and right is calculated according to Equation 5-2. For our example with a filter size of 3×3, there are two rows and two columns to be padded.

$$Padding_{rows} = floor(Filter_{rows}/2) \qquad \text{(Equation 5-1)}$$

$$Padding_{cols} = floor(Filter_{cols}/2) \qquad \text{(Equation 5-2)}$$

In most cases, the number of rows and columns in the filter is an odd number. This helps localize a center pixel at which the SOP will be inserted.

The second solution is to avoid working with the image borders. In this case, the resulting image will have a size less than that of the original image. The number of rows and columns in the output image is calculated according to Equations 5.3 and 5.4, respectively. For our input image of size 8×8, the size of the resultant image is 6×6.

$$NewSize_{rows} = OldSize_{rows} - 2xPadding_{rows} \qquad \text{(Equation 5-3)}$$

$$NewSize_{cols} = OldSize_{cols} - 2xPadding_{cols} \qquad \text{(Equation 5-4)}$$

Assuming that no padding is used, then the first pixel to work with is the pixel located in the second row and second column with value 103. Centering the filter at this pixel and multiplying each element by its corresponding pixels, the SOP is as follows:

$$sop = 65(1) + 84(0) + 215(-1) + 162(1) + 103(0) + 70(-1) + 150(1) + 40(0) + 106(-1) = -14$$

This result is inserted in a new image at the pixel located at the top-left row and top-left column. After calculating the output for one pixel, the next step is to shift the filter to get another pixel. The number of shifts required is called stride. A stride of 1 shifts the filter one column/row at a time. In the current step, it will move the filter to the right just one column and center the filter over the pixel in the second row and third column with a value of 70. A stride of 2 shifts the filter two columns/rows at a time, and thus the current pixel will be 97.

Using a stride of 1, we will continue calculating the SOP for all pixels in the first row starting from column 2 to column 7, each time calculating the SOP. After that, the filter is shifted one row down, and thus the current pixel will be 40 located at the third row and second column. The final result without padding and using a stride of 1 is shown in Figure 5-29.

-14	-92	6	-114	184	69
94	-10	-118	-152	293	57
-61	-122	-255	-212	281	6
-250	-122	85	-100	55	39
-317	-82	-24	195	-83	-74
-260	30	14	346	93	-71

Figure 5-29. *Convolution output between an image of size 8×8 and a 3×3 filter*

Max Pooling Operation Example

Assuming that there is a conv layer that produced the previous result in Figure 5-29 and that this layer is connected with a max pooling layer, let's work on calculating its output.

The max pooling layer selects a group of pixels to summarize into a single pixel by just keeping their maximum value. If a mask of size 2×2 is used, it will start from the top-left 4 pixels marked in gray in Figure 5-29. Their maximum value is 94, which is the output. Similar to convolution, max pooling will shift the mask to work on another 4 pixels, and thus it needs a stride. The stride value for the pooling layer is equal to 2 at the minimum. The reason is that a stride of 1 will duplicate values without the output, which is not helpful. In the highlighted pixels in black in Figure 5-29, the result of the max pooling operation for the first two columns will be 30. Using a stride of 1 and shifting the mask to the right by one column, the result of this operation for the last two columns highlighted in black is also 30. As a result, a value of 30 appeared twice. Is it helpful to return the same value more than once? A value of 30 returned the first time means that there is a match between the convolution filter and the image that equals 30. So, we got that information. There is no need to repeat it again. Working with a stride of 1 will use more parameters to return repeated results we are not interested in. As a result, a stride of 2 will be helpful.

The result of applying the max pooling operation over the convolution result in Figure 5-29 is shown in Figure 5-30.

94	6	293
-61	85	281
30	364	93

Figure 5-30. *Max pooling output using a mask of size 2×2*

Building a CNN Using NumPy from Scratch

CNN is the state-of-the-art technique for analyzing multidimensional signals such as images. There are different libraries that already implement CNN such as TensorFlow (TF) and Keras. These libraries isolate the developer from some details and just give an abstract application program interface (API) to make life easier and avoid complexity in the implementation. But in practice, such details might make a difference. Sometimes, the data scientist has to go through such details to enhance the performance. The solution in this situation is to build every piece of the model yourself. This gives the highest possible level of control over the network.

It is recommended to implement such models to have a better understanding of them. Some ideas seem to be clear, but that may not actually be the case until programming. It will be easy to do that after learning how CNNs work. This section shows how a CNN is implemented from scratch just using NumPy. So, let's implement it and compare its outputs with TF to validate the implementation.

In this section, a CNN is created using only the NumPy library. Three layers are created: convolution (conv for short), ReLU, and max/average pooling. The major steps involved are as follows:

1. Reading the input image.

2. Preparing the filters.

3. Conv layer: Convolving each filter with the input image.

4. ReLU layer: Applying the ReLU activation function on the feature maps (output of conv layer).

5. Max pooling layer: Applying the pooling operation on the output of ReLU layer.

6. Stacking conv, ReLU, and max pooling layers.

Reading the Input Image

Listing 5-1 reads an already existing image from the skimage Python library and converts it into gray.

Listing 5-1. Reading an Image

```
import skimage.data
# Reading the image
img = skimage.data.chelsea()
# Converting the image into gray.
img = skimage.color.rgb2gray(img)
```

This example uses an already existing image within the skimage Python library. The image is called using `skimage.data.chelsea()`. Note that this call implicitly reads an image file named "chelsea.png" within the skimage library installation directory. The image could also be read by passing its path to the `skimage.data.imread(fname)`. For example, if the library is located in "Lib\site-packages\skimage\data\", then we could read it as follows:

```
img = skimage.data.chelsea("\AhmedGad\Anaconda3\Lib\site-packages\skimage\
data\chelsea.png")
```

Reading image is the first step because the next steps depend on the input size. The image after being converted into gray is in Figure 5-31.

Figure 5-31. *Original gray image read using skimage.data.chelsea()*

Preparing Filters

The following line prepares the filter bank for the first conv layer (**l1** for short):

```
l1_filter = numpy.zeros((2,3,3))
```

A zero array is created according to the number of filters and the size of each filter. Two filters of size **3×3** are created; that is why the zero array is of size (**2**=num_filters, **3**=num_rows_filter, **3**=num_columns_filter). The size of the filter is selected to be a 2D array without depth because the input image is gray and has no depth (i.e., 2D). If the image is RGB with three channels, the filter size must be (3, 3, **3**=depth).

The size of the filter bank is specified by the preceding zero array but not the actual values of the filters. It is possible to override the values as follows to detect vertical and horizontal edges.

```
l1_filter[0, :, :] = numpy.array([[[-1, 0, 1],
                                    [-1, 0, 1],
                                    [-1, 0, 1]]])
l1_filter[1, :, :] = numpy.array([[[1,   1,  1],
                                    [0,   0,  0],
                                    [-1, -1, -1]]])
```

Conv Layer

After preparing the filters, the next step is to convolve the input image by them. The next line convolves the image with the filter bank using a function called **conv**:

```
l1_feature_map = conv(img, l1_filter)
```

This function accepts just two arguments, the image and the filter bank, as implemented in Listing 5-2.

Listing 5-2. Convolving the Image by a Single Filter

```
def conv(img, conv_filter):
    if len(img.shape) > 2 or len(conv_filter.shape) > 3: # Check if number
    of image channels matches the filter depth.
```

```python
    if img.shape[-1] != conv_filter.shape[-1]:
        print("Error: Number of channels in both image and filter must
        match.")
        sys.exit()
if conv_filter.shape[1] != conv_filter.shape[2]:
    print('Error: Filter must be a square matrix, i.e., number of rows
    and columns must match.')
    sys.exit()
if conv_filter.shape[1]%2==0: # Check if filter dimensions are odd.
    print('Error: Filter must have an odd size, i.e., number of rows
    and columns must be odd.')
    sys.exit()

# An empty feature map to hold the output of convolving the filter(s)
with the image.
feature_maps = numpy.zeros((img.shape[0]-conv_filter.shape[1]+1,
                            img.shape[1]-conv_filter.shape[1]+1,
                            conv_filter.shape[0]))

# Convolving the image by the filter(s).
for filter_num in range(conv_filter.shape[0]):
    print("Filter ", filter_num + 1)
    curr_filter = conv_filter[filter_num, :] # getting a filter from
    the bank.

    # Checking if there are multiple channels for the single filter.
    # If so, then each channel will convolve the image.
    # The result of all convolutions is summed to return a single
    feature map.

    if len(curr_filter.shape) > 2:
        conv_map = conv_(img[:, :, 0], curr_filter[:, :, 0]) # Array
        holding the sum of all feature maps.
        for ch_num in range(1, curr_filter.shape[-1]): # Convolving
        each channel with the image and summing the results.
            conv_map = conv_map + conv_(img[:, :, ch_num],
                            curr_filter[:, :, ch_num])
```

```
    else: # There is just a single channel in the filter.
        conv_map = conv_(img, curr_filter)
    feature_maps[:, :, filter_num] = conv_map # Holding feature map
    with the current filter.
return feature_maps # Returning all feature maps.
```

The function starts by ensuring that the depth of each filter is equal to the number of image channels. In the following code, the outer if checks if the channel and the filter have a depth. If a depth already exists, then the inner if checks their inequality. If there is no match, then the script will exit.

```
if len(img.shape) > 2 or len(conv_filter.shape) > 3: # Check if number of
image channels matches the filter depth.
    if img.shape[-1] != conv_filter.shape[-1]:
        print("Error: Number of channels in both image and filter must
        match.")
        sys.exit()
```

Moreover, the size of the filter should be odd and filter dimensions should be equal (i.e., number of rows and columns are odd and equal). This is checked according to the following two **if** blocks. If these conditions don't meet, the script will exit.

```
if conv_filter.shape[1] != conv_filter.shape[2]: # Check if filter
dimensions are equal.
    print('Error: Filter must be a square matrix, i.e., number of rows and
    columns must match.')
    sys.exit()
if conv_filter.shape[1]%2==0:
    print('Error: Filter must have an odd size, i.e., number of rows and
    columns must be odd.')
    sys.exit()
```

Not satisfying any of the conditions in the preceding is a proof that the filter depth is suitable with the image, and convolution is ready to be applied. Convolving the image by the filter starts by initializing an array to hold the outputs of convolution (i.e., feature maps) by specifying its size according to the following code:

```
# An empty feature map to hold the output of convolving the filter(s) with
the image.
feature_maps = numpy.zeros((img.shape[0]-conv_filter.shape[1]+1,
                            img.shape[1]-conv_filter.shape[1]+1,
                            conv_filter.shape[0]))
```

Because there is no stride or padding, the feature map size will be equal to (img_rows-filter_rows+1, image_columns-filter_columns+1, num_filters) as in the preceding code. Note that there is an output feature map for every filter in the bank. That is why the number of filters in the filter bank (**conv_filter.shape[0]**) is used to specify the size as a third argument. After preparing the inputs and outputs of the convolution operation, the next step is to apply it according to Listing 5-3.

Listing 5-3. Convolving the Image by Filters

```
# Convolving the image by the filter(s).
for filter_num in range(conv_filter.shape[0]):
    print("Filter ", filter_num + 1)
    curr_filter = conv_filter[filter_num, :] # getting a filter from
    the bank.

    # Checking if there are multiple channels for the single filter.
    # If so, then each channel will convolve the image.
    # The result of all convolutions is summed to return a single
    feature map.

    if len(curr_filter.shape) > 2:
        conv_map = conv_(img[:, :, 0], curr_filter[:, :, 0]) # Array
        holding the sum of all feature maps.
        for ch_num in range(1, curr_filter.shape[-1]): # Convolving
        each channel with the image and summing the results.
            conv_map = conv_map + conv_(img[:, :, ch_num],
                                curr_filter[:, :, ch_num])
    else: # There is just a single channel in the filter.
        conv_map = conv_(img, curr_filter)
    feature_maps[:, :, filter_num] = conv_map # Holding feature map
    with the current filter.
return feature_maps # Returning all feature maps.
```

The outer loop iterates over each filter in the filter bank and returns it for further steps according to this line:

```
curr_filter = conv_filter[filter_num, :] # getting a filter from the bank.
```

If the image to be convolved has more than one channel, then the filter must have a depth equal to this number of channels. Convolution, in this case, is done by convolving each image channel with its corresponding channel in the filter. Finally, the sum of the results will be the output feature map. If the image has just a single channel, then convolution will be straightforward. Determining this behavior is done in an if-else block:

```
if len(curr_filter.shape) > 2:
    conv_map = conv_(img[:, :, 0], curr_filter[:, :, 0]) # Array holding
    the sum of all feature map
    for ch_num in range(1, curr_filter.shape[-1]): # Convolving each
    channel with the image and summing the results.
        conv_map = conv_map + conv_(img[:, :, ch_num],
                                    curr_filter[:, :, ch_num])
else: # There is just a single channel in the filter.
    conv_map = conv_(img, curr_filter)
```

You might notice that the convolution is applied by a function called **conv_**, which is different from the **conv** function. The function **conv** just accepts the input image and the filter bank but doesn't apply convolution its own. It just passes each set of input-filter pairs to be convolved to the **conv_** function. This is just for making the code simpler to investigate. Listing 5-4 gives the implementation of the **conv_** function.

Listing 5-4. Convolving the Image by All Filters

```
def conv_(img, conv_filter):
    filter_size = conv_filter.shape[1]
    result = numpy.zeros((img.shape))
    #Looping through the image to apply the convolution operation.
    for r in numpy.uint16(numpy.arange(filter_size/2.0,
                          img.shape[0]-filter_size/2.0+1)):
        for c in numpy.uint16(numpy.arange(filter_size/2.0,
                                          img.shape[1]-filter_
                                          size/2.0+1)):
```

```
        # Getting the current region to get multiplied with the filter.
        # How to loop through the image and get the region based on
        # the image and filer sizes is the most tricky part of
        convolution.

        curr_region = img[r-numpy.uint16(numpy.floor(filter_
        size/2.0)):r+numpy.uint16(numpy.ceil(filter_size/2.0)),
                       c-numpy.uint16(numpy.floor(filter_
                       size/2.0)):c+numpy.uint16(numpy.ceil(filter_
                       size/2.0))]
        #Element-wise multiplication between the current region and the
        filter.
        curr_result = curr_region * conv_filter
        conv_sum = numpy.sum(curr_result) #Summing the result of
        multiplication.
        result[r, c] = conv_sum #Saving the summation in the
        convolution layer feature map.

    #Clipping the outliers of the result matrix.
    final_result = result[numpy.uint16(filter_size/2.0):result.shape[0]-
    numpy.uint16(filter_size/2.0),
                     numpy.uint16(filter_size/2.0):result.shape[1]-
                     numpy.uint16(filter_size/2.0)]
    return final_result
```

It iterates over the image and extracts regions of equal size to the filter according to this line:

```
curr_region = img[r-numpy.uint16(numpy.floor(filter_size/2.0)):r+numpy.
uint16(numpy.ceil(filter_size/2.0)),
                       c-numpy.uint16(numpy.floor(filter_
                       size/2.0)):c+numpy.uint16(numpy.ceil(filter_
                       size/2.0))]
```

Then it applies element-wise multiplication between the region and the filter and sums them to get a single value as the output according to these lines:

```
#Element-wise multiplication between the current region and the filter.
curr_result = curr_region * conv_filter
conv_sum = numpy.sum(curr_result)
result[r, c] = conv_sum
```

After convolving each filter by the input, the feature maps are returned by the **conv** function. Figure 5-32 shows the feature maps returned by this conv layer. At the end of this chapter, Listing 5-9 shows the results of all layers discussed in the code.

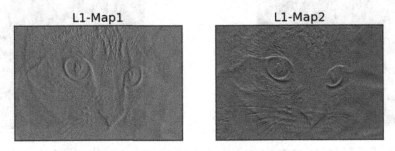

Figure 5-32. *Output feature maps of the first conv layer*

The output of such a layer will be applied to the ReLU layer.

ReLU Layer

The ReLU layer applies the ReLU activation function over each feature map returned by the conv layer. It is called using the **relu** function according to the following line of code:

```
l1_feature_map_relu = relu(l1_feature_map)
```

The **relu** function is implemented in Listing 5-5.

Listing 5-5. ReLU Implementation

```
def relu(feature_map):
    #Preparing the output of the ReLU activation function.
    relu_out = numpy.zeros(feature_map.shape)
    for map_num in range(feature_map.shape[-1]):
```

```
    for r in numpy.arange(0,feature_map.shape[0]):
        for c in numpy.arange(0, feature_map.shape[1]):
            relu_out[r, c, map_num] = numpy.max([feature_map[r, c, map_
            num], 0])
return relu_out
```

It is very simple. Just loop through each element in the feature map and return the original value in the feature map if it is larger than 0. Otherwise, return 0. The outputs of the ReLU layer are shown in Figure 5-33.

Figure 5-33. *ReLU layer output applied to the output of the first conv layer*

The output of the ReLU layer is applied to the max pooling layer.

Max Pooling Layer

The max pooling layer accepts the output of the ReLU layer and applies the max pooling operation according to the following line:

```
l1_feature_map_relu_pool = pooling(l1_feature_map_relu, 2, 2)
```

It is implemented using the **pooling** function according to Listing 5-6.

Listing 5-6. Max Pooling Implementation

```
def pooling(feature_map, size=2, stride=2):
    #Preparing the output of the pooling operation.
    pool_out = numpy.zeros((numpy.uint16((feature_map.shape[0]-size+1)/
    stride+1), numpy.uint16((feature_map.shape[1]-size+1)/stride+1),
    feature_map.shape[-1]))
```

```
for map_num in range(feature_map.shape[-1]):
    r2 = 0
    for r in numpy.arange(0,feature_map.shape[0]-size+1, stride):
        c2 = 0
        for c in numpy.arange(0, feature_map.shape[1]-size+1, stride):
            pool_out[r2, c2, map_num] = numpy.max([feature_
            map[r:r+size,  c:c+size]])
            c2 = c2 + 1
        r2 = r2 +1
return pool_out
```

The function accepts three inputs: the output of the ReLU layer, pooling mask size, and stride. It simply creates an empty array, as previously, that holds the output of the layer. The size of the array is specified according to the size and stride arguments, as in the following line:

```
pool_out = numpy.zeros((numpy.uint16((feature_map.shape[0]-size+1)/
stride+1),
                        numpy.uint16((feature_map.shape[1]-size+1)/
                        stride+1),
                        feature_map.shape[-1]))
```

Then it loops through the input channel by channel according to the outer loop, which uses the looping variable **map_num**. For each channel in the input, max pooling operation is applied. According to the stride and size used, the region is clipped and the max of it is returned in the output array according to this line:

```
pool_out[r2, c2, map_num] = numpy.max(feature_map[r:r+size,  c:c+size])
```

The outputs of the pooling layer are shown in Figure 5-34. Note that the size of the pooling layer output is smaller than its input even if they seem identical in their graphs.

L1-Map1ReLUPool

L1-Map2ReLUPool

Figure 5-34. Pooling layer output applied to the output of the first ReLU layer

Stacking Layers

Up to this point, the CNN architecture with conv, ReLU, and max pooling layers is complete. There might be some other layers to be stacked in addition to the previous ones, as given in Listing 5-7.

Listing 5-7. Building CNN Architecture

```
# Second conv layer
l2_filter = numpy.random.rand(3, 5, 5, l1_feature_map_relu_pool.shape[-1])
print("\n**Working with conv layer 2**")
l2_feature_map = conv(l1_feature_map_relu_pool, l2_filter)
print("\n**ReLU**")
l2_feature_map_relu = relu(l2_feature_map)
print("\n**Pooling**")
l2_feature_map_relu_pool = pooling(l2_feature_map_relu, 2, 2)
print("**End of conv layer 2**\n")
```

The previous conv layer uses **three** filters, with their values generated randomly. That is why there will be **three** feature maps resulting from the conv layer. This is also the same for the successive ReLU and pooling layers. Outputs of the layers are shown in Figure 5-35.

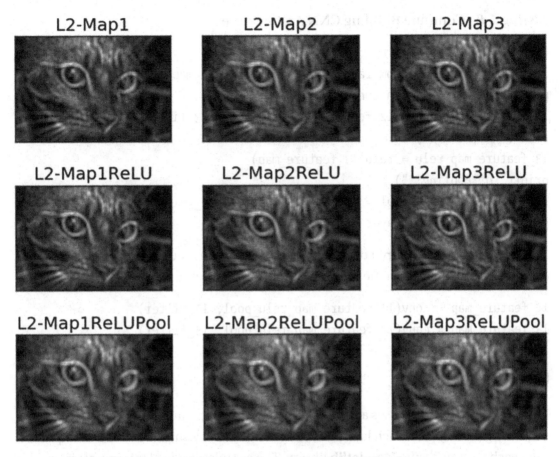

Figure 5-35. *The output of the second conv-ReLU-pooling layers*

The CNN architecture is extended by adding extra conv, ReLU, and pooling layers according to Listing 5-8. Figure 5-36 shows the outputs of these layers. The conv layer accepts just a single filter. That is why there is only one feature map as output.

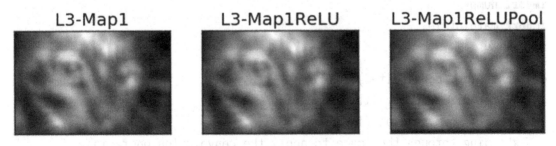

Figure 5-36. *Outputs of the third conv-ReLU-pooling layers*

Listing 5-8. Continue Building CNN Architecture

```
# Third conv layer
l3_filter = numpy.random.rand(1, 7, 7, l2_feature_map_relu_pool.shape[-1])
print("\n**Working with conv layer 3**")
l3_feature_map = conv(l2_feature_map_relu_pool, l3_filter)
print("\n**ReLU**")
l3_feature_map_relu = relu(l3_feature_map)
print("\n**Pooling**")
l3_feature_map_relu_pool = pooling(l3_feature_map_relu, 2, 2)
print("**End of conv layer 3**\n")
```

But remember, the output of each previous layer is the input to the next layer. For example, these lines accept the previous outputs as their inputs.

```
l2_feature_map = conv(l1_feature_map_relu_pool, l2_filter)
l3_feature_map = conv(l2_feature_map_relu_pool, l3_filter)
```

Complete Code

The presented code discusses and gives an example of implementing a CNN with visualizing the results of each layer. The code contains the visualization of the outputs from each layer using the **Matplotlib** library. The complete code of this project is available at **GitHub** (https://github.com/ahmedfgad/NumPyCNN).

Listing 5-9. Complete Code for Implementing CNN

```
import skimage.data
import numpy
import matplotlib
import sys

def conv_(img, conv_filter):
    filter_size = conv_filter.shape[1]
    result = numpy.zeros((img.shape))
    #Looping through the image to apply the convolution operation.
    for r in numpy.uint16(numpy.arange(filter_size/2.0,
                          img.shape[0]-filter_size/2.0+1)):
```

```
    for c in numpy.uint16(numpy.arange(filter_size/2.0,
                                      img.shape[1]-filter_
                                      size/2.0+1)):

        # Getting the current region to get multiplied with the filter.
        # How to loop through the image and get the region based on
        # the image and filer sizes is the most tricky part of
        convolution.

        curr_region = img[r-numpy.uint16(numpy.floor(filter_
        size/2.0)):r+numpy.uint16(numpy.ceil(filter_size/2.0)),
                       c-numpy.uint16(numpy.floor(filter_
                       size/2.0)):c+numpy.uint16(numpy.ceil(filter_
                       size/2.0))]
        #Element-wise multiplication between the current region and the
        filter.
        curr_result = curr_region * conv_filter
        conv_sum = numpy.sum(curr_result) #Summing the result of
        multiplication.
        result[r, c] = conv_sum #Saving the summation in the
        convolution layer feature map.

    #Clipping the outliers of the result matrix.
    final_result = result[numpy.uint16(filter_size/2.0):result.shape[0]-
                   numpy.uint16(filter_size/2.0), numpy.uint16(filter_
                   size/2.0):result.shape[1]-numpy.uint16(filter_size/2.0)]
    return final_result
def conv(img, conv_filter):
    if len(img.shape) > 2 or len(conv_filter.shape) > 3:
        if img.shape[-1] != conv_filter.shape[-1]:
            print("Error: Number of channels in both image and filter must
            match.")
            sys.exit()
    if conv_filter.shape[1] != conv_filter.shape[2]:
        print('Error: Filter must be a square matrix, i.e., number of rows
        and columns must match.')
        sys.exit()
```

```python
    if conv_filter.shape[1]%2==0:
        print('Error: Filter must have an odd size, i.e., number of rows
        and columns must be odd.')
        sys.exit()

    # An empty feature map to hold the output of convolving the filter(s)
    with the image.
    feature_maps = numpy.zeros((img.shape[0]-conv_filter.shape[1]+1,
                                img.shape[1]-conv_filter.shape[1]+1,
                                conv_filter.shape[0]))

    # Convolving the image by the filter(s).
    for filter_num in range(conv_filter.shape[0]):
        print("Filter ", filter_num + 1)
        curr_filter = conv_filter[filter_num, :] # getting a filter from
        the bank.

        # Checking if there are multiple channels for the single filter.
        # If so, then each channel will convolve the image.
        # The result of all convolutions is summed to return a single
        feature map.

        if len(curr_filter.shape) > 2:
            conv_map = conv_(img[:, :, 0], curr_filter[:, :, 0]) # Array
            holding the sum of all feature maps.
            for ch_num in range(1, curr_filter.shape[-1]): # Convolving
            each channel with the image and summing the results.
                conv_map = conv_map + conv_(img[:, :, ch_num],
                                    curr_filter[:, :, ch_num])
        else: # There is just a single channel in the filter.
            conv_map = conv_(img, curr_filter)
        feature_maps[:, :, filter_num] = conv_map # Holding feature map
        with the current filter.
    return feature_maps # Returning all feature maps.

def pooling(feature_map, size=2, stride=2):
    #Preparing the output of the pooling operation.
```

```python
    pool_out = numpy.zeros((numpy.uint16((feature_map.shape[0]-size+1)/
    stride+1), numpy.uint16((feature_map.shape[1]-size+1)/stride+1),
    feature_map.shape[-1]))
    for map_num in range(feature_map.shape[-1]):
        r2 = 0
        for r in numpy.arange(0,feature_map.shape[0]-size+1, stride):
            c2 = 0
            for c in numpy.arange(0, feature_map.shape[1]-size+1, stride):
                pool_out[r2, c2, map_num] = numpy.max([feature_
                map[r:r+size,  c:c+size]])
                c2 = c2 + 1
            r2 = r2 +1
    return pool_out

def relu(feature_map):
    #Preparing the output of the ReLU activation function.
    relu_out = numpy.zeros(feature_map.shape)
    for map_num in range(feature_map.shape[-1]):
        for r in numpy.arange(0,feature_map.shape[0]):
            for c in numpy.arange(0, feature_map.shape[1]):
                relu_out[r, c, map_num] = numpy.max([feature_map[r, c, map_
                num], 0])
    return relu_out

# Reading the image
#img = skimage.io.imread("fruits2.png")
img = skimage.data.chelsea()
# Converting the image into gray.
img = skimage.color.rgb2gray(img)

# First conv layer
#l1_filter = numpy.random.rand(2,7,7)*20 # Preparing the filters randomly.
l1_filter = numpy.zeros((2,3,3))
l1_filter[0, :, :] = numpy.array([[[-1, 0, 1],
                                   [-1, 0, 1],
                                   [-1, 0, 1]]])
```

```
l1_filter[1, :, :] = numpy.array([[[1,   1,  1],
                                   [0,   0,  0],
                                   [-1, -1, -1]]])

print("\n**Working with conv layer 1**")
l1_feature_map = conv(img, l1_filter)
print("\n**ReLU**")
l1_feature_map_relu = relu(l1_feature_map)
print("\n**Pooling**")
l1_feature_map_relu_pool = pooling(l1_feature_map_relu, 2, 2)
print("**End of conv layer 1**\n")

# Second conv layer
l2_filter = numpy.random.rand(3, 5, 5, l1_feature_map_relu_pool.shape[-1])
print("\n**Working with conv layer 2**")
l2_feature_map = conv(l1_feature_map_relu_pool, l2_filter)
print("\n**ReLU**")
l2_feature_map_relu = relu(l2_feature_map)
print("\n**Pooling**")
l2_feature_map_relu_pool = pooling(l2_feature_map_relu, 2, 2)
print("**End of conv layer 2**\n")

# Third conv layer
l3_filter = numpy.random.rand(1, 7, 7, l2_feature_map_relu_pool.shape[-1])
print("\n**Working with conv layer 3**")
l3_feature_map = conv(l2_feature_map_relu_pool, l3_filter)
print("\n**ReLU**")
l3_feature_map_relu = relu(l3_feature_map)
print("\n**Pooling**")
l3_feature_map_relu_pool = pooling(l3_feature_map_relu, 2, 2)
print("**End of conv layer 3**\n")

# Graphing results
fig0, ax0 = matplotlib.pyplot.subplots(nrows=1, ncols=1)
ax0.imshow(img).set_cmap("gray")
ax0.set_title("Input Image")
```

```
ax0.get_xaxis().set_ticks([])
ax0.get_yaxis().set_ticks([])
matplotlib.pyplot.savefig("in_img.png", bbox_inches="tight")
matplotlib.pyplot.close(fig0)

# Layer 1
fig1, ax1 = matplotlib.pyplot.subplots(nrows=3, ncols=2)
ax1[0, 0].imshow(l1_feature_map[:, :, 0]).set_cmap("gray")
ax1[0, 0].get_xaxis().set_ticks([])
ax1[0, 0].get_yaxis().set_ticks([])
ax1[0, 0].set_title("L1-Map1")

ax1[0, 1].imshow(l1_feature_map[:, :, 1]).set_cmap("gray")
ax1[0, 1].get_xaxis().set_ticks([])
ax1[0, 1].get_yaxis().set_ticks([])
ax1[0, 1].set_title("L1-Map2")

ax1[1, 0].imshow(l1_feature_map_relu[:, :, 0]).set_cmap("gray")
ax1[1, 0].get_xaxis().set_ticks([])
ax1[1, 0].get_yaxis().set_ticks([])
ax1[1, 0].set_title("L1-Map1ReLU")

ax1[1, 1].imshow(l1_feature_map_relu[:, :, 1]).set_cmap("gray")
ax1[1, 1].get_xaxis().set_ticks([])
ax1[1, 1].get_yaxis().set_ticks([])
ax1[1, 1].set_title("L1-Map2ReLU")

ax1[2, 0].imshow(l1_feature_map_relu_pool[:, :, 0]).set_cmap("gray")
ax1[2, 0].get_xaxis().set_ticks([])
ax1[2, 0].get_yaxis().set_ticks([])
ax1[2, 0].set_title("L1-Map1ReLUPool")

ax1[2, 1].imshow(l1_feature_map_relu_pool[:, :, 1]).set_cmap("gray")
ax1[2, 0].get_xaxis().set_ticks([])
ax1[2, 0].get_yaxis().set_ticks([])
ax1[2, 1].set_title("L1-Map2ReLUPool")

matplotlib.pyplot.savefig("L1.png", bbox_inches="tight")
matplotlib.pyplot.close(fig1)
```

```
# Layer 2
fig2, ax2 = matplotlib.pyplot.subplots(nrows=3, ncols=3)
ax2[0, 0].imshow(l2_feature_map[:, :, 0]).set_cmap("gray")
ax2[0, 0].get_xaxis().set_ticks([])
ax2[0, 0].get_yaxis().set_ticks([])
ax2[0, 0].set_title("L2-Map1")

ax2[0, 1].imshow(l2_feature_map[:, :, 1]).set_cmap("gray")
ax2[0, 1].get_xaxis().set_ticks([])
ax2[0, 1].get_yaxis().set_ticks([])
ax2[0, 1].set_title("L2-Map2")

ax2[0, 2].imshow(l2_feature_map[:, :, 2]).set_cmap("gray")
ax2[0, 2].get_xaxis().set_ticks([])
ax2[0, 2].get_yaxis().set_ticks([])
ax2[0, 2].set_title("L2-Map3")

ax2[1, 0].imshow(l2_feature_map_relu[:, :, 0]).set_cmap("gray")
ax2[1, 0].get_xaxis().set_ticks([])
ax2[1, 0].get_yaxis().set_ticks([])
ax2[1, 0].set_title("L2-Map1ReLU")

ax2[1, 1].imshow(l2_feature_map_relu[:, :, 1]).set_cmap("gray")
ax2[1, 1].get_xaxis().set_ticks([])
ax2[1, 1].get_yaxis().set_ticks([])
ax2[1, 1].set_title("L2-Map2ReLU")

ax2[1, 2].imshow(l2_feature_map_relu[:, :, 2]).set_cmap("gray")
ax2[1, 2].get_xaxis().set_ticks([])
ax2[1, 2].get_yaxis().set_ticks([])
ax2[1, 2].set_title("L2-Map3ReLU")

ax2[2, 0].imshow(l2_feature_map_relu_pool[:, :, 0]).set_cmap("gray")
ax2[2, 0].get_xaxis().set_ticks([])
ax2[2, 0].get_yaxis().set_ticks([])
ax2[2, 0].set_title("L2-Map1ReLUPool")

ax2[2, 1].imshow(l2_feature_map_relu_pool[:, :, 1]).set_cmap("gray")
ax2[2, 1].get_xaxis().set_ticks([])
```

```
ax2[2, 1].get_yaxis().set_ticks([])
ax2[2, 1].set_title("L2-Map2ReLUPool")

ax2[2, 2].imshow(l2_feature_map_relu_pool[:, :, 2]).set_cmap("gray")
ax2[2, 2].get_xaxis().set_ticks([])
ax2[2, 2].get_yaxis().set_ticks([])
ax2[2, 2].set_title("L2-Map3ReLUPool")

matplotlib.pyplot.savefig("L2.png", bbox_inches="tight")
matplotlib.pyplot.close(fig2)

# Layer 3
fig3, ax3 = matplotlib.pyplot.subplots(nrows=1, ncols=3)
ax3[0].imshow(l3_feature_map[:, :, 0]).set_cmap("gray")
ax3[0].get_xaxis().set_ticks([])
ax3[0].get_yaxis().set_ticks([])
ax3[0].set_title("L3-Map1")

ax3[1].imshow(l3_feature_map_relu[:, :, 0]).set_cmap("gray")
ax3[1].get_xaxis().set_ticks([])
ax3[1].get_yaxis().set_ticks([])
ax3[1].set_title("L3-Map1ReLU")

ax3[2].imshow(l3_feature_map_relu_pool[:, :, 0]).set_cmap("gray")
ax3[2].get_xaxis().set_ticks([])
ax3[2].get_yaxis().set_ticks([])
ax3[2].set_title("L3-Map1ReLUPool")
```

There are more layers available in CNN, and it is easy to add them to the preceding layers. For example, a dropout layer could be implemented by dropping a percentage of the neurons in the last layer. An FC layer is just converting the results of the last layer into a 1D vector.

Now that the chapter is complete, it is expected that you have good background information about CNN.

CHAPTER 6

TensorFlow Recognition Application

Building a DL model such as CNN from scratch using NumPy as we did helps us have a better understanding of how each layer works in detail. For practical applications, it is not recommended to use such implementation. One reason is that it is computationally intensive in its calculations and needs efforts to optimize the code. Another is that it does not support distributed processing, GPUs, and many more features. On the other hand, there are different already existing libraries that support these features in a time-efficient manner. These libraries include TF, Keras, Theano, PyTorch, Caffe, and more.

This chapter starts with introducing the TF DL library from scratch by building and visualizing the computational graph for a simple linear model and a two-class classifier using ANN. The computational graph is visualized using TensorBoard (TB). Using TF-Layers API, a CNN model is created to apply the concepts previously discussed for recognizing images from the CIFAR10 dataset.

Introduction to TF

There are different programming paradigms or styles for building software programs. They include sequential, which builds the programs as a set of sequential lines that the program follows from the beginning until the end; functional, which organizes the code into a set of functions that can be called multiple times; imperative, which tells the computer about every detailed step about how the program works; and more. One programming language might support different paradigms. But these paradigms have the disadvantage of being dependent on the language being written in.

229

© Ahmed Fawzy Gad 2018
A. F. Gad, *Practical Computer Vision Applications Using Deep Learning with CNNs*,
https://doi.org/10.1007/978-1-4842-4167-7_6

Another paradigm is dataflow. Dataflow languages represent their programs as text instructions that describe computational steps from receiving the data until returning the results. A dataflow program could be visualized as a graph that shows the operations in addition to their inputs and outputs. Dataflow languages support parallel processing because it is much easier to deduce the independent operations that could be executed at the same time.

The name "TensorFlow" consists of two words. The first is "tensor," which is the data unit that TF uses in its computations. The second word is "flow," reflecting that it uses the dataflow paradigm. As a result, TF builds a computational graph that consists of data represented as tensors and the operations applied to them. To make things easier to understand, just remember that rather than using variables and methods, TF uses tensors and operations.

Here are some advantages of using dataflow with TF:

- **Parallelism**: It is easier to identify the operations that can be executed in parallel.

- **Distributed Execution**: The TF program can be partitioned across multiple devices (CPUs, GPUs, and TF Processing Units [TPUs]). TF itself handles the necessary work for communication and cooperation between the devices.

- **Portability**: The dataflow graph is a language-independent representation of the code of the model. The dataflow graph can be created using Python, get saved, and then be restored in the C++ program.

TF provides multiple APIs; each supports a different level of control. The lowest-level API is called TF Core, which gives the programmer the ability to control every piece of code and have much better control over the created models.

But there are also a number of higher-level APIs in TF that make things easier by just providing a simple interface for frequently used tasks, such as Estimators, TF-Layers, and TF-Learn. All higher-level APIs are built on top of TF Core. For example, TF Estimators is a high-level API in TF that creates models much easier than TF Core.

Tensor

Tensor is the basic data unit in TF; it is similar to arrays in NumPy. Tensor consists of a set of primitive data types, such as integer, floating point, character, and string, which are shaped into an array.

A tensor has both rank and shape. Table 6-1 gives some tensor examples showing their ranks and shapes.

Table 6-1. *Ranks and Shapes of TF Tensors*

Tensor	Rank	Shape
5	0	()
[4, 8]	1	(2)
[[3, 1, 7], [1, 5, 2]]	2	(2,2)
[[[8, 3]], [[11, 9]]]]	2	(2,1,2)

The rank of a tensor is the number of dimensions. The tensor shape is similar to NumPy array shape. The NumPy array shape returns the number of elements within each dimension, and this is how tensor shape works. But tensor rank returns just the number of dimensions, which is similar to the ndim property of a NumPy array. Tensor rank is just a scalar value representing the number of dimensions in the tensor, while the shape is a tuple such as (4, 3) representing an array with two dimensions, where the sizes of these dimensions are 4 and 3, respectively.

Let's get started in TF Core.

TF Core

In order to create TF Core programs, there are two steps:

1. Building the computational graph.

2. Running the computational graph.

TF uses a dataflow graph to represent the computations in the program. After specifying the sequence of computations, it gets executed within a TF session on local or remote machines. Assume that Figure 6-1 represents a graph that has four operations, A, B, C, and D, where the inputs are fed into operation A and then propagated to operation D.

It is possible for the graph to just execute a selected part of it, and it is not required to run the complete graph. For example, by specifying that the target of session execution is operation C, then the program will run until reaching the operation C result only. That way will not execute operation D. Also, if operation B is the target, then operations C and D will not get executed.

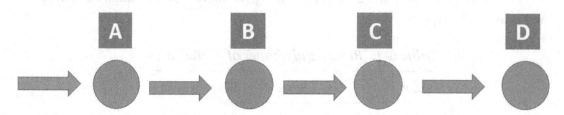

Figure 6-1. *A graph with four operations*

Working with TF Core API requires understanding of how dataflow graphs and sessions work. Working with high-level APIs such as Estimators hides some of the overhead from the user. But understanding how graphs and sessions work is useful for understanding in turn how such high-level APIs are implemented.

Dataflow Graph

A dataflow graph consists of nodes and edges. Nodes represent units of operation. Edges represent inputs to and outputs from an operation node. For example, the method tensorflow.matmul() accepts two input tensors, multiples them, and returns an output tensor. The operation itself is represented with a single node connected to two edges, one for each input tensor. There is also an edge that represents the output tensor. Later, we will see how to build the computational graph using TB.

A special kind of node is the constant, which accepts zero tensors as input. The output that the constant node returns is a value stored internally. Listing 6-1 creates a single constant node of type float32 and prints it.

Listing 6-1. Constant Node

```
import tensorflow
tensor1 = tensorflow.constant(3.7, dtype=tensorflow.float32)
print(tensor1)
```

When printing the constant node, the result is

```
Tensor("Const:0", shape=(), dtype=float32)
```

Based on the output of the print statement, there are three things to note:

- The shape is (), which means that the tensor is of rank 0.

- The output tensor has a string equal to "Const:0". This string is the name of the tensor. The tensor name is an important property because it is used to retrieve the tensor value from the graph. It is also the label printed in the TF graph. The default name for constant tensors is "Const". The 0 appended to this string defines it as the first output returned. There are some operations that return more than one output. The first output is given 0, the second one is given 1, and so on.

- The print statement does not print the value 3.7 but prints the node itself. The value will get printed only after evaluating the nodes.

Tensor Names

There might be multiple constant tensors within the graph. For this reason, TF appends the string "Const" with a number that identifies the constant among all constants in the graph. Listing 6-2 gives an example of three constants and prints them.

Listing 6-2. Creating Three Constants

```
import tensorflow

tensor1 = tensorflow.constant(value=3.7, dtype=tensorflow.float32)
tensor2 = tensorflow.constant(value=[[0.5], [7]], dtype=tensorflow.float32)
tensor3 = tensorflow.constant(value=[[12, 9]], dtype=tensorflow.float32)
print(tensor1)
print(tensor2)
print(tensor3)
```

Here is the result of the three print statements:

```
Tensor("Const:0", shape=(), dtype=float32)
Tensor("Const_1:0", shape=(2, 1), dtype=float32)
Tensor("Const_2:0", shape=(1, 2), dtype=float32)
```

The first tensor name is "Const:0". To differentiate it from other tensors, the string "Const" is appended by an underscore and a number. For example, the second tensor name is "Const_1:0". The number "1" is the identifier to that constant in the graph. But we can change the name of a tensor by using the name attribute as in Listing 6-3.

Listing 6-3. Setting Names of the Tensors Using the Name Attribute

```
import tensorflow

tensor1 = tensorflow.constant(value=3.7, dtype=tensorflow.float32,
name"firstConstant")
tensor2 = tensorflow.constant(value=[[0.5], [7]], dtype=tensorflow.float32,
name"secondConstant")
tensor3 = tensorflow.constant(value=[[12, 9]], dtype=tensorflow.float32,
name"thirdConstant")
print(tensor1)
print(tensor2)
print(tensor3)
```

The results of the three print statements are as follows:

```
Tensor("firstConstant:0", shape=(), dtype=float32)
Tensor("secondConstant:0", shape=(2, 1), dtype=float32)
Tensor("thirdConstant:0", shape=(1, 2), dtype=float32)
```

Because each tensor is given a unique name, there are no appended numbers to the string. If the same value of the name attribute is used for more than one tensor, the number will be used as in Listing 6-4. The first two tensors are given the value myConstant and thus the second tensor is appended by a number "1".

Listing 6-4. Two Tensors with the Same Value for the Name Attribute

```
import tensorflow

tensor1 = tensorflow.constant(value=3.7, dtype=tensorflow.float32,
name"myConstant")
tensor2 = tensorflow.constant(value=[[0.5], [7]], dtype=tensorflow.float32,
name"myConstant")
```

```
tensor3 = tensorflow.constant(value=[[12, 9]], dtype=tensorflow.float32,
name"thirdConstant")
print(tensor1)
print(tensor2)
print(tensor3)
```

The results of Listing 6-4 are as follows:

```
Tensor("myConstant:0", shape=(), dtype=float32)
Tensor("myConstant_1:0", shape=(2, 1), dtype=float32)
Tensor("thirdConstant:0", shape=(1, 2), dtype=float32)
```

In Listing 6-5, the operation `tensorflow.nn.top_k` is used to return the largest K values for a vector. In other words, this operation returns multiple values as outputs. Based on the output string, the two outputs are given the string "TopKV2" but with a different number after the colon. The first output is given number "0" and the second output is given "1".

Listing 6-5. Operation Returning Multiple Outputs

```
import tensorflow
aa = tensorflow.nn.top_k([1, 2, 3, 4], 2)
print(aa)
```

The print output is

```
TopKV2(values=<tf.Tensor 'TopKV2:0' shape=(2,) dtype=int32>, indices=<tf.
Tensor 'TopKV2:1' shape=(2,) dtype=int32>)
```

Up to this point, we have been able to print the tensor but not evaluate its result. Let's create a TF session for evaluating the operations.

Creating a TF Session

TF uses the `tensorflow.Session` class to represent a connection between the client program (typically a Python program) and the runtime environment. A `tensorflow.Session` object provides access to devices in the local machine and to remote devices using the distributed TF runtime environment. It also caches information about the `tensorflow.Graph` so that we can efficiently rerun the same graph. Listing 6-6 creates a TF session for evaluating the results of a single constant tensor. The tensor to be evaluated is assigned to the fetches attribute.

The session is created and returned into a variable named sess. After running the session using the tensorflow.Session.run() method to evaluate the tensor tensor1, the result will be 3.7, which is the constant value. This method runs the tensorflow. Operation and evaluates the tensorflow.Tensor. This method could accept more than one tensor for evaluation by typing them in a list and assigning this list to the fetches attribute.

Listing 6-6. Evaluating a Single Constant Tensor

```
import tensorflow

tensor1 = tensorflow.constant(value=3.7, dtype=tensorflow.float32)
sess = tensorflow.Session()
print(sess.run(fetches=tensor1))
sess.close()
```

As the tensorflow.Session owns physical resources such as CPUs, GPUs, and network connections, it must free these resources after finishing execution. According to Listing 6-6, we have to manually exit the session using the tensorflow.Session. close() to free resources. There is also another way to create a session, in which it gets closed automatically. This is by creating it using the with block as in Listing 6-7. When the session is created within the with block, it will get closed automatically after getting outside the block.

Listing 6-7. Creating a Session Using the With Block

```
import tensorflow

tensor1 = tensorflow.constant(value=3.7, dtype=tensorflow.float32)

with tensorflow.Session() as sess:
    print(sess.run(fetches=tensor1))
```

We can also specify more than one tensor in the tensorflow.Session.run() method to get their outputs, as in Listing 6-8.

Listing 6-8. Evaluating More Than One Tensor

```
import tensorflow

tensor1 = tensorflow.constant(value=3.7, dtype=tensorflow.float32)
tensor2 = tensorflow.constant(value=[[0.5], [7]], dtype=tensorflow.float32)
tensor3 = tensorflow.constant(value=[[12, 9]], dtype=tensorflow.float32)

with tensorflow.Session() as sess:
    print(sess.run(fetches=[tensor1, tensor2, tensor3]))
```

Here are the outputs of the three evaluated tensors.

```
3.7
array([[ 0.5], [7.]], dtype=float32)
array([[ 12.,    9.]], dtype=float32)
```

The previous examples just print the evaluated results for tensors. It is possible to store such values and reuse them in the program. Listing 6-9 returns the evaluation results in the results tensor.

Listing 6-9. Evaluating More Than One Tensor

```
import tensorflow

node1 = tensorflow.constant(value=3.7, dtype=tensorflow.float32)
node2 = tensorflow.constant(value=7.7, dtype=tensorflow.float32)
node3 = tensorflow.constant(value=9.1, dtype=tensorflow.float32)

with tensorflow.Session() as sess:
    results = sess.run(fetches=[node1, node2, node3])

vIDX = 0
for value in results:
    print("Value ", vIDX, " : ", value)
    vIDX = vIDX + 1
```

Because there are three tensors to be evaluated, all three outputs will be stored into the results tensor, which is a list. Using for loop, we can iterate and print each output separately. The outputs are as follows:

```
Value  0  :  3.7
Value  1  :  7.7
Value  2  :  9.1
```

The previous examples just evaluated the value of constant tensors without applying any operation. We can apply some operations over such tensors. Listing 6-10 creates two tensors and adds them together using the tensorflow.add operation. This operation accepts two tensors and adds them together. Both tensors must have the same data type (i.e., dtype attribute). It returns a new tensor of the same type as the input tensors. Using the + operator is identical to using the tensorflow.add() method.

Listing 6-10. Adding Two Tensors Using the tensorflow.add Operation

```
import tensorflow

tensor1 = tensorflow.constant(value=3.7, dtype=tensorflow.float32)
tensor2 = tensorflow.constant(value=7.7, dtype=tensorflow.float32)

add_op = tensorflow.add(tensor1, tensor2)

with tensorflow.Session() as sess:
    add_result = sess.run(fetches=[add_op])

print("Result of addition : ", add_result)
```

The output of the print statement is

```
Result of addition :  [11.4]
```

In Figure 6-2, the graph of the program in Listing 6-10 is visualized using TB. Note that all nodes and edges are given labels. These labels are the name of each tensor and operation. The default values are used. Later in this chapter, we will learn how to visualize graphs in TB.

Figure 6-2. *Visualization of the graph using TB*

The name of the operation is descriptive and reflects its job, but the names of the tensors are not. We can change them to num1 and num2 and visualize the graph as in Figure 6-3.

Figure 6-3. *Changing the name of the tensors*

Parameterized Graph Using Placeholder

The previous graph is static because it uses constant tensors. It always accepts the same inputs and generates the same output each time it gets evaluated. To be able to modify the inputs each time the program runs, we can use tensorflow.placeholder. In other words, for evaluating the same operation but using different inputs, you should use tensorflow.placeholder. Note that placeholder can get its value changed only by rerunning the graph.

The tensorflow.placeholderaccepts three arguments as follows:

- dtype: Data type of elements the tensor will accept.

- shape (Optional – default None): Shape of the array within the tensor. If not specified, then you can feed the tensor with any shape.

- name (Optional – default None): Name for the operation.

It returns a tensor with these specifications.

We can modify the previous example in Listing 6-10 to use tensorflow.placeholder as in Listing 6-11. When running the session previously, the tensorflow.Session.run() accepts only the operations to be evaluated. When using placeholders, this method will also accept the initial values of the placeholders in the feed_dict argument. The feed_dict argument accepts the values as a dictionary that maps the name of each placeholder to its value.

Listing 6-11. Parameterized Graph Using a Placeholder

```
import tensorflow

tensor1 = tensorflow.placeholder(dtype=tensorflow.float32, shape=(),
name="num1")
tensor2 = tensorflow.placeholder(dtype=tensorflow.float32, shape=(),
name="num2")

add_op = tensorflow.add(tensor1, tensor2, name="Add_Op")

with tensorflow.Session() as sess:
    add_result = sess.run(fetches=[add_op], feed_dict={tensor1: 3.7,
    tensor2: 7.7})

print("Result of addition : ", add_result)
```

Assigning the placeholders the same values used by the constants in Listing 6-10, the same result will be returned. The benefit of using placeholders is that their values can be changed even within the program, but constants cannot be changed once created.

After using a third placeholder and a multiply operation, Listing 6-12 runs the session multiple times with different values for placeholders. It uses a for loop iterating through a list of five numbers returned by the range() native Python function. Values of all tensors are set equal to the list values, one value at each iteration. Values of the first two tensors are added using the tensorflow.add operation. The result of the addition is returned into the add_op tensor. Its value is then multiplied by the third tensor using the tensorflow.multiply operation. The multiplication result is returned in the mul_op tensor. Using the * operator is identical to using the tensorflow.add() method. The fetches argument in Listing 6-11 is a set of add_op compared to mul_op in Listing 6-12.

Listing 6-12. Running the Session for Different Values for the Placeholders

```
import tensorflow

tensor1 = tensorflow.placeholder(dtype=tensorflow.float32, shape=(),
name="num1")
tensor2 = tensorflow.placeholder(dtype=tensorflow.float32, shape=(),
name="num2")
tensor3 = tensorflow.placeholder(dtype=tensorflow.float32, shape=(),
name="num3")
```

```
add_op = tensorflow.add(tensor1, tensor2, name="Add_Op")
mul_op = tensorflow.multiply(add_op, tensor3, name="Add_Op")

with tensorflow.Session() as sess:
    for num in range(5):
result = sess.run(fetches=[mul_op], feed_dict={tensor1: num, tensor2: num,
tensor3: num})
        print("Result at iteration ", num, " : ", result)
```

The output of the print statement is as follows:

```
Result at iteration  0  :  [0.0]
Result at iteration  1  :  [2.0]
Result at iteration  2  :  [8.0]
Result at iteration  3  :  [18.0]
Result at iteration  4  :  [32.0]
```

A visualization of the previous graph is given in Figure 6-4. Note that all operations and tensors are renamed. The first two tensors num1 and num2 are connected with the first operation Add_Op. The result of this operation is used as input, with the third tensor num3 as input to the second operation Mul_Op.

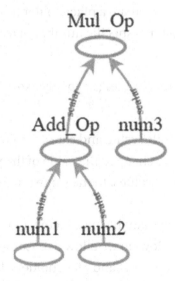

Figure 6-4. *Visualization of the graph in Listing 6-12 using TB*

The mul_op tensor is selected to be a member of the fetches list in Listing 6-12. Why not just select just add_op? The answer is that the last tensor in the graph chain is selected for evaluation. Evaluating mul_op will implicitly evaluate all other tensors in the graph. If "add_op" is selected for evaluation, then mul_op will not be evaluated because add_op doesn't depend on mul_op, and we have nothing to do for evaluating it. But mul_op is what depends on add_mul and all other tensors. Thus, mul_op is selected for evaluation. Remember that it is possible to use more than one tensor for evaluation.

TF Variables

Placeholders are used to allocate memory for future use. Their main use is for feeding input data for a model to get trained with. If the same operation is to be applied for different input data, then place the input data into a placeholder and run the session by assigning different values to the placeholder.

Placeholders are not initialized and their value is assigned only during runtime; in other words, only after calling the tensorflow.Session.run() are the placeholders assigned values. A placeholder allows the creation of an unconstrained shape tensor, which makes it suitable for use to hold the training data.

Suppose that you want to assign the training data to the placeholder and you just know that each sample gets described by 35 features. We have not decided yet how many samples to use for training. We can create a placeholder that accepts a tensor with an unspecified number of samples but a specific number of features (columns) per sample as follows:

```
data_tensor = tensorflow.placeholder(dtype=tensorflow.float16,
shape=[None, 35])
```

The placeholder just accepts the value and cannot get changed after being assigned. Remember that in Listing 6-12 we changed the value of the placeholders only by rebuilding the graph with the new values. In the same graph, it is not possible to change the placeholder value.

ML models have a number of trainable parameters that are changed multiple times until reaching their best values. How do we allow a tensor to change its values multiple times? This is not provided by constants and placeholders, but by variables (tensorflow. Variable()).

TF variables are identical to the normal variables used in other languages. They are assigned initial values, and such a value can be updated during the execution of

242

the program based on the operations applied to it. A placeholder doesn't allow data modifications once assigned during execution time.

Constant tensors have their values initialized once the tensorflow.constant() is called, but variables won't be initialized after calling tensorflow.Variable(). There is an easy way to initialize all global variables within the program by running the tensorflow.global_variables_initializer() operation within the session. Note that initializing the variable does not mean it is evaluated. The variable needs to be evaluated after being initialized. Listing 6-13 gives an example of creating a single variable named "Var1" where its value is initialized, then the variable is evaluated, and finally, its value is printed.

Listing 6-13. Creating, Initializing, and Evaluating the Variable

```
import tensorflow

var1 = tensorflow.Variable(initial_value=5.8, dtype=tensorflow.float32,
name="Var1")

with tensorflow.Session() as sess:
    init = tensorflow.global_variables_initializer()
    sess.run(fetches=init)
    var_value = sess.run(fetches=var1)
    print("Variable value : ", var_value)
```

The print statement will return:

```
Variable value :5.8
```

Note that there are two runs to the session: the first for initializing all variables and the second for evaluating the variable. Remember that placeholder is a function but variable is a class, and thus its name starts with uppercase.

Variables can be initialized by a tensor of any type and shape. The type and shape of this tensor will define the type and shape of the variable, which cannot be changed. The variable value can be changed. Working with a distributed environment, variables can be stored once and get shared across all devices. They have a state that helps in debugging. Moreover, the variable value can be saved and restored when required.

Variable Initialization

There are different ways to initialize a variable. All variable initialization methods have can set both the shape and data type of the variable. One way is by using the initial value of a previously initialized variable. For example, the variable named "Var1" in Listing 6-13 is initialized by a rank 0 tensor of value 5.8. This initialized variable can be used to initialize other variables. Note that the initial value of a variable can be returned using the initialized_value() method of the tensorflow.Variable class. The initial value can be assigned to another variable as in the following. The variable "var3" is initialized by multiplying the initial value of "var1" by 5.

```
var2 = tensorflow.Variable(initial_value=var1.initialized_value(),
dtype=tensorflow.float32)
var3 = tensorflow.Variable(initial_value=var1.initialized_value()*5,
dtype=tensorflow.float32)
```

A variable can be initialized based on another tensor created by one of the build-in operations in TF. There are different operations to generate tensors, including the following:

- tensorflow.lin_space(start, stop, num, name=None)

- tensorflow.range(start, limit=None, delta=1, dtype=None, name='range')

- tensorflow.zeros(shape, dtype=tf.float32, name=None)

- tensorflow.ones(shape, dtype=tf.float32, name=None)

- tensorflow.constant(value, dtype=None, shape=None, name='Const', verify_shape=False)

They have the same meaning as their corresponding methods in NumPy. All of these operations return the tensor of the specified data type and shape. For example, we can create a tensorflow.Variable() whose values are initialized using tensorflow.zeros(), which returns a 1D row vector with 12 elements as follows:

```
var1 = tensorflow.Variable(tensorflow.zeros([12]))
```

Graph Visualization Using TB

TF is designed to work with deep models trained with large amounts of data. TF supports a suite of visualization tools called TB to help to optimize and to debug TF programs easier. The computational dataflow graph is visualized as a set of nodes representing the operations, which are connected together with edges representing the input and output tensors.

Here are the summarized steps for visualizing a simple graph using TB:

1. Build the dataflow graph.

2. Write the graph in a directory using tensorflow.summary. FileWriter.

3. Launch TB within the directory of the saved graph.

4. Access TB from a web browser.

5. Visualize the graph.

Let's use the code in Listing 6-14 for visualization. This code creates six variables that are fed into nine operations. After writing the instructions for building the graph, next is to save it using FileWriter. The tensorflow.summary.FileWriter() constructor accepts two important arguments: "graph" and "logdir". The "graph" argument accepts the session graph, which is returned by "sess.graph" assuming that the session variable is named "sess". The graph is exported into the directory specified using the "logdir" argument. Change the "logdir" to match your system. Note that we do not have to initialize the variables nor run the session because our target is not to execute the graph but just to visualize it.

Listing 6-14. Saving Dataflow Graph for Visualization Using TB

```
import tensorflow

tensor1 = tensorflow.Variable(initial_value=4, dtype=tensorflow.float32,
name="Var1")
tensor2 = tensorflow.Variable(initial_value=15, dtype=tensorflow.float32,
name="Var2")
tensor3 = tensorflow.Variable(initial_value=-2, dtype=tensorflow.float32,
name="Var3")
```

```
tensor4 = tensorflow.Variable(initial_value=1.8, dtype=tensorflow.float32,
name="Var4")
tensor5 = tensorflow.Variable(initial_value=14, dtype=tensorflow.float32,
name="Var5")
tensor6 = tensorflow.Variable(initial_value=8, dtype=tensorflow.float32,
name="Var6")

op1 = tensorflow.add(x=tensor1, y=tensor2, name="Add_Op1")
op2 = tensorflow.subtract(x=op1, y=tensor1, name="Subt_Op1")
op3 = tensorflow.divide(x=op2, y=tensor3, name="Divide_Op1")
op4 = tensorflow.multiply(x=op3, y=tensor4, name="Mul_Op1")
op5 = tensorflow.multiply(x=op4, y=op1, name="Mul_Op2")
op6 = tensorflow.add(x=op5, y=2, name="Add_Op2")
op7 = tensorflow.subtract(x=op6, y=op2, name="Subt_Op2")
op8 = tensorflow.multiply(x=op7, y=tensor6, name="Mul_Op3")
op9 = tensorflow.multiply(x=op8, y=tensor5, name="Mul_Op4")

with tensorflow.Session() as sess:
    writer = tensorflow.summary.FileWriter(logdir="\\AhmedGad\\
TensorBoard\\", graph=sess.graph)
    writer.close()
```

After exporting the graph, the next step is to launch TB to access the graph. Launching TB differs a bit based on whether TF is installed in a separate virtual environment (venv) or as a regular library within the site-packages directory.

If it is installed into a venv, then TF must be activated using the activate.bat file located under the Scripts directory of the Python installation. Assuming that the Scripts directory is added to either the user or system PATH variable environment and the venv folder is named "tensorflow", then TF will be activated according to the following command:

```
activate tensorflow
```

After activating TF, next is to launch TB into the directory at which the graph is saved according to this command:

```
tensorBoard --logdir=\\AhmedGad\\TensorBoard\\
```

In case the TF is installed within the site-packages directory, then it can be activated by issuing this command:

```
python -m tensorboard.main --logdir="\\AhmedGad\\TensorBoard\\"
```

This will activate TB, and we will then be ready to visualize the graph by navigating to "http://localhost:6006" from a web browser. The graph is shown in Figure 6-5. It is easier to debug the graph in this case. For example, an isolated node that is not connected to any other node of the graph is easily detected in the graph than the code.

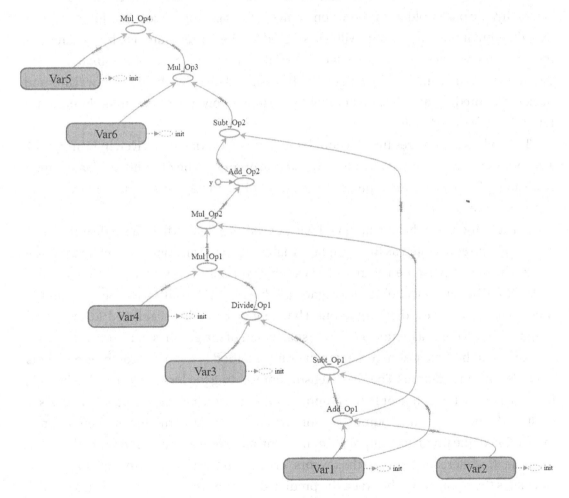

Figure 6-5. *Visualization of a dataflow graph using TB*

Linear Model

A linear model has the general form in Equation 6-1. There are n input variables x_n, and each variable is assigned a weight w_n for a total of n weights. A bias b is added to the SOP of each input and its corresponding bias.

$$y = w_1x_1+w_2x_2+\cdots+w_nx_n+b \qquad \text{(Equation 6-1)}$$

For a simple linear model, there are input data, weights, and biases. Which is the most suitable option between placeholders and variables to hold each of these? Generally, the placeholder is used when applying the same operation multiple times over different inputs. The inputs will be assigned for the placeholder one by one and the operation will get applied to each one. Variables are used for storing trainable parameters. As a result, the input data is to be assigned to a placeholder, but weights and biases are stored in variables. Remember to use tensorflow.global_variables_initializer() for initializing the variables.

The code that prepares the placeholder and the two variables is given in Listing 6-15. The input samples have just one input x_1 and one output y. The placeholder "data_input_placeholder" represents the input, and the placeholder "data_output_placeholder" represents the output.

Because there is only one input variable per sample, there will be a single weight w_1. The weight is represented as the "weight_variable" variable and assigned an initial value of 0.2. The bias, represented as the "bias_variable" variable, is assigned an initial value of 0.1. Note that the placeholder is assigned a value inside the tensorflow.Session.run() method using the "feed_dict" argument. The input placeholder is assigned 2.0 and the output placeholder is assigned 5.0. The visualization of the graph is in Figure 6-6.

Note that the "fetches" argument of the run() method is set to a list of three elements: "loss", "error", and "output". The "loss" tensor representing the loss function is fetched because it is the target tensor in the graph. All other tensors will be evaluated once it is evaluated. The "error" and "output" tensors are fetched just to print the prediction error in addition to the predicted output as in the print statement at the end of the code.

Note the difference between the tensors "error" and "loss". The "error" tensor calculates the square error between the predicted and desired outputs for each sample. To just summarize all errors in a single value, the tensor "loss" is used. It calculates the summation of all square errors.

Listing 6-15. Preparing Inputs, Weight, and Bias for a Linear Model

```
import tensorflow

data_input_placeholder = tensorflow.placeholder(dtype=tensorflow.float32,
name="DataInput")
data_output_placeholder = tensorflow.placeholder(dtype=tensorflow.float32,
name="DataOutput")
weight_variable = tensorflow.Variable(initial_value=0.1, dtype=tensorflow.
float32, name="Weight")
bias_variable = tensorflow.Variable(initial_value=0.2, dtype=tensorflow.
float32, name="Bias")

output = tensorflow.multiply(x=data_input_placeholder, y=weight_variable)
output = tensorflow.add(x=output, y=bias_variable)

diff = tensorflow.subtract(x=output, y=data_output_placeholder,
name="Diff")
error = tensorflow.square(x=diff, name="PredictError")
loss = tensorflow.reduce_sum(input_tensor=error, name="Loss")

with tensorflow.Session() as sess:
    writer = tensorflow.summary.FileWriter(logdir="\\AhmedGad\\
    TensorBoard\\", graph=sess.graph)
    init = tensorflow.global_variables_initializer()
    sess.run(fetches=init)
loss, predict_error, predicted_output = sess.run(fetches=[loss, error,
output], feed_dict={data_input_placeholder: 2.0,data_output_placeholder:
5.0})
    print("Loss : ", loss, "\nPredicted output : ", predicted_output,"\
    nPrediction error : ", predict_error)
    writer.close()
```

Based on the values assigned to the placeholders and the variables, the output of the print message is as follows:

```
Loss :  21.16
Predicted output :  0.4
Prediction error :  21.16
```

The predicted output is 0.4 and the desired output is 5.0. There is an error equal to 21.16. There is only one value returned in the fetched tensors because the program is working with just one sample. Also, the loss value is equal to the error value because there is just one sample. We can run the program for multiple samples.

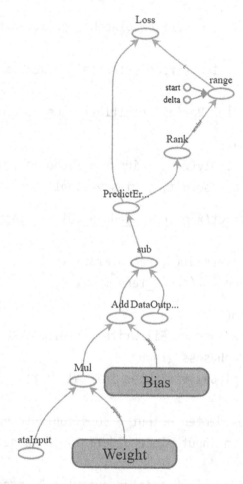

Figure 6-6. *Visualization of a dataflow graph of a linear model with one input*

Rather than assigning just a single value to the placeholder "data_input_placeholder", we can assign multiple values enclosed in a list. This also applies to the "data_output_placeholder" placeholder. Note that they must have identical shapes. The modified program after using two samples is in Listing 6-16. The print message is as follows:

```
Loss :  51.41
Predicted output :  [ 0.4  0.5]
Prediction error :  [21.16  30.25]
```

This means the prediction errors are 21.16 and 30.25 for the first and second samples, respectively. The sum of all square errors is 51.41. Because there is a high value for the loss function, we have to update the parameters (weights and bias) in order to minimize the prediction error.

Listing 6-16. Running the TF Program for Multiple Samples

```
import tensorflow

data_input_placeholder = tensorflow.placeholder(dtype=tensorflow.float32,
name="DataInput")
data_output_placeholder = tensorflow.placeholder(dtype=tensorflow.float32,
name="DataOutput")
weight_variable = tensorflow.Variable(initial_value=0.1, dtype=tensorflow.
float32, name="Weight")
bias_variable = tensorflow.Variable(initial_value=0.2, dtype=tensorflow.
float32, name="Bias")

output = tensorflow.multiply(x=data_input_placeholder, y=weight_variable)
output = tensorflow.add(x=output, y=bias_variable)

diff = tensorflow.subtract(x=output, y=data_output_placeholder,
name="Diff")
error = tensorflow.square(x=diff, name="PredictError")
loss = tensorflow.reduce_sum(input_tensor=error, name="Loss")

with tensorflow.Session() as sess:
    init = tensorflow.global_variables_initializer()
    sess.run(fetches=init)
loss, predict_error, predicted_output = sess.run(fetches=[loss, error,
output], feed_dict={data_input_placeholder: [2.0, 3.0],data_output_
placeholder: [5.0, 6.0]})
    print("Loss : ", loss, "\nPredicted output : ", predicted_output,
    "\nPrediction error : ", predict_error)
```

Currently, there is no way to update the parameters. A number of optimizers already exist in TF for doing that job.

GD Optimizer from TF Train API

There are a number of optimizers that TF provides for optimizing model parameters automatically. GD is an example that changes the values of each parameter slowly until reaching the value that minimizes the loss. GD modifies each variable according to the magnitude of the derivative of loss with respect to the variable. This is identical to what is discussed in Chapter 3 in the backward pass of training ANN. The "tensorflow.train" API has a class called "GradientDescentOptimizer" that can both calculate the derivatives and optimize the parameters. The program after using "GradientDescentOptimizer" is in Listing 6-17.

Listing 6-17. Using GD for Optimizing the Model Parameters

```
import tensorflow

data_input_placeholder = tensorflow.placeholder(dtype=tensorflow.float32,
name="DataInput")
data_output_placeholder = tensorflow.placeholder(dtype=tensorflow.float32,
name="DataOutput")
weight_variable = tensorflow.Variable(initial_value=0.1, dtype=tensorflow.
float32, name="Weight")
bias_variable = tensorflow.Variable(initial_value=0.2, dtype=tensorflow.
float32, name="Bias")

output = tensorflow.multiply(x=data_input_placeholder, y=weight_variable,
name="Multiply")
output = tensorflow.add(x=output, y=bias_variable, name="Add")

diff = tensorflow.subtract(x=output, y=data_output_placeholder,
name="Diff")
error = tensorflow.square(x=diff, name="PredictError")
loss = tensorflow.reduce_sum(input_tensor=error, name="Loss")
train_optim = tensorflow.train.GradientDescentOptimizer(learning_rate=0.01,
name="Optimizer")
minimizer = train_optim.minimize(loss=loss, name="Minimizer")

with tensorflow.Session() as sess:
```

```
writer = tensorflow.summary.FileWriter(graph=sess.graph, logdir=
"\\AhmedGad\\TensorBoard\\")
init = tensorflow.global_variables_initializer()
sess.run(fetches=init)
for k in range(1000):
    _, data_loss, predict_error, predicted_output = sess.
    run(fetches=[minimizer,loss, error, output], feed_dict={data_input_
    placeholder: [1.0, 2.0],data_output_placeholder: [5.0, 6.0]})

print("Loss : ", data_loss,"\nPredicted output : ", predicted_output,
"\nPrediction error : ", predict_error)
writer.close()
```

The program uses a loop that iterates through 1,000 iterations. For each iteration, the current parameters are used for predicting the outputs, the loss is calculated, and the GD optimizer updates the parameters to minimize the loss. Note that the "minimize()" operation returns an operation that minimizes the loss.

After the end of the iterations, the print statement is executed. Here are its outputs:

```
Loss :  0.00323573
Predicted output :  [ 4.951612    6.02990532]
Prediction error :  [ 0.0023414   0.00089433]
```

Thanks to GD, the loss is reduced from 51.41 to just 0.0032. The graph of the previous program in Listing 6-17 is available in Figure 6-7.

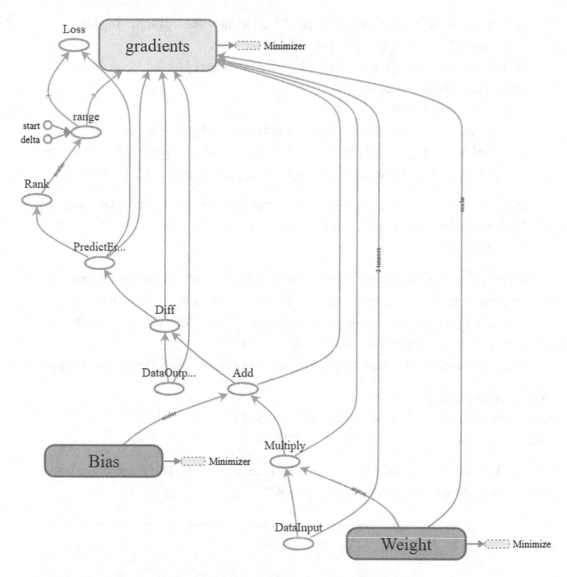

Figure 6-7. *Dataflow graph of a linear model optimized using GD*

Locating Parameters to Optimize

An important question now arises: How does the optimizer know the parameters to change their values? Let's see how it knows that.

After running the session, the "minimizer" operation will be executed. TF will follow the chain of graph nodes to evaluate such an operation. TF found that the "minimizer" operation depends on a single argument, which is the "loss" tensor. Thus, our goal is to minimize the value of such a tensor. How can we minimize that tensor? We have to follow the graph back.

The "loss" tensor is evaluated using the "tensorflow.reduce_sum()" operation. As a result, our goal is to minimize the result of the "tensorflow.reduce_sum()" operation.

Stepping back, this operation is evaluated using the "error" tensor. As a result, our goal now is to minimize the "error" tensor. Stepping back again, we find that the "error" tensor depends on the "tensorflow.square()" operation. As a result, we have to minimize "tensorflow.square()" the operation. The input tensor to this operation is the "diff" tensor. Thus, our goal is to minimize the "diff" tensor. Because the "diff" tensor is the result of the "tensorflow.subtract()" operation, then our goal is to minimize this operation.

Minimizing the "tensorflow.subtract()" asks us to minimize its input tensors, which are "output" and "data_output_placeholder". Looking at these two tensors, which one can be modified? Only the variable tensors can be modified. Because "data_output_placeholder" is not a variable but a placeholder, we can't modify it. Thus, we have only the "output" tensor to minimize in order to minimize the result.

The "output" tensor is calculated according to Equation 6-1. It has three inputs: input, weight, and bias, which are represented by the tensors "data_input_placeholder", "weight_variable", and "bias_variable", respectively. Looking for these three tensors, only "weight_variable" and "bias_variable" can be changed because they are variables. Thus, finally we know that our goal is to minimize "weight_variable" and "bias_variable" tensors.

In order to minimize the "tensorflow.train.GradientDescentOptimizer.minimize()" operation, we have to change the values of the "weight_variable" and "bias_variable" tensors. This is how TF deduced that to minimize the loss it should minimize the weight and bias parameters.

Building FFNN

In this section, two basic feed-forward ANNs (FFNNs) will be created for classification using TF Core API. We will follow the same steps used previously to build an ANN using NumPy but with changes.

The summarized steps are as follows:

1. Reading the training data (inputs and outputs).

2. Building the neural network layers and preparing their parameters (weights, biases, and activation functions).

3. Building a loss function to assess the prediction error.

4. Create a training loop for training the network and updating its parameters.

5. Assessing the accuracy of the trained ANN using new unseen test data.

We will start by building a single-layer FFANN.

Linear Classification

Table 6-2 gives the data of the first classification problem. It is a binary classification problem to classify the RGB colors into either red or blue based on the color channels red, green, and blue.

Table 6-2. *RGB Color Classification Problem*

Class	Red	Green	Blue
Red	255	0	0
	248	80	68
Blue	0	9	255
	67	15	210

According to Listing 6-18, two placeholders ("training_inputs" and "training_outputs") are created for holding the training data inputs and outputs. Their data type is set to "float32" but they do not have a specific shape. The shape of the "training_inputs" placeholder is N×3. What does that mean?

Regularly, placeholders are used to hold the training data of the model. The size of the training data is not always fixed. There might be a change in the number of samples, the number of features, or both. For example, we might train a model with 100 samples, where each sample is represented by 15 features. The shape of the placeholder, in this case, is 100×15. Assume that we later decided to change the number of training samples to be 50. The shape of the placeholder must get changed to be 50×15.

Listing 6-18. Placeholders for the Training Data Inputs and Outputs

```
import tensorflow
training_inputs = tensorflow.placeholder(shape=[None, 3], dtype=tensorflow.
float32)
training_outputs = tensorflow.placeholder(shape=[None, 1],
dtype=tensorflow.float32)
```

To make life easier, TF supports creating placeholders of variable shape. The placeholder shape is determined based on the data assigned to it. The shape might be variable across all dimensions or for just some dimensions. If we decided to use 30 features but had not decided on the number of training samples, then the shape is N×15, where N is the number of samples. Feeding 20 samples to the placeholder, N will be set to 20. This is the case for the two placeholders in Listing 6-18. To leave the placeholder generic for holding any number of training samples, its shape is set to (None, 3). None means that this dimension (representing the number of samples) does not have a static size.

After preparing the inputs and the outputs, the next step is to decide the network architecture for preparing their parameters (weights and bias). Because the data is simple, we could plot it. Listing 6-19 gives the code used to plot the data. Note that the data has three dimensions, and thus the plot is 3D as in Figure 6-8.

Listing 6-19. 3D Scatter Plot of the Training Data

```
import matplotlib.pyplot
import mpl_toolkits.mplot3d

figure3D = matplotlib.pyplot.figure()
axis3D = mpl_toolkits.mplot3d.Axes3D(figure3D)

red = [255, 248, 0, 67]
green = [0, 80, 9, 15]
blue = [0, 68, 255, 210]

axis3D.scatter(red, green, blue, color="black")
axis3D.set_xlabel(xlabel="Red")
```

```
axis3D.set_ylabel(ylabel="Green")
axis3D.set_zlabel(zlabel="Blue")
matplotlib.pyplot.show()
```

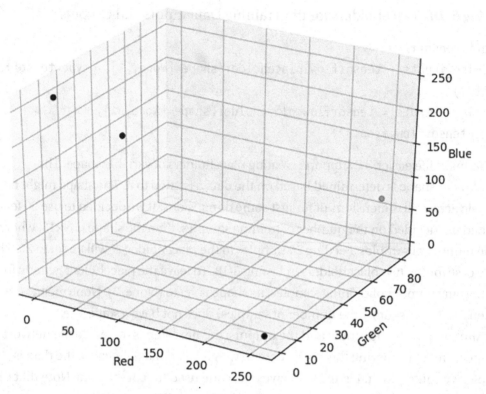

Figure 6-8. *3D scatter plot of the training data*

Based on Figure 6-8, it is obvious that the two classes can be separated linearly. The two samples of the class red are located on the right of the plot, and the blue samples are on the left. Knowing it is a linear problem guides us to not use any hidden layer. Thus, the network architecture will just have input and output layers. Because each sample is represented using three features, then the input layer will have just three inputs, one for each feature. The network architecture is in Figure 6-9, where $X_0 = 1.0$ is the bias input and W_0 is the bias. W_1, W_2, and W_3 are the weights for the three inputs R (Red), G (Green), and B (Blue).

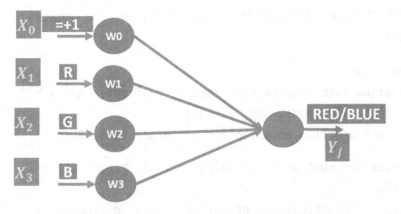

Figure 6-9. *ANN architecture for classifying RGB colors linearly*

Listing 6-20 prepares the variables holding these parameters. Because there are three inputs and each input has a weight, the shape of the weights is 3×1 according to the "weights" variable. The shape is 3×1 to make matrix multiplication between the inputs and the weights valid. The input data of shape N×3 could be multiplied by the weights of shape 3×1, and the result will be N×1. There is just one bias according to the "bias" variable.

Listing 6-20. Preparing ANN Parameter Variables

```
import tensorflow
weights = tensorflow.Variable(initial_value=[[0.003], [0.001], [0.008]],
dtype=tensorflow.float32)
bias = tensorflow.Variable(initial_value=[0.001], dtype=tensorflow.float32)
```

After preparing the data, network architecture, and the parameters, next is to feed the training input data into the network, predict their outputs, and calculate the loss according to Listing 6-21. The input data matrix is multiplied by the weights vector using the "matmul()" operation and the result is stored in the "sop" tensor. According to Equation 6-1, the result of the multiplication is added to the bias. The result of the addition is stored in the "sop_bias" tensor. The result is then applied to the sigmoid function defined by the "tensorflow.nn.sigmoid()" operation and returned into the "predictions" tensor.

Listing 6-21. Using the Network Parameters to Predict the Outputs of the Training Data

```
import tensorflow
sop = tensorflow.matmul(a=training_inputs, b=weights, name="SOPs")
sop_bias = tensorflow.add(x=sop, y=bias)
predictions = tensorflow.nn.sigmoid(x=sop_bias, name="Sigmoid")

error = tensorflow.subtract(x=training_outputs, y=predictions,
name="Error")
square_error = tensorflow.square(x=error, name="SquareError")
loss = tensorflow.reduce_sum(square_error, name="Loss")

train_optim = tensorflow.train.GradientDescentOptimizer(learning_rate=0.05,
name="GradientDescent")
minimizer = train_op.minimize(loss, name="Minimizer")
```

After predicting the outputs, next is to measure the loss. At first, the difference between the predicted and the correct outputs are calculated using the "subtract()" operation, and the result is stored in the "error" tensor. The square of that error is then calculated using the "square" tensor and the result is stored into the "square_error" tensor. Finally, the squared errors are reduced into a single value by summing them all. The result is stored into the "loss" tensor.

The loss is calculated to learn how we far we currently are from the optimal results where the loss is 0. Based on the loss, the GD optimizer is initialized in the "train_optim" tensor to update the network parameters in order to minimize the loss. The update operation is returned into the "minimizer" tensor.

Up to this point, the network architecture is complete and ready for training using the input and output data. Two Python lists are created in Listing 6-22 to hold the training data inputs and outputs. Note that the red class label is "1.0" and the blue one is "0.0". The lists are assigned to the placeholders "training_inputs" and "training_outputs" using the "feed_dict" argument inside the "tensorflow.Session.run()" operation. Note that the target of execution is the "minimizer" operation. The session goes through a number of iterations to update the ANN parameters.

Listing 6-22. Training Data Inputs and Outputs

```
training_inputs_data = [[255, 0, 0],
                        [248, 80, 68],
                        [0, 0, 255],
                        [67, 15, 210]]
training_outputs_data = [[1.0],
                         [1.0],
                         [0.0],
                         [0.0]]

with tensorflow.Session() as sess:
    init = tensorflow.global_variables_initializer()
    sess.run(init)

    for step in range(10):
        sess.run(fetches=minimizer, feed_dict={training_inputs: training_
        inputs_data, training_outputs: training_outputs_data})
```

The complete code for building a single-layer ANN for classifying the two-class problem in Table 6-2 is in Listing 6-23.

Listing 6-23. The Complete Code for Classifying the Two-Class RGB Color Problem

```
import tensorflow

# Preparing a placeholder for the training data inputs of shape (N, 3)
training_inputs = tensorflow.placeholder(shape=[None, 3], dtype=tensorflow.
float32, name="Inputs")

# Preparing a placeholder for the training data outputs of shape (N, 1)
training_outputs = tensorflow.placeholder(shape=[None, 1],
dtype=tensorflow.float32, name="Outputs")

# Initializing neural network weights of shape (3, 1)
weights = tensorflow.Variable(initial_value=[[0.003], [0.001], [0.008]],
dtype=tensorflow.float32, name="Weights")
```

```
# Initializing the ANN bias
bias = tensorflow.Variable(initial_value=[0.001], dtype=tensorflow.float32,
name="Bias")

# Calculating the SOPs by multiplying the weights matrix by the data inputs
matrix
sop = tensorflow.matmul(a=training_inputs, b=weights, name="SOPs")

# Adding the bias to the SOPs
sop_bias = tensorflow.add(x=sop, y=bias, name="AddBias")

# Sigmoid activation function of the output layer neuron
predictions = tensorflow.nn.sigmoid(x=sop_bias, name="Sigmoid")

# Calculating the difference (error) between the ANN predictions and the
correct outputs
error = tensorflow.subtract(x=training_outputs, y=predictions,
name="Error")

# Square error.
square_error = tensorflow.square(x=error, name="SquareError")

# Measuring the prediction error of the network after being trained
loss = tensorflow.reduce_sum(square_error, name="Loss")

# Minimizing the prediction error using gradient descent optimizer
train_optim = tensorflow.train.GradientDescentOptimizer(learning_rate=0.05,
name="GradientDescent")
minimizer = train_optim.minimize(loss, name="Minimizer")

# Training data inputs of shape (N, 3)
training_inputs_data = [[255, 0, 0],
                        [248, 80, 68],
                        [0, 0, 255],
                        [67, 15, 210]]

# Training data desired outputs
training_outputs_data = [[1.0],
                         [1.0],
                         [0.0],
                         [0.0]]
```

```
# Creating a TensorFlow Session
with tensorflow.Session() as sess:
    writer = tensorflow.summary.FileWriter(logdir="\\AhmedGad\\
    TensorBoard\\", graph=sess.graph)
    # Initializing the TensorFlow Variables (weights and bias)
    init = tensorflow.global_variables_initializer()
    sess.run(init)

    # Training loop of the neural network
    for step in range(10):
        sess.run(fetches=minimizer, feed_dict={training_inputs: training_
        inputs_data, training_outputs: training_outputs_data})

    # Class scores of training data
    print("Expected Outputs for Train Data:\n", sess.
    run(fetches=[predictions, weights, bias], feed_dict={training_inputs:
    training_inputs_data}))

    # Class scores of new test data
    print("Expected Outputs for Test Data:\n", sess.
    run(fetches=predictions, feed_dict={training_inputs: [[230, 60, 76],
    [93, 52, 180]]}))
    writer.close()
```

After all training iterations, the trained network is used to predict the output of both the training samples and the two other unseen test samples. The following is the output of the print statements at the end of Listing 6-23. The network is able to predict all training and test samples correctly.

```
Expected Outputs for Train Data:
 [[ 1.]
 [ 1.]
 [ 0.]
 [ 0.]]
Expected Outputs for Test Data:
 [[ 1.]
 [ 0.]]
```

The weighs and bias after training the network are as follows:

```
Weights:[[1.90823114], [0.11530305], [-4.13670015]],
Bias: [-0.00771546].
```

Figure 6-10 visualizes the graph created in Listing 6-23.

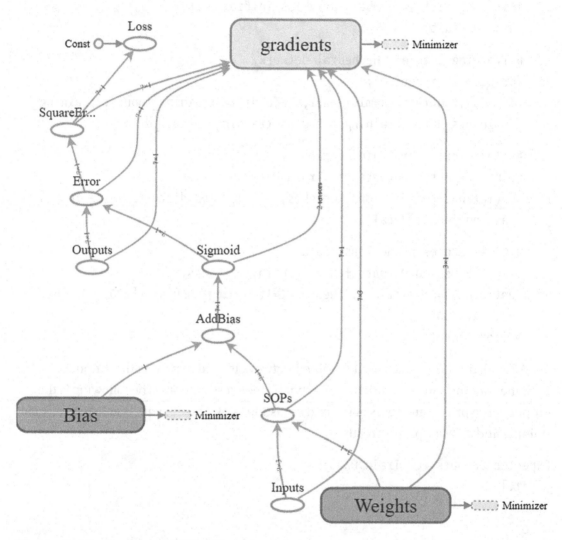

Figure 6-10. *Graph of ANN with a single layer*

Nonlinear Classification

Now we are going to build an ANN that simulates the operation of an XOR gate with two inputs. The truth table for the problem is in Table 6-3. Because the problem is simple, we can plot it as in Figure 6-11 to know whether the classes are linearly or nonlinearly separable.

Table 6-3. *The Truth Table of Two-Input XOR Gate*

Output	A	B
1	1	0
	0	1
0	0	0
	1	1

Based on the graph, it is obvious that the classes are nonlinearly separable. Thus, we have to use hidden layers. According to the first example in section **Designing ANN** of Chapter 3, we know that just a single hidden layer with two neurons is sufficient.

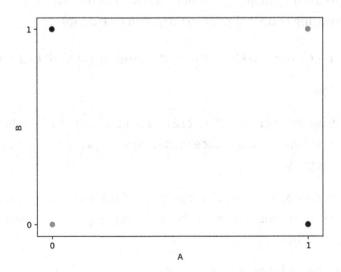

Figure 6-11. *Graph of two-input XOR gate*

The network architecture is in Figure 6-12. That hidden layer accepts the inputs from the input layer. Based on its weights and biases, its two activation functions will produce two outputs. The outputs of the hidden layer will be regarded as the inputs to the output layer. Using its activation function, the output layer produces the final expected class of the input sample.

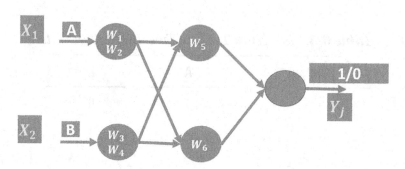

Figure 6-12. *Network architecture for XOR gate with two inputs*

The complete code is in Listing 6-24. There are some changes compared to the previous example. The initial parameters are randomly generated using "tensorflow. truncated_normal()" operation. The output tensor of the hidden layer "hidden_sigmoid" is used as input to the output layer. The output tensor of the output layer is the predicted outputs. The remaining code is similar to the previous example.

Listing 6-24. The Complete Code for ANN Simulating XOR Gate with Two Inputs

```
import tensorflow
```

```
# Preparing a placeholder for the training data inputs of shape (N, 3)
training_inputs = tensorflow.placeholder(shape=[4, 2], dtype=tensorflow.
float32, name="Inputs")
```

```
# Preparing a placeholder for the training data outputs of shape (N, 1)
training_outputs = tensorflow.placeholder(shape=[4, 1], dtype=tensorflow.
float32, name="Outputs")
```

```
# Initializing the weights of the hidden layer of shape (2, 2)
hidden_weights = tensorflow.Variable(initial_value=tensorflow.truncated_
normal(shape=(2,2), name="HiddenRandomWeights"), dtype=tensorflow.float32,
name="HiddenWeights")
```

```
# Initializing the bias of the hidden layer of shape (1,2)
hidden_bias = tensorflow.Variable(initial_value=tensorflow.truncated_
normal(shape=(1,2), name="HiddenRandomBias"), dtype=tensorflow.float32,
name="HiddenBias")

# Calculating the SOPs by multiplying the weights matrix of the hidden
layer by the data inputs matrix
hidden_sop = tensorflow.matmul(a=training_inputs, b=hidden_weights,
name="HiddenSOPs")

# Adding the bias to the SOPs of the hidden layer
hidden_sop_bias = tensorflow.add(x=hidden_sop, y=hidden_bias,
name="HiddenAddBias")

# Sigmoid activation function of the hidden layer outputs
hidden_sigmoid = tensorflow.nn.sigmoid(x=hidden_sop_bias,
name="HiddenSigmoid")

# Initializing the weights of the output layer of shape (2, 1)
output_weights = tensorflow.Variable(initial_value=tensorflow.truncated_
normal(shape=(2,1), name="OutputRandomWeights"), dtype=tensorflow.float32,
name="OutputWeights")

# Initializing the bias of the output layer of shape (1,1)
output_bias = tensorflow.Variable(initial_value=tensorflow.truncated_
normal(shape=(1,1), name="OutputRandomBias"), dtype=tensorflow.float32,
name="OutputBias")

# Calculating the SOPs by multiplying the weights matrix of the hidden
layer by the outputs of the hidden layer
output_sop = tensorflow.matmul(a=hidden_sigmoid, b=output_weights,
name="Output_SOPs")

# Adding the bias to the SOPs of the hidden layer
output_sop_bias = tensorflow.add(x=output_sop, y=output_bias,
name="OutputAddBias")

# Sigmoid activation function of the output layer outputs. These are the
predictions.
```

```python
predictions = tensorflow.nn.sigmoid(x=output_sop_bias,
name="OutputSigmoid")

# Calculating the difference (error) between the ANN predictions and the
correct outputs
error = tensorflow.subtract(x=training_outputs, y=predictions,
name="Error")

# Square error.
square_error = tensorflow.square(x=error, name="SquareError")

# Measuring the prediction error of the network after being trained
loss = tensorflow.reduce_sum(square_error, name="Loss")

# Minimizing the prediction error using gradient descent optimizer
train_optim = tensorflow.train.GradientDescentOptimizer(learning_rate=0.01,
name="GradientDescent")
minimizer = train_optim.minimize(loss, name="Minimizer")

# Training data inputs of shape (4, 2)
training_inputs_data = [[1, 0],
                        [0, 1],
                        [0, 0],
                        [1, 1]]

# Training data desired outputs
training_outputs_data = [[1.0],
                         [1.0],
                         [0.0],
                         [0.0]]

# Creating a TensorFlow Session
with tensorflow.Session() as sess:
    writer = tensorflow.summary.FileWriter(logdir="\\AhmedGad\\
    TensorBoard\\", graph=sess.graph)
    # Initializing the TensorFlow Variables (weights and bias)
    init = tensorflow.global_variables_initializer()
    sess.run(init)
```

```
# Training loop of the neural network
for step in range(100000):
    print(sess.run(fetches=minimizer, feed_dict={training_inputs:
    training_inputs_data, training_outputs: training_outputs_data}))

# Class scores of training data
print("Expected Outputs for Train Data:\n", sess.
run(fetches=[predictions, hidden_weights, output_weights, hidden_bias,
output_bias], feed_dict={training_inputs: training_inputs_data}))

writer.close()
```

After completing the training process, the samples are correctly classified. Here are the predicted outputs:

```
[[0.96982265],
 [0.96998841],
 [0.0275135],
 [0.0380362]]
```

The parameters of the network after training are as follows:

- Hidden layer weights: [-6.27943468, -4.30125761], [-6.38489389, -4.31706429]]

- Hidden layer bias: [[-8.8601017], [8.70441246]]

- Output layer weights: [[2.49879336, 6.37831974]]

- Output layer bias: [[-4.06760359]]

Figure 6-13 visualizes the graph of Listing 6-24.

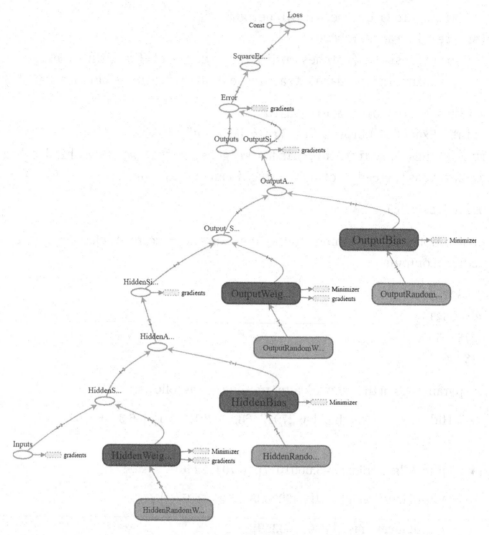

Figure 6-13. *Graph of ANN simulating XOR gate with two inputs*

CIFAR10 Recognition Using CNN

The previous examples we discussed help us learn the basics of TF and build good knowledge. This section extends this knowledge by using TF to build a CNN to recognize images from the CIFAR10 dataset.

Preparing Training Data

The binary data of the CIFAR10 dataset is available for download for Python from this page: www.cs.toronto.edu/~kriz/cifar.html. The dataset has 60,000 images split into training and testing sets. There are five binary files containing the training data, where each file has 10,000 images. The images are RGB of size 32×32×3. The training files are named "data_batch_1", "data_batch_2", and so on. There is a single file for the test data named "test_batch" with 10,000 images. A metadata file named "batches.meta" is available, giving details about the dataset such as the class labels, which are airplane, automobile, bird, cat, deer, dog, frog, horse, ship, and truck.

Because each file in the dataset is binary, we have to decode it in order to retrieve the actual image data. To do this job, a function called "unpickle_patch" is created, as defined in Listing 6-25.

Listing 6-25. Decoding the CIFAR10 Binary Data

```
def unpickle_patch(file):
    patch_bin_file = open(file, 'rb')#Reading the binary file.
    patch_dict = pickle.load(patch_bin_file, encoding='bytes')#Loading the
    details of the binary file into a dictionary.
    return patch_dict#Returning the dictionary.
```

The method accepts the binary file path and returns the details about this file into the "patch_dict" dictionary. The dictionary has the image data for all 10,000 samples within the file in addition to their class labels.

There are five training data files. In order to decode the entire training data, a new function called "get_dataset_images" is created as in Listing 6-26. That function accepts the dataset path and decodes the data of just the five training files. Firstly, it lists all files under the dataset directory using the "os.listdir()" function. All file names are returned into the "files_names" list.

Because all train and test files are located within the same directory, this function filters the files under this path to just return the training files. The function uses an "if" statement to just return files starting with "data_batch_" as it is discriminative to the train file names. Note that the test data is prepared later after building and training the CNN.

Listing 6-26. Decoding All Training Files

```
def get_dataset_images(dataset_path, im_dim=32, num_channels=3):
    num_files = 5#Number of training binary files in the CIFAR10 dataset.
    images_per_file = 10000#Number of samples within each binary file.
    files_names = os.listdir(patches_dir)#Listing the binary files in the
    dataset path.

    dataset_array = numpy.zeros(shape=(num_files * images_per_file, im_dim,
    im_dim, num_channels))
    dataset_labels = numpy.zeros(shape=(num_files * images_per_file),
    dtype=numpy.uint8)

    index = 0#Index variable to count number of training binary files being
    processed.
    for file_name in files_names:
        if file_name[0:len(file_name) - 1] == "data_batch_":
            print("Working on : ", file_name)
            data_dict = unpickle_patch(dataset_path+file_name)

            images_data = data_dict[b"data"]
            #Reshaping all samples in the current binary file to be of
            32x32x3 shape.
            images_data_reshaped = numpy.reshape(images_data,
            newshape=(len(images_data), im_dim, im_dim, num_channels))
            #Appending the data of the current file after being reshaped.
            dataset_array[index * images_per_file:(index + 1) * images_per_
            file, :, :, :] = images_data_reshaped
            #Appending the labels of the current file.
            dataset_labels[index * images_per_file:(index + 1) * images_
            per_file] = data_dict[b"labels"]
            index = index + 1#Incrementing the counter of the processed
            training files by 1 to accept new file.
    return dataset_array, dataset_labels#Returning the training input data
    and output labels.
```

Each training file is decoded by calling the "unpickle_patch" function, and its image data and their labels are returned into the "data_dict" dictionary. There are five training files, and thus there are five classes to such a function, where each call returns a dictionary.

Based on the dictionary returned by this function, the "get_dataset_images" function concatenates the details (image data and class labels) of all files into a NumPy array. The image data could be retrieved from that dictionary using the "data" key and stored into the "dataset_array" NumPy array, which stores all decoded images across all training files. Class labels are retrieved using the "labels" key and returned into the "dataset_labels" NumPy array, which stores all labels across all images in the training data. The "dataset_array" and "dataset_labels" are returned by the function.

When decoded, the data of each image returns as a 1D vector of length 32×32×3=3,072 pixels. This vector should be reshaped of the original shape with three dimensions. This is because CNN layers created in TF accepts the images of this shape. For this reason, the "get_dataset_images" function has arguments for accepting the size of each dimension for the dataset images. The first one is "im_dim" representing the number of rows/columns (they are equal) in addition to the "num_channels" representing the number of channels.

After preparing the training data, we can build and train the CNN model using TF.

Building the CNN

The dataflow graph of the CNN is created inside a function called "create_CNN" as in Listing 6-27. It creates a stack of convolution (conv), ReLU, max pooling, dropout, and FC layers. The architecture of the CNN is illustrated in Figure 6-14. It has three conv-relu-pool groups followed by a dropout layer and finally two FC layers.

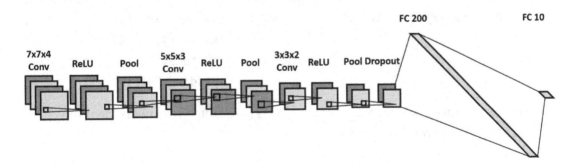

Figure 6-14. CNN architecture

The function returns the results of the last FC layer. As regularly, the output of each layer is the input to the next layer. This requires consistency between the sizes of the outputs and inputs of neighboring layers. Note that for each conv, ReLU, and max pooling layer, there are some parameters to get specified, such as strides across each dimension and padding.

Listing 6-27. Building the CNN Structure

```
def create_CNN(input_data, num_classes, keep_prop):
    filters1, conv_layer1 = create_conv_layer(input_data=input_data,
    filter_size=7, num_filters=4)
    relu_layer1 = tensorflow.nn.relu(conv_layer1)
    max_pooling_layer1 = tensorflow.nn.max_pool(value=relu_layer1,
                                                ksize=[1, 2, 2, 1],
                                                strides=[1, 1, 1, 1],
                                                padding="VALID")

    filters2, conv_layer2 = create_conv_layer(input_data=max_pooling_
    layer1, filter_size=5, num_filters=3)
    relu_layer2 = tensorflow.nn.relu(conv_layer2)
    max_pooling_layer2 = tensorflow.nn.max_pool(value=relu_layer2,
                                                ksize=[1, 2, 2, 1],
                                                strides=[1, 1, 1, 1],
                                                padding="VALID")

    filters3, conv_layer3 = create_conv_layer(input_data=max_pooling_
    layer2, filter_size=3, num_filters=2)
    relu_layer3 = tensorflow.nn.relu(conv_layer3)
    max_pooling_layer3 = tensorflow.nn.max_pool(value=relu_layer3,
                                                ksize=[1, 2, 2, 1],
                                                strides=[1, 1, 1, 1],
                                                padding="VALID")

    flattened_layer = dropout_flatten_layer(previous_layer=max_pooling_
    layer3, keep_prop=keep_prop)
```

274

```
fc_result1 = fc_layer(flattened_layer=flattened_layer, num_
inputs=flattened_layer.get_shape()[1:].num_elements(),
                        num_outputs=200)

fc_result2 = fc_layer(flattened_layer=fc_result1, num_inputs=fc_
result1.get_shape()[1:].num_elements(),
                        num_outputs=num_classes)
print("Fully connected layer results : ", fc_result2)
return fc_result2#Returning the result of the last FC layer.
```

The first layer in the CNN works directly on the input data. Thus, the "create_CNN" function accepts the input data as an input argument called "input_data". This data is what returned by the "get_dataset_images" function. The first layer is a convolution layer, which is created using the "create_conv_layer" function according to Listing 6-28.

The "create_conv_layer" function accepts the input data, filter size, and the number of filters. It returns the result of convolving the input data with the set of filters. The filters in the set have their depth set according to the number of channels of the input data. Because the number of channels is the last element in a NumPy array, index –1 is used to return the number of channels. The set of filters are returned into the "filters" variable.

Listing 6-28. Building Convolution Layer

```
def create_conv_layer(input_data, filter_size, num_filters):
    filters = tensorflow.Variable(tensorflow.truncated_
    normal(shape=(filter_size, filter_size, tensorflow.cast(input_data.
    shape[-1], dtype=tensorflow.int32), num_filters), stddev=0.05))

    conv_layer = tensorflow.nn.conv2d(input=input_data,
                                      filter=filters,
                                      strides=[1, 1, 1, 1],
                                      padding="VALID")
    return filters, conv_layer#Returning the filters and the convolution
    layer result.
```

The convolution layer is built by specifying the input data, filters, and strides along each of the four dimensions, and the padding to the "tensorflow.nn.conv2D" operation. A padding value of "VALID" means that some borders of the input image will be lost in the result, based on the filter size.

The result of any conv layer is fed into a ReLU layer created using the "tensorflow. nn.relu" operation. It accepts the conv layer output and returns a tensor of the same number of features after applying the ReLU activation function. Remember that activation functions help to create a nonlinear relationship between the inputs and the outputs. The result of the ReLU layer is then fed to a max pooling layer created using the "tensorflow.nn.max_pool" operation. Remember that the goal of pooling layers is to make the recognition translation invariant.

The "create_CNN" function accepts an argument named "keep_prop" representing the probability of keeping neurons in the dropout layer, which helps to avoid overfitting. The dropout layer is implemented using the "dropout_flatten_layer" function, as in Listing 6-29. This function returns a flattened array that is used as the input to the FC layers.

Listing 6-29. Building Dropout Layer

```
def dropout_flatten_layer(previous_layer, keep_prop):
    dropout = tensorflow.nn.dropout(x=previous_layer, keep_prob=keep_prop)
    num_features = dropout.get_shape()[1:].num_elements()
    layer = tensorflow.reshape(previous_layer, shape=(-1, num_
    features))#Flattening the results.
    return layer
```

Because the last FC layer should have a number of output neurons equal to the number of dataset classes, the number of dataset classes is used as another input argument named "num_classes" to the "create_CNN" function. The FC layer is created using the "fc_layer" function, defined according to Listing 6-30. This function accepts the flattened result of the dropout layer, the number of features in the flattened result, and the number of output neurons from the FC layer. Based on the number of inputs and outputs, a tensor named "fc_weights" represents the weights for the FC layer that is created. It gets multiplied by the flattened layer to get the returned result of the FC layer.

Listing 6-30. Building FC Layer

```
def fc_layer(flattened_layer, num_inputs, num_outputs):
    fc_weights = tensorflow.Variable(tensorflow.truncated_
    normal(shape=(num_inputs, num_outputs), stddev=0.05))
```

```
fc_result1 = tensorflow.matmul(flattened_layer, fc_weights)
return fc_result1#Output of the FC layer (result of matrix
multiplication).
```

The computational graph after being visualized using TB is shown in Figure 6-15. Part a gives the architecture of the CNN until the final max pooling layer, while part b shows the remaining steps.

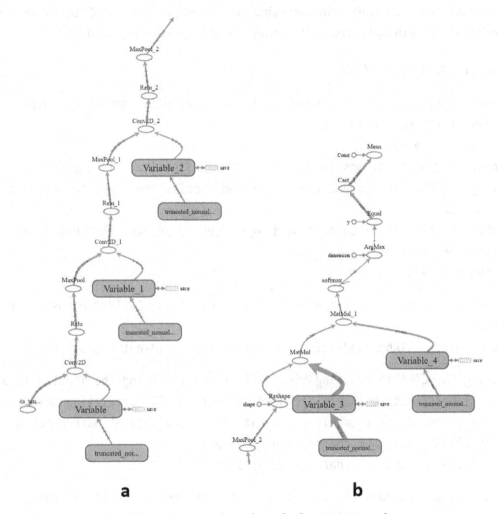

a   b

Figure 6-15. *Graph of the CNN used to classify the CIFAR10 dataset*

Training CNN

After building the computational graph of the CNN, next is to train it against the previously prepared training data. The training is done according to Listing 6-31. The code starts by preparing the path of the dataset and the data placeholders. Note that the path should be changed to be suitable for your system. Then it calls the previously discussed functions. The predictions of the trained CNN are used to measure the cost of the network, which is to be minimized using the GD optimizer. Some of the tensors have descriptive names to make it easier to retrieve them later when testing the CNN.

Listing 6-31. Training CNN

```
#Number of classes in the dataset. Used to specify the number of outputs in
the last fully connected layer.
num_dataset_classes = 10
#Number of rows & columns in each input image. The image is expected to be
rectangular Used to reshape the images and specify the input tensor shape.
im_dim = 32
#Number of channels in each input image. Used to reshape the images and
specify the input tensor shape.
num_channels = 3

#Directory at which the training binary files of the CIFAR10 dataset are
saved.
patches_dir = "\\AhmedGad\\cifar-10-python\\cifar-10-batches-py\\"

#Reading the CIFAR10 training binary files and returning the input data and
output labels. Output labels are used to test the CNN prediction accuracy.
dataset_array, dataset_labels = get_dataset_images(dataset_path=patches_
dir, im_dim=im_dim, num_channels=num_channels)
print("Size of data : ", dataset_array.shape)

# Input tensor to hold the data read in the preceding. It is the entry
point of the computational graph.
# The given name of 'data_tensor' is useful for retrieving it when
restoring the trained model graph for testing.
```

```
data_tensor = tensorflow.placeholder(tensorflow.float32, shape=[None, im_
dim, im_dim, num_channels], name='data_tensor')

# Tensor to hold the outputs label.
# The name "label_tensor" is used for accessing the tensor when testing the
saved trained model after being restored.

label_tensor = tensorflow.placeholder(tensorflow.float32, shape=[None],
name='label_tensor')

#The probability of dropping neurons in the dropout layer. It is given a
name for accessing it later.
keep_prop = tensorflow.Variable(initial_value=0.5, name="keep_prop")

#Building the CNN architecture and returning the last layer which is the
fully connected layer.
fc_result2 = create_CNN(input_data=data_tensor, num_classes=num_dataset_
classes, keep_prop=keep_prop)

# Predictions propabilities of the CNN for each training sample.
# Each sample has a probability for each of the 10 classes in the dataset.
# Such a tensor is given a name for accessing it later.

softmax_propabilities = tensorflow.nn.softmax(fc_result2, name="softmax_
probs")

# Predictions labels of the CNN for each training sample.
# The input sample is classified as the class of the highest probability.
# axis=1 indicates that maximum of values in the second axis is to be
returned. This returns that maximum class probability of each sample.

softmax_predictions = tensorflow.argmax(softmax_propabilities, axis=1)

#Cross entropy of the CNN based on its calculated propabilities.
cross_entropy = tensorflow.nn.softmax_cross_entropy_with_
logits(logits=tensorflow.reduce_max(input_tensor=softmax_propabilities,
reduction_indices=[1]), labels=label_tensor)
```

```
#Summarizing the cross entropy into a single value (cost) to be minimized
by the learning algorithm.
cost = tensorflow.reduce_mean(cross_entropy)
#Minimizing the network cost using the Gradient Descent optimizer with a
learning rate is 0.01.
error = tensorflow.train.GradientDescentOptimizer(learning_rate=.01).
minimize(cost)

#Creating a new TensorFlow Session to process the computational graph.
sess = tensorflow.Session()
#Writing summary of the graph to visualize it using TensorBoard.
tensorflow.summary.FileWriter(logdir="\\AhmedGad\\TensorBoard\\",
graph=sess.graph)
#Initializing the variables of the graph.
sess.run(tensorflow.global_variables_initializer())

# Because it may be impossible to feed the complete data to the CNN on
normal machines, it is recommended to split the data into a number of
patches.
# A subset of the training samples is used to create each path. Samples for
each path can be randomly selected.

num_patches = 5#Number of patches
for patch_num in numpy.arange(num_patches):
    print("Patch : ", str(patch_num))
    percent = 80 #percent of samples to be included in each path.

    #Getting the input-output data of the current path.
    shuffled_data, shuffled_labels = get_patch(data=dataset_array,
    labels=dataset_labels, percent=percent)

    #Data required for cnn operation. 1)Input Images, 2)Output Labels, and
    3)Dropout probability
    cnn_feed_dict = {data_tensor: shuffled_data,
                    label_tensor: shuffled_labels,
                    keep_prop: 0.5}
```

```
# Training the CNN based on the current patch.
# CNN error is used as input in the run to minimize it.
# SoftMax predictions are returned to compute the classification accuracy.
    softmax_predictions_, _ = sess.run([softmax_predictions, error], feed_
    dict=cnn_feed_dict)
    #Calculating number of correctly classified samples.
    correct = numpy.array(numpy.where(softmax_predictions_ == shuffled_
    labels))
    correct = correct.size
    print("Correct predictions/", str(percent * 50000/100), ' : ', correct)

#Closing the session
sess.close()
```

Rather than feeding the entire training data to the CNN, just a subset of the data is returned. This helps adjust the data to the amount of memory available. The subset is returned using the "get_patch" function according to Listing 6-32. This function accepts the input data, labels, and percentage of samples to be returned from the data. It then returns a subset of the data according to the specified percentage.

Listing 6-32. Splitting Dataset into Patches

```
def get_patch(data, labels, percent=70):
    num_elements = numpy.uint32(percent*data.shape[0]/100)
    shuffled_labels = labels#Temporary variable to hold the data after
    being shuffled.
    numpy.random.shuffle(shuffled_labels)#Randomly reordering the labels.

    return data[shuffled_labels[:num_elements], :, :, :], shuffled_
    labels[:num_elements]
```

Saving the Trained Model

After training the CNN, the model is saved for reuse later for testing according to Listing 6-33. You should also change the path where the model is saved to be suitable for your system.

Listing 6-33. Saving the Trained CNN Model

```
#Saving the model after being trained.
saver = tensorflow.train.Saver()
save_model_path = "\\AhmedGad\\model\\"
save_path = saver.save(sess=sess, save_path=save_model_path+"model.ckpt")
print("Model saved in : ", save_path)
```

Complete Code to Build and Train CNN

After going through all parts of the project from reading the data until saving the trained model, a summary of the steps is given in Figure 6-16. Listing 6-34 gives the complete code for training the CNN. After saving the trained model, it will be used to predict the class labels of the test data.

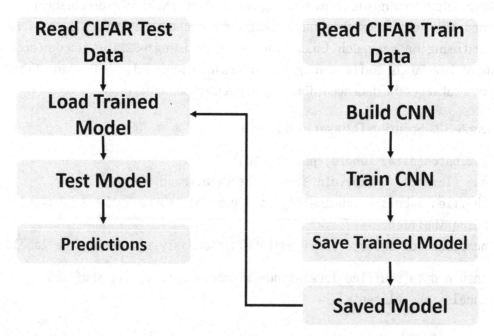

Figure 6-16. *Summary of steps for building a CNN trained using CIFAR10 dataset*

Listing 6-34. Complete Code to Train CNN for CIFAR10 Dataset

```python
import pickle
import tensorflow
import numpy
import matplotlib.pyplot
import scipy.misc
import os

def get_dataset_images(dataset_path, im_dim=32, num_channels=3):
    """

    This function accepts the dataset path, reads the data, and returns it
    after being reshaped to match the requirements of the CNN.
    :param dataset_path:Path of the CIFAR10 dataset binary files.
    :param im_dim:Number of rows and columns in each image. The image is
    expected to be rectangular.
    :param num_channels:Number of color channels in the image.
    :return:Returns the input data after being reshaped and output labels.
    """

    num_files = 5#Number of training binary files in the CIFAR10 dataset.
    images_per_file = 10000#Number of samples within each binary file.
    files_names = os.listdir(patches_dir)#Listing the binary files in the
    dataset path.
# Creating an empty array to hold the entire training data after being
reshaped. The dataset has 5 binary files holding the data. Each binary
file has 10,000 samples. Total number of samples in the dataset is
5*10,000=50,000.
# Each sample has a total of 3,072 pixels. These pixels are reshaped to
form a RGB image of shape 32x32x3.
# Finally, the entire dataset has 50,000 samples and each sample of shape
32x32x3 (50,000x32x32x3).
    dataset_array = numpy.zeros(shape=(num_files * images_per_file, im_dim,
    im_dim, num_channels))
    #Creating an empty array to hold the labels of each input sample. Its
    size is 50,000 to hold the label of each sample in the dataset.
```

```
    dataset_labels = numpy.zeros(shape=(num_files * images_per_file),
    dtype=numpy.uint8)
    index = 0#Index variable to count number of training binary files being
    processed.
    for file_name in files_names:
# Because the CIFAR10 directory does not only contain the desired training
files and has some  other files, it is required to filter the required
files. Training files start by 'data_batch_' which is used to test whether
the file is for training or not.
        if file_name[0:len(file_name) - 1] == "data_batch_":
            print("Working on : ", file_name)
# Appending the path of the binary files to the name of the current file.
# Then the complete path of the binary file is used to decoded the file and
return the actual pixels values.
            data_dict = unpickle_patch(dataset_path+file_name)
# Returning the data using its key 'data' in the dictionary.
# Character b is used before the key to tell it is binary string.
            images_data = data_dict[b"data"]
            #Reshaping all samples in the current binary file to be of
            32x32x3 shape.
            images_data_reshaped = numpy.reshape(images_data,
            newshape=(len(images_data), im_dim, im_dim, num_channels))
            #Appending the data of the current file after being reshaped.
            dataset_array[index * images_per_file:(index + 1) * images_per_
            file, :, :, :] = images_data_reshaped
            #Appending the labels of the current file.
            dataset_labels[index * images_per_file:(index + 1) * images_
            per_file] = data_dict[b"labels"]
            index = index + 1#Incrementing the counter of the processed
            training files by 1 to accept new file.
    return dataset_array, dataset_labels#Returning the training input data
    and output labels.

def unpickle_patch(file):
    """
```

```
    Decoding the binary file.
    :param file:File path to decode its data.
    :return: Dictionary of the file holding details including input data
    and output labels.
    """
    patch_bin_file = open(file, 'rb')#Reading the binary file.
    patch_dict = pickle.load(patch_bin_file, encoding='bytes')#Loading the
    details of the binary file into a dictionary.
    return patch_dict#Returning the dictionary.

def get_patch(data, labels, percent=70):
    """
    Returning patch to train the CNN.
    :param data: Complete input data after being encoded and reshaped.
    :param labels: Labels of the entire dataset.
    :param percent: Percent of samples to get returned in each patch.
    :return: Subset of the data (patch) to train the CNN model.
    """
    #Using the percent of samples per patch to return the actual number of
    samples to get returned.
    num_elements = numpy.uint32(percent*data.shape[0]/100)
    shuffled_labels = labels#Temporary variable to hold the data after
    being shuffled.
    numpy.random.shuffle(shuffled_labels)#Randomly reordering the labels.
# The previously specified percent of the data is returned starting from
the beginning until meeting the required number of samples.
# The labels indices are also used to return their corresponding input
images samples.
    return data[shuffled_labels[:num_elements], :, :, :], shuffled_
    labels[:num_elements]

def create_conv_layer(input_data, filter_size, num_filters):
    """
    Builds the CNN convolution (conv) layer.
    :param input_data:patch data to be processed.
```

```
    :param filter_size:#Number of rows and columns of each filter. It is
    expected to have a rectangular filter.
    :param num_filters:Number of filters.
    :return:The last fully connected layer of the network.
    """

# Preparing the filters of the conv layer by specifying  its shape.
# Number of channels in both input image and each filter must match.
# Because number of channels is specified in the shape of the input image
as the last value, index of -1 works fine.
    filters = tensorflow.Variable(tensorflow.truncated_
    normal(shape=(filter_size, filter_size, tensorflow.cast(input_data.
    shape[-1], dtype=tensorflow.int32), num_filters), stddev=0.05))
    print("Size of conv filters bank : ", filters.shape)

# Building the convolution layer by specifying the input data, filters,
strides along each of the 4 dimensions, and the padding.
# Padding value of 'VALID' means the some borders of the input image will
be lost in the result based on the filter size.
    conv_layer = tensorflow.nn.conv2d(input=input_data,
                                      filter=filters,
                                      strides=[1, 1, 1, 1],
                                      padding="VALID")
    print("Size of conv result : ", conv_layer.shape)
    return filters, conv_layer#Returning the filters and the convolution
    layer result.

def create_CNN(input_data, num_classes, keep_prop):
    """

    Builds the CNN architecture by stacking conv, relu, pool, dropout, and
    fully connected layers.
    :param input_data:patch data to be processed.
    :param num_classes:Number of classes in the dataset. It helps to
    determine the number of outputs in the last fully connected layer.
    :param keep_prop:probability of keeping neurons in the dropout layer.
    :return: last fully connected layer.
    """
```

```
#Preparing the first convolution layer.
filters1, conv_layer1 = create_conv_layer(input_data=input_data,
filter_size=7, num_filters=4)
```
Applying ReLU activation function over the conv layer output.
It returns a new array of the same shape as the input array.
```
relu_layer1 = tensorflow.nn.relu(conv_layer1)
print("Size of relu1 result : ", relu_layer1.shape)
```
Max-pooling is applied to the ReLU layer result to achieve translation invariance. It returns a new array of a different shape from the input array relative to the strides and kernel size used.
```
max_pooling_layer1 = tensorflow.nn.max_pool(value=relu_layer1,
                                            ksize=[1, 2, 2, 1],
                                            strides=[1, 1, 1, 1],
                                            padding="VALID")
print("Size of maxpool1 result : ", max_pooling_layer1.shape)

#Similar to the previous conv-relu-pool layers, new layers are just
stacked to complete the CNN architecture.
#Conv layer with 3 filters and each filter is of size 5x5.
filters2, conv_layer2 = create_conv_layer(input_data=max_pooling_
layer1, filter_size=5, num_filters=3)
relu_layer2 = tensorflow.nn.relu(conv_layer2)
print("Size of relu2 result : ", relu_layer2.shape)
max_pooling_layer2 = tensorflow.nn.max_pool(value=relu_layer2,
                                            ksize=[1, 2, 2, 1],
                                            strides=[1, 1, 1, 1],
                                            padding="VALID")
print("Size of maxpool2 result : ", max_pooling_layer2.shape)

#Conv layer with 2 filters and a filter size of 5x5.
filters3, conv_layer3 = create_conv_layer(input_data=max_pooling_
layer2, filter_size=3, num_filters=2)
relu_layer3 = tensorflow.nn.relu(conv_layer3)
print("Size of relu3 result : ", relu_layer3.shape)
```

287

```
        max_pooling_layer3 = tensorflow.nn.max_pool(value=relu_layer3,
                                            ksize=[1, 2, 2, 1],
                                            strides=[1, 1, 1, 1],
                                            padding="VALID")
    print("Size of maxpool3 result : ", max_pooling_layer3.shape)

    #Adding dropout layer before the fully connected layers to avoid
    overfitting.
    flattened_layer = dropout_flatten_layer(previous_layer=max_pooling_
    layer3, keep_prop=keep_prop)

    #First fully connected (FC) layer. It accepts the result of the dropout
    layer after being flattened (1D).
    fc_result1 = fc_layer(flattened_layer=flattened_layer, num_
    inputs=flattened_layer.get_shape()[1:].num_elements(),
                        num_outputs=200)
    #Second fully connected layer accepting the output of the previous
    fully connected layer. Number of outputs is equal to the number of
    dataset classes.
    fc_result2 = fc_layer(flattened_layer=fc_result1, num_inputs=fc_
    result1.get_shape()[1:].num_elements(),
                        num_outputs=num_classes)
    print("Fully connected layer results : ", fc_result2)
    return fc_result2#Returning the result of the last FC layer.

def dropout_flatten_layer(previous_layer, keep_prop):
    """

    Applying the dropout layer.
    :param previous_layer: Result of the previous layer to the dropout
    layer.
    :param keep_prop: Probability of keeping neurons.
    :return: flattened array.
    """

    dropout = tensorflow.nn.dropout(x=previous_layer, keep_prob=keep_prop)
    num_features = dropout.get_shape()[1:].num_elements()
```

```
        layer = tensorflow.reshape(previous_layer, shape=(-1, num_features))
        #Flattening the results.
        return layer

def fc_layer(flattened_layer, num_inputs, num_outputs):
        """
        building a fully connected (FC) layer.
        :param flattened_layer: Previous layer after being flattened.
        :param num_inputs: Number of inputs in the previous layer.
        :param num_outputs: Number of outputs to be returned in such FC layer.
        :return:
        """
        #Preparing the set of weights for the FC layer. It depends on the
        number of inputs and number of outputs.
        fc_weights = tensorflow.Variable(tensorflow.truncated_
        normal(shape=(num_inputs, num_outputs), stddev=0.05))
        #Matrix multiplication between the flattened array and the set of
        weights.
        fc_result1 = tensorflow.matmul(flattened_layer, fc_weights)
        return fc_result1#Output of the FC layer (result of matrix
        multiplication).

#***********************************************************
#Number of classes in the dataset. Used to specify number of outputs in the
last FC layer.
num_dataset_classes = 10
#Number of rows & columns in each input image. The image is expected to be
rectangular Used to reshape the images and specify the input tensor shape.
im_dim = 32
# Number of channels in each input image. Used to reshape the images and
specify the input tensor shape.
num_channels = 3

#Directory at which the training binary files of the CIFAR10 dataset are
saved.
patches_dir = "\\AhmedGad\\cifar-10-python\\cifar-10-batches-py\\"
```

```
#Reading the CIFAR10 training binary files and returning the input data and
output labels. Output labels are used to test the CNN prediction accuracy.
dataset_array, dataset_labels = get_dataset_images(dataset_path=patches_
dir, im_dim=im_dim, num_channels=num_channels)
print("Size of data : ", dataset_array.shape)

# Input tensor to hold the data read in the preceding. It is the entry
point of the computational graph.
# The given name of 'data_tensor' is useful for retrieving it when
restoring the trained model graph for testing.
data_tensor = tensorflow.placeholder(tensorflow.float32, shape=[None, im_
dim, im_dim, num_channels], name='data_tensor')

# Tensor to hold the outputs label.
# The name "label_tensor" is used for accessing the tensor when testing the
saved trained model after being restored.
label_tensor = tensorflow.placeholder(tensorflow.float32, shape=[None],
name='label_tensor')

#The probability of dropping neurons in the dropout layer. It is given a
name for accessing it later.
keep_prop = tensorflow.Variable(initial_value=0.5, name="keep_prop")

#Building the CNN architecture and returning the last layer which is the FC
layer.
fc_result2 = create_CNN(input_data=data_tensor, num_classes=num_dataset_
classes, keep_prop=keep_prop)

# Predictions propabilities of the CNN for each training sample.
# Each sample has a probability for each of the 10 classes in the dataset.
# Such a tensor is given a name for accessing it later.
softmax_propabilities = tensorflow.nn.softmax(fc_result2, name="softmax_
probs")

# Predictions labels of the CNN for each training sample.
# The input sample is classified as the class of the highest probability.
# axis=1 indicates that maximum of values in the second axis is to be
returned. This returns that maximum class probability of each sample.
```

```
softmax_predictions = tensorflow.argmax(softmax_propabilities, axis=1)
```

```
#Cross entropy of the CNN based on its calculated propabilities.
cross_entropy = tensorflow.nn.softmax_cross_entropy_with_
logits(logits=tensorflow.reduce_max(input_tensor=softmax_propabilities,
reduction_indices=[1]),labels=label_tensor)
#Summarizing the cross entropy into a single value (cost) to be minimized
by the learning algorithm.
cost = tensorflow.reduce_mean(cross_entropy)
#Minimizing the network cost using the Gradient Descent optimizer with a
learning rate is 0.01.
ops = tensorflow.train.GradientDescentOptimizer(learning_rate=.01).
minimize(cost)
```

```
#Creating a new TensorFlow Session to process the computational graph.
sess = tensorflow.Session()
#Writing summary of the graph to visualize it using TensorBoard.
tensorflow.summary.FileWriter(logdir="\\AhmedGad\\TensorBoard\\",
graph=sess.graph)
#Initializing the variables of the graph.
sess.run(tensorflow.global_variables_initializer())
```

Because it may be impossible to feed the complete data to the CNN on normal machines, it is recommended to split the data into a number of patches. A subset of the training samples is used to create each path. Samples for each path can be randomly selected.

```
num_patches = 5#Number of patches
for patch_num in numpy.arange(num_patches):
    print("Patch : ", str(patch_num))
    percent = 80 #percent of samples to be included in each path.
    #Getting the input-output data of the current path.
    shuffled_data, shuffled_labels = get_patch(data=dataset_array,
    labels=dataset_labels, percent=percent)
    #Data required for cnn operation. 1)Input Images, 2)Output Labels,
    and 3)Dropout probability
```

```
        cnn_feed_dict = {data_tensor: shuffled_data,
                         label_tensor: shuffled_labels,
                         keep_prop: 0.5}
```

```
# Training the CNN based on the current patch.
# CNN error is used as input in the run to minimize it.
# SoftMax predictions are returned to compute the classification accuracy.
```

```
        softmax_predictions_, _ = sess.run([softmax_predictions, ops], feed_
        dict=cnn_feed_dict)
        #Calculating number of correctly classified samples.
        correct = numpy.array(numpy.where(softmax_predictions_ == shuffled_
        labels))
        correct = correct.size
        print("Correct predictions/", str(percent * 50000/100), ' : ', correct)
```

```
#Closing the session
sess.close()
```

```
#Saving the model after being trained.
saver = tensorflow.train.Saver()
save_model_path = " \\AhmedGad\\model\\"
save_path = saver.save(sess=sess, save_path=save_model_path+"model.ckpt")
print("Model saved in : ", save_path)
```

Preparing Test Data

Before testing the trained model, it is required to prepare the test data and restore the previously trained model. Test data preparation is similar to what happened with the training data except that there is just a single binary file to be decoded. The test file is decoded according to the modified "get_dataset_images" function according to Listing 6-35. Note that it has the same name as the function used to decode the training data because it is assumed that there are two separate scripts, one for training and another for testing. This function calls the "unpickle_patch" function exactly as done before with training data.

Listing 6-35. Saving the Trained CNN Model

```
def get_dataset_images(test_path_path, im_dim=32, num_channels=3):
    data_dict = unpickle_patch(test_path_path)
    images_data = data_dict[b"data"]
    dataset_array = numpy.reshape(images_data, newshape=(len(images_data),
    im_dim, im_dim, num_channels))
    return dataset_array, data_dict[b"labels"]
```

Testing the Trained CNN Model

According to Figure 6-16, the saved model will be used to predict the labels for the test data. After preparing the test data and restoring the trained model, we can start testing the model according to Listing 6-36. It's worth mentioning that when training the CNN, the session runs to minimize the cost. In testing, we are not interested in minimizing the cost anymore and just we would like to return the predictions for the data samples. This is why the TF session runs to return just the predictions by fetching the "softmax_propabilities" and "softmax_predictions" tensors.

When the graph is restored, the tensor named "data_tensor" in the training phase will be assigned the testing data, while the tensor named "label_tensor" will be assigned the sample labels.

Another interesting point is that the keep probability "keep_prop" of the dropout layer is now set to 1.0. That means do not drop any neuron (i.e., use all neurons). This is because we are just using the pretrained model after settling on what neurons to drop. Now we just use what the model did before and are not interested in making any modifications.

Listing 6-36. Testing the Trained CNN

```
#Dataset path containing the testing binary file to be decoded.
patches_dir = "\\AhmedGad\\cifar-10-python\\cifar-10-batches-py\\"
dataset_array, dataset_labels = get_dataset_images(test_path_path=patches_
dir + "test_batch", im_dim=32, num_channels=3)
print("Size of data : ", dataset_array.shape)

sess = tensorflow.Session()
```

```
#Restoring the previously saved trained model.
saved_model_path = '\\AhmedGad\\model\\'
saver = tensorflow.train.import_meta_graph(saved_model_path+'model.ckpt.meta')
saver.restore(sess=sess, save_path=saved_model_path+'model.ckpt')

#Initializing the variables.
sess.run(tensorflow.global_variables_initializer())

graph = tensorflow.get_default_graph()


softmax_propabilities = graph.get_tensor_by_name(name="softmax_probs:0")
softmax_predictions = tensorflow.argmax(softmax_propabilities, axis=1)
data_tensor = graph.get_tensor_by_name(name="data_tensor:0")
label_tensor = graph.get_tensor_by_name(name="label_tensor:0")
keep_prop = graph.get_tensor_by_name(name="keep_prop:0")

#keep_prop is equal to 1 because there is no more interest to remove
neurons in the testing phase.
feed_dict_testing = {data_tensor: dataset_array,
                     label_tensor: dataset_labels,
                     keep_prop: 1.0}

#Running the session to predict the outcomes of the testing samples.
softmax_propabilities_, softmax_predictions_ = sess.run([softmax_
propabilities, softmax_predictions], feed_dict=feed_dict_testing)

#Assessing the model accuracy by counting number of correctly classified
samples.
correct = numpy.array(numpy.where(softmax_predictions_ == dataset_labels))
correct = correct.size
print("Correct predictions/10,000 : ", correct)

#Closing the session
sess.close()
```

At this point, we have successfully built the CNN model for classifying images of the CIFAR10 dataset. In the next chapter, the saved trained CNN model is deployed to a web server created using Flask for being accessed from Internet users.

CHAPTER 7

Deploying Pretrained Models

In the pipeline of building DL models, creating the model is the hardest step, but it is not the end. In order to benefit from the created models, users should remotely access them. Users' feedback will help improve the model performance.

This chapter discusses how to deploy pretrained models online to be accessed by Internet users. Using Flask micro web framework, a web application is created using Python. Using HTML (HyperText Markup Language), CSS (Cascading Style Sheet), and JavaScript, simple web pages are built to allow the user to send and receive HTTP (HyperText Transfer Protocol) requests to the server. Using a web browser, the user accesses the application and is able to upload an image to the server. Based on the deployed model, the image is classified and its class label is returned back to the user. Moreover, an Android application is created to access the web server. This chapter assumes the reader has a basic knowledge of HTML, CSS, JavaScript, and Android. Readers can follow the instructions in this link for installing Flask (`http://flask.pocoo.org/docs/1.0/installation/`).

Application Overview

The target application of this chapter is summarized in Figure 7-1 which extends the steps in Chapter 6: the dataflow graph of a CNN using TF is built and then trained using the CIFAR10 dataset; finally, the trained model is saved to be ready for deployment. Using Flask, a web application that listens to HTTP requests from clients is created. Clients access the web application from web pages created using HTML, CSS, and JavaScript.

© Ahmed Fawzy Gad 2018
A. F. Gad, *Practical Computer Vision Applications Using Deep Learning with CNNs*,
https://doi.org/10.1007/978-1-4842-4167-7_7

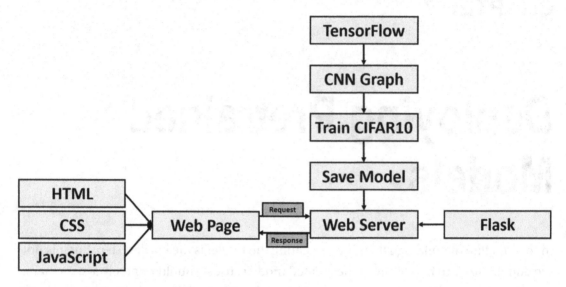

Figure 7-1. *Overview of the application*

The server loads the saved model, opens a session, and waits for incoming requests from the clients. The client uses a web browser to open a web page that allows uploading an image to the server for classification. The server ensures that the image belongs to the CIFAR10 dataset based on the size. After that, the image is fed into the model for classification. The predicted label by the model is returned in a response to the client. Finally, the client displays the label on the web page. For being customized to Android devices, an Android application to send HTTP requests to the server and receive the classification label is created.

In this chapter, each of the steps involved in the application will be covered until successful completion.

Introduction to Flask

Flask is a microframework for building web applications. Despite being micro, it does not support some functionalities that other frameworks do. It is called "micro" because it comes with the core requirements required to build an application. Later using extensions, you can add the functionalities needed. Flask gives the user the decision about what to use. For example, it does not come with a specific database and gives the user the freedom about which database to use.

Flask uses the WSGI (Web Server Gateway Interface). WSGI is how the server handles requests from the Python web applications. It is regarded as the communication channel between the server and the application. After the server receives a request, the WSGI processes the request and sends it to the application written in Python. WSGI receives the response of the application and returns it to the server. The server then responds to the client. Flask uses Werkzeug, which is an SWGI utility for implementing the requests and responses. Flask also uses jinja2, which is the template engine used to build template web pages that are later filled dynamically with data.

In order to get started in Flask, let's discusses the minimal Flask application according to Listing 7-1. The first thing to do in order to build a Flask application is to create an instance from the Flask class. The app instance is created using the class constructor. The mandatory import_name parameter of the constructor is very important. It is used to locate application resources. If the application is found in FlaskApp\ firstApp.py, then set this argument to FlaskApp. For example, if there is a CSS file to be located under the application directory, this parameter is used to locate the file.

Listing 7-1. Minimal Flask Application

```
import flask

app = flask.Flask(import_name="FlaskApp")

@app.route(rule="/")
def testFunc():
    return "Hello"

app.run()
```

The Flask application consists of a set of functions, each associated with a URL (Universal Resource Locator). When the client navigates to a URL, the server sends a request to the applications to respond to the client. The application uses a view function associated with that URL to respond. The return of the view function is the response rendered on the web page. This leaves a question: How do we associate a function with a URL? Fortunately, the answer is simple.

route() Decorator

At first, the function is a regular Python function that can accept arguments. In Listing 7-1, the function is called testFunc() but is not accepting any arguments yet. It returns the string Hello. This means that when the client visits the URL associated with that function, the string Hello will be rendered on the screen. The URL is associated with the function using the route() decorator. It is called "route" because it works like a router. A router receives an input message and decides which output interface to follow. Also, the decorator receives an input URL and decides which function to call.

The route() decorator accepts an argument named rule representing the URL associated with the view function exactly below the decorator. According to Listing 7-1, the route() decorator associates the URL / representing the homepage to the view function named testFunc().

After completing this simple application, the next step is to make it active by running the script using the run() method of the Flask class. The result of running the application is in Figure 7-2. According to the output, the server by default listens to the IP (Internet Protocol) address 127.0.0.1, which is a loopback address. This means the server is just listening to requests from the local host on port 5000.

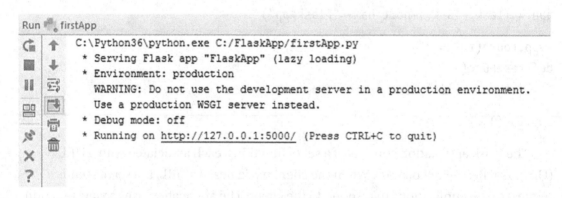

Figure 7-2. Console output after running the first Flask app

When visiting the server at the 127.0.0.1:5000/ address using a web browser, the testFunc() function will be called. Its output is rendered on the web browser according to Figure 7-3.

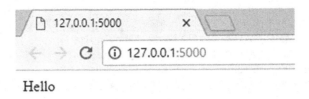

Hello

Figure 7-3. *Visiting the URL associated with the* testFunc() *function*

We can override the default values of the IP and port using the host and port arguments of the run() method. The run() method is as follows after overriding the default values of these arguments:

```
app.run(host="127.0.0.5", port=6500)
```

Figure 7-4 shows the result after setting the host to 127.0.0.5 and the port number to 6500. Just make sure no application is using the port selected.

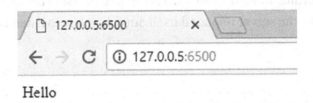

Hello

Figure 7-4. *Listening to a different host and port by overriding the default values of the* run() *method*

For each request received by the server, the method of the HTTP request, URL, and the response code are printed on the console. For example, when visiting the homepage, the request returned 200, which means the page was successfully located. Visiting a page that does not exist such as 127.0.0.5:6500/abc returns 404 as the response code, meaning that the page was not found. This helps in debugging the application.

```
Run      firstApp
 G    ↑    C:\Python36\python.exe C:/FlaskApp/firstApp.py
 ■    ↓     * Serving Flask app "FlaskApp" (lazy loading)
 II   ⇄     * Environment: production
              WARNING: Do not use the development server in a production environment.
 ⊞    ⤓      Use a production WSGI server instead.
 ⛶    ⎙     * Debug mode: off
 ✕    🗑     * Running on http://127.0.0.5:6500/ (Press CTRL+C to quit)
 ?          127.0.0.1 - - [04/Sep/2018 22:25:42] "GET / HTTP/1.1" 200 -
            127.0.0.1 - - [04/Sep/2018 22:25:47] "GET /abc HTTP/1.1" 404 -
```

Figure 7-5. *Requests received by the server*

Another useful argument to the run() method is named debug. It is a boolean argument used to decide whether to print debugging information or not. It defaults to False. When such an argument is set to True, then we do not have to restart the server for each change in the code. This is useful in the development of the application. Just save the Python file of the application after each change and the server will reload itself automatically. According to Figure 7-6, the server started using port number 6500. After it is changed to 6300, the server reloaded itself automatically to listen for the new port.

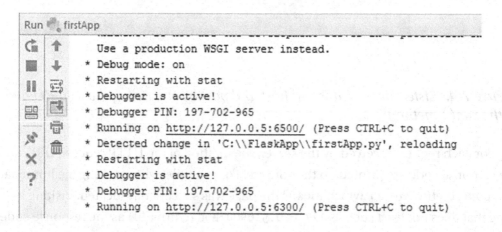

```
Run      firstApp
 G    ↑         Use a production WSGI server instead.
 ■    ↓      * Debug mode: on
 II   ⇄      * Restarting with stat
             * Debugger is active!
 ⊞    ⤓      * Debugger PIN: 197-702-965
 ⛶    ⎙      * Running on http://127.0.0.5:6500/ (Press CTRL+C to quit)
 ✕    🗑      * Detected change in 'C:\\FlaskApp\\firstApp.py', reloading
 ?           * Restarting with stat
             * Debugger is active!
             * Debugger PIN: 197-702-965
             * Running on http://127.0.0.5:6300/ (Press CTRL+C to quit)
```

Figure 7-6. *Automatic reload of the server after each change when debugging is active*

300

add_rule_url Method

Previously, the URL has been bound to the function using the route() decorator. The decorator internally calls the add_url_rule() method inside the Flask class. This method does the same job as any other decorator. We can directly use this method according to Listing 7-2. It accepts the rule argument as before but in addition to the view_func argument. It specifies which view function is associated with that rule. It is set to the function name, which is testFunc. When we used the route() decorator, the function is implicitly known. The function is exactly below the decorator. Note that the call to this method does not have to be exactly below the function. Running this code returns the same results as before.

Listing 7-2. Using the add_url_rule() Method

```
import flask

app = flask.Flask(import_name="FlaskApp")

def testFunc():
    return "Hello"
app.add_url_rule(rule="/", view_func=testFunc)

app.run(host="127.0.0.5", port=6300, debug=True)
```

Variable Rules

The previous rules are static. It is possible to add a variable part to the rule. It is regarded as a parameter. The variable part is added after the static part of the rule between two angle brackets <>. We can modify the previous code to accept a variable parameter representing the name according to Listing 7-3. The rule for the homepage is now /<name> rather than just /. If the client navigates to the URL 127.0.0.5:6300/Gad, then the name is set to Gad.

Listing 7-3. Adding Variable Part to the Rule

```
import flask

app = flask.Flask(import_name="FlaskApp")

def testFunc(name):
    return "Hello : " + name
app.add_url_rule(rule="/<name>", view_func=testFunc, endpoint="home")

app.run(host="127.0.0.5", port=6300, debug=True)
```

Note that there must be an argument in the view function to accept the variable part of the URL. For this reason, the testFunc() is modified to accept an argument named the same as defined in the rule. The return of the function is modified to also return the value of the name argument. Figure 7-7 shows the result after using the variable rule. Changing the variable part and visiting the homepage will change the output.

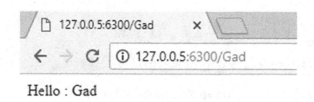

Figure 7-7. *Using variable part in the rule*

It is possible to use multiple variable parts in the rule. According to Listing 7-4, the rule accepts two parameters representing the first and last names separated by -.

Listing 7-4. Using More Than One Variable Part

```
import flask

app = flask.Flask(import_name="FlaskApp")

def testFunc(fname, lname):
    return "Hello : " + fname + " " + lname
```

```
app.add_url_rule(rule="/<fname>-<lname>", view_func=testFunc,
endpoint="home")

app.run(host="127.0.0.5", port=6300, debug=True)
```

Visiting the URL 127.0.0.5:6300/Ahmed-Gad sets the fname to Ahmed and lname to Gad. The result is shown in Figure 7-8.

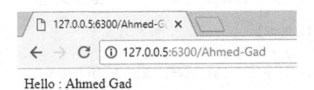

Figure 7-8. *More than one variable part in the rule*

Endpoint

The add_url_rule() method accepts a third argument named endpoint. It is an identifier to the rule and helps reuse the same rule multiple times. Note that this argument also exists in the route() decorator. The value of the endpoint is set to the view function by default. Here is a scenario in which the endpoint is important.

Assume that the website has two pages with one rule assigned to each page. The first rule is / and the second rule is /addNums/<num1>-<num2>. The second page has two parameters representing two numbers. These numbers are added together, and the result is returned to the homepage for rendering it. Listing 7-5 gives the code for creating these rules and their view functions. The testFunc() view function is given an endpoint value equal to home.

The add_func() view function accepts two arguments, which are the variable parts of the rule it is associated with. Because the values of these arguments come as strings, their values are converted into integers using the int() function. Then they get added together into the num3 variable. The return of this function is not the number but redirection to another page using the redirect() method. Such a method accepts the redirect location.

Listing 7-5. Using Endpoint to Redirect Between Pages

```
import flask

app = flask.Flask(import_name="FlaskApp")

def testFunc(result):
    return "Result is : " + result
app.add_url_rule(rule="/<result>", view_func=testFunc, endpoint="home")

def add_func(num1, num2):
    num3 = int(num1) + int(num2)
    return flask.redirect(location=flask.url_for("home", result=num3))
app.add_url_rule(rule="/addNums/<num1>-<num2>", view_func=add_func)

app.run(host="127.0.0.5", port=6300, debug=True)
```

Rather than hard-coding the URL, we can simply use the endpoint to return it. The URL is returned from the endpoint using the `from_url()` method. It accepts the endpoint of a rule in addition to any variables accepted by that rule. Because the homepage rule accepts a variable named `result`, then we have to add an argument named `result` inside the `from_url()` method and assign a value to it. The value assigned to such a variable is `num3`. By navigating to the URL `127.0.0.5:6300/addNums/1-2`, the numbers 1 and 2 are added, and the result is 3. The function then redirects to the homepage, where the `result` variable of the rule is set equal to 3.

Using endpoints makes life easier than hard-coding the URLs. We can simply assign the `location` argument of the `redirect()` method to the rule / but this is not recommended. Assume that the URL of the homepage changed from / to /home, then we have to apply that change in every reference to the homepage. Moreover, assume that the URL is long, such as `127.0.0.5:6300/home/page1`. Typing this URL each time we need to reference it is tiresome. The endpoints are regarded as an abstraction to the URL.

Another case that proves the importance of using endpoints it that the site administrator might decide to change the address of a page. If the page is referenced multiple times by copying and pasting its URL, then we have to change the URL everywhere. Using endpoints avoids that problem. The endpoint is not as frequently changed as the URLs are, and thus the site will remain active even with changes to the pages' URLs. Note that redirecting without using the endpoint makes it difficult to pass the variable parts to the rule.

The code in Listing 7-5 accepts the input numbers to be added from the URL. We can create a simple HTML form allowing the user to enter these numbers.

HTML Form

The add_url_rule() method (and of course route() decorator) accepts another argument called methods. It accepts a list specifying the HTTP methods the rule responds to. The rule can respond to multiple types of methods.

There are two common HTTP methods: GET and POST. The GET method is the default method and sends the data unencrypted. The POST method is used to send the HTML form data to the server. Let's create a simple form that accepts two numbers and send them to the Flask application for addition and rendering.

Listing 7-6 gives the HTML code that creates a form with two inputs of type number in addition to an input of type submit. The form method is set to post. Its action is the URL http://127.0.0.5:6300/form. The action represents the page to which the form data will be sent. There is a rule that associates that URL with a view function that fetches the numbers from the form, adds them, and renders the result. The names of the form elements are very important because only elements with name attribute are sent to the server after the form gets submitted. The element names are used as identifiers to retrieve the element data within the Flask application.

Listing 7-6. HTML Form

```
<html>
<header>
<title>HTML Form</title>
</header>
<body>

<form method="post" action="http://127.0.0.5:6300/form">
<span>Num1 </span>
<input type="number" name="num1"><br>
<span>Num2 </span>
<input type="number" name="num2"><br>
```

```
<input type="submit" name="Add">
</form>

</body>
</html>
```

The HTML form is shown in Figure 7-9.

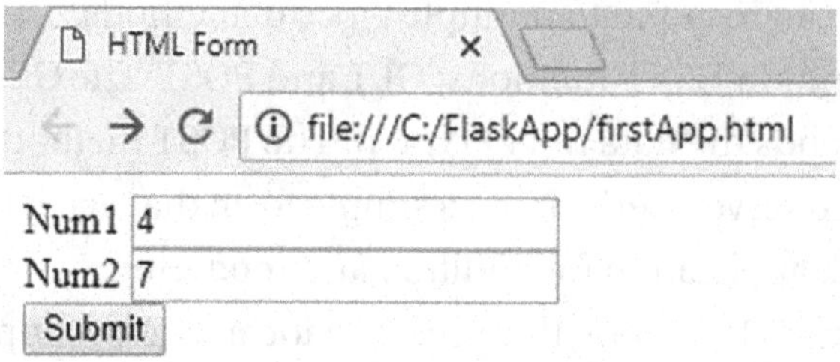

Figure 7-9. *HTML form with two numeric inputs*

After submitting the form, the Flask application in Listing 7-7 retrieves the form data. The rule /form is associated with the handle_form() function. The rule just responds to HTTP messages of type POST. Inside the function, the form elements are returned using the flask.request.form dictionary. The name of each HTML form element is used as an index to that object in order to return their values. For example, the value of the first form element of the name num1 is returned using by using flask.request. form["num1"].

Listing 7-7. Flask Application to Retrieve the HTML Form Data

```
import flask

app = flask.Flask(import_name="FlaskApp")

def handle_form():
    num1 = flask.request.form["num1"]
    num1 = int(num1)
    num2 = flask.request.form["num2"]
    num2 = int(num2)

    result = num1 + num2
    result = str(result)
```

```
    return "Result is : " + result
app.add_url_rule(rule="/form", view_func=handle_form, methods=["POST"])

app.run(host="127.0.0.5", port=6300, debug=True)
```

Because the value returned by indexing the flask.request.form object is a string, it must get converted into an integer using the int() function. After adding the two numbers, their result is stored in the result variable. This variable is converted into a string in order to concatenate its value with a string. The concatenated string is returned by the handle_form view function. The rendered result is shown in Figure 7-10.

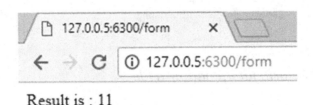

Figure 7-10. *The result of adding the two numeric HTML form elements*

File Upload

Uploading files in Flask is very simple and similar to the previous example except with some changes. An input of type file is created in the HTML form. Also, the form encryption type attribute enctype is set to multipart/form-data. The code of the HTML form for uploading a file is in Listing 7-8. A screenshot of the form is available in Figure 7-11.

Listing 7-8. HTML Form for Uploading a File

```
<html>
<header>
<title>HTML Form</title>
</header>
<body>

<form method="post" enctype="multipart/form-data"
action="http://127.0.0.5:6300/form">
<span>Select File to Upload</span><br>
```

307

```
<input type="file" name="fileUpload"><br>
<input type="submit" name="Add">
</form>

</body>
</html>
```

Figure 7-11. *HTML form for uploading a file*

After selecting the image to be uploaded, it is sent to the Flask application created according to Listing 7-9. The rule is again set to respond only to HTTP messages of type POST. Previously, we used the flask.request.form object to retrieve the data fields. Now, we use the flask.request.files to return the details of the files to be uploaded. The name of the form input fileUpload is used as an index to that object to return the file to be uploaded. Note that the flask.request is a global object that receives the data from the client web page.

In order to save the file, its name is retrieved using the filename property. It is not recommended to save the file according to its name submitted by the user. Some file names are set to hurt the server. To secure saving the file, the werkzeug.secure_filename() function is used. Remember to import the werkzeug module.

Listing 7-9. Flask Application to Upload Files to the Server

```
import flask, werkzeug

app = flask.Flask(import_name="FlaskApp")

def handle_form():
    file = flask.request.files["fileUpload"]
    file_name = file.filename
    secure_file_name = werkzeug.secure_filename(file_name)
    file.save(dst=secure_file_name)
```

```
    return "File uploaded successfully."
app.add_url_rule(rule="/form", view_func=handle_form, methods=["POST"])

app.run(host="127.0.0.5", port=6300, debug=True)
```

The secure file name is returned to the secure_file_name variable. Finally, the file is saved permanently by calling the save() method. Such a method accepts the destination at which the file will be saved. Because just the file name is used, it will be saved in the current directory of the Flask application Python file.

HTML Inside Flask Application

The return output from the previous view function is just a text that appears on the web page without any formatting. Flask supports generating HTML content within the Python code, which helps to render the results better. Listing 7-10 gives an example in which the return result of the tesFunc() view function is HTML code in which the <h1> element renders the result. Figure 7-12 shows the result.

Listing 7-10. Generating HTML Inside Python

```
import flask, werkzeug

app = flask.Flask(import_name="FlaskApp")

def testFunc():
    return "<html><body><h1>Hello</h1></body></html>"
app.add_url_rule(rule="/", view_func=testFunc)

app.run(host="127.0.0.5", port=6300, debug=True)
```

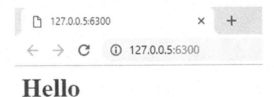

Figure 7-12. *Formatting the output of the view function using HTML code*

Generating HTML within the Python code makes it difficult to debug the code. It is better to separate Python from HTML. This is why Flask supports templates using the Jinja2 template engine.

Flask Templates

Rather than typing the HTML code within the Python file, a separate HTML file (i.e., template) is created. Such a template is rendered within Python using the render_template() method. The HTML file is called template because it is not a static file. The template can be used multiple times with different data inputs.

In order to locate the Flask templates within the Python code, a folder named templates is created holding all HTML files. Assuming that the Flask Python file is named firstApp.py and the HTML file is named hello.html, the project structure is illustrated in Figure 7-13. In Listing 7-11, the hello.html file is created to print the Hello message exactly the same as in Listing 7-10.

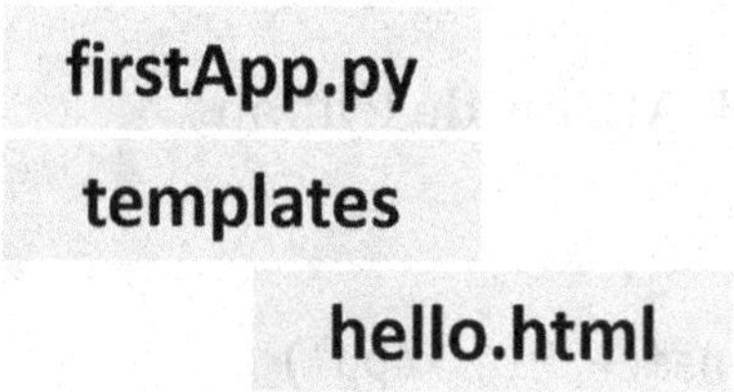

firstApp.py

templates

hello.html

Figure 7-13. *Project structure after using templates*

Listing 7-11. Template to Print Hello Message

```
<html>
<header>
<title>HTML Template</title>
</header>
<body>

<h1>Hello</h1>

</body>
</html>
```

The Python code rendering this template is given in Listing 7-12. The return result of the view function associated with the homepage is the output of the render_template() method. This method accepts an argument named template_name_or_list specifying the template file name. Note that the argument may accept a single name or a list of names. When a list is specified with multiple names, the first template existing will be rendered. The rendered result of this example is identical to Figure 7-12.

Listing 7-12. Python Code to Render an HTML Template

```python
import flask, werkzeug

app = flask.Flask(import_name="FlaskApp")

def testFunc():
    return flask.render_template(template_name_or_list="hello.html")
app.add_url_rule(rule="/", view_func=testFunc)

app.run(host="127.0.0.5", port=6300, debug=True)
```

Dynamic Templates

The templates are currently static, as they get rendered the same each time. We can make them dynamic by using variable data. Jinja2 supports adding placeholders inside the template. When rendering the template, these placeholders are replaced by the output of evaluating a Python expression. At the place at which the expression output is to be printed, enclose the expression by {{...}}. Listing 7-13 gives the HTML code in which the variable name is used.

Listing 7-13. HTML Code with an Expression

```html
<html>
<header>
<title>HTML Template with an Expression</title>
</header>
<body>

<h1>Hello {{name}}</h1>

</body>
</html>
```

Next is to render that template after passing the value for the variable name according to Listing 7-14. The variables inside the template to be rendered are passed as arguments inside the render_template along with their values. The result of visiting the homepage is in Figure 7-14.

Listing 7-14. Rendering Flask Template with an Expression

```
import flask, werkzeug

app = flask.Flask(import_name="FlaskApp")

def testFunc():
    return flask.render_template(template_name_or_list="hello.html",
    name="Ahmed")
app.add_url_rule(rule="/", view_func=testFunc)

app.run(host="127.0.0.5", port=6300, debug=True)
```

Figure 7-14. *The result of rendering a template with an expression*

The value of the variable name is statically typed, but it could be generated dynamically using either a variable rule or an HTML form. Listing 7-15 gives the code used to create a variable rule accepting a name. The view function must have an argument named according to the variable part of the rule. The value of this argument is then assigned to the name argument of the render_template() method. The value is then passed to the template to be rendered according to Figure 7-15.

Listing 7-15. Variable Rule to Pass Value to Flask Template

```
import flask, werkzeug

app = flask.Flask(import_name="FlaskApp")

def testFunc(name):
    return flask.render_template(template_name_or_list="hello.html",
    name=name)
app.add_url_rule(rule="/<name>", view_func=testFunc)

app.run(host="127.0.0.5", port=6300, debug=True)
```

Figure 7-15. *Passing the value received from a variable rule to Flask template*

We can also insert Python statements, comments, and line statements inside the HTML code, each with a different placeholder. Statements are enclosed between {% ... %}, comments are enclosed by {# ... #}, and line statements are enclosed by # ... ##. Listing 7-16 gives an example in which a Python for loop is inserted to print five numbers from 0 to 4, each inside <h1> HTML element. Each statement within the loop is enclosed by {%...%}.

Python uses indentation to define blocks. Because there is no indentation inside HTML, the end of the for loop is marked with endfor. The result of rendering this file is given in Figure 7-16.

Listing 7-16. Embedding a Python Loop Inside Flask Template

```
<html>
<header>
<title>HTML Template with Expression</title>
</header>
<body>
```

313

```
{%for k in range(5):%}
<h1>{%print(k)%}</h1>
{%endfor%}

</body>
</html>
```

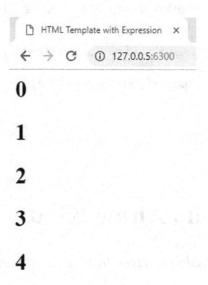

Figure 7-16. *Rendering a template with a Python loop*

Static Files

Static files such as CSS and JavaScript files are used to style web pages and make them dynamic. Similar to the templates, there is a folder created to store the static files. The folder name is static. If we are to create a CSS file named style.css and a JavaScript file named simpeJS.js, the project structure will be as given in Figure 7-17.

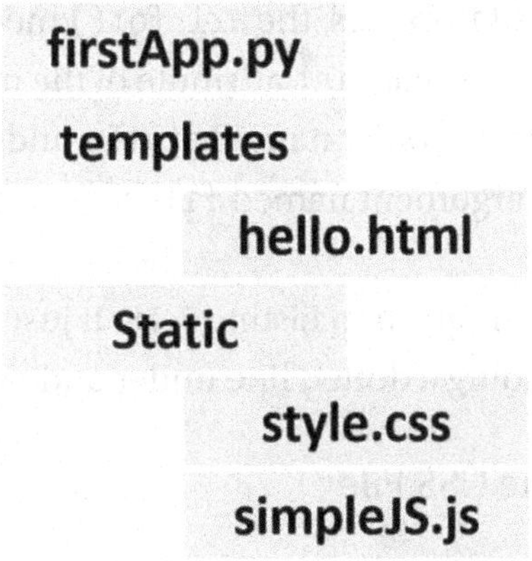

firstApp.py

templates

hello.html

Static

style.css

simpleJS.js

Figure 7-17. *Project structure with both templates and static files*

The Python code is identical to the code in Listing 7-15 without using the variable part of the rule. Listing 7-17 shows the content of the hello.html file. It's worth mentioning how the HTML file is linked to the JavaScript and CSS files. As regularly, the JavaScript file is added using the <script> tag, where the type attribute is text/javascript. Also, the CSS file is added using the <link> tag, where the rel attribute is set to stylesheet. What is new is how these files are located.

Listing 7-17. HTML File Linked with CSS and JavaScript Files

```
<html>
<header>
<title>HTML Template with Expression</title>
<script type="text/javascript" src="{{url_for(endpoint='static',
filename='simpleJS.js')}}"></script>
<link rel="stylesheet" href="{{url_for(endpoint='static', filename='style.
css')}}">
</header>
<body>

{%for k in range(5):%}
<h1 onclick="showAlert({{k}})">{%print(k)%}</h1>
{%endfor%}
</body>
</html>
```

Within the <script> and <link> tags, the url_for() method is used within an expression to locate the files. The endpoint attribute of the method is set to static, which means that you should look at the folder named static under the project structure. The method accepts another argument named filename, which refers to the file name of the static file.

The content of the CSS file is given in Listing 7-18. It just targets any <h1> elements and decorates their text by adding a dotted line under and over it.

Listing 7-18. Content of the CSS File

```
h1 {
text-decoration: underline overline;
}
```

Listing 7-19 gives the content of the JavaScript file. It has a single function named showAlert, which accepts an argument that is concatenated to a string and printed in an alert. When any of the <h1> elements representing the five numbers inside the HTML template are clicked, this function is called. The number associated with the element is passed as an argument to the function in order to get printed.

Listing 7-19. Content of the JavaScript File

```
function showAlert(num){
alert("Number is " + num)
}
```

When the number <h1> element with the text 1 is clicked, the output is as given in Figure 7-18.

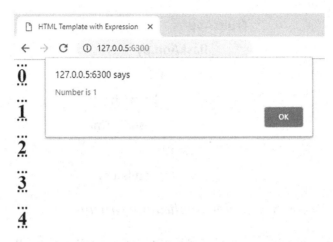

Figure 7-18. *The result of clicking on the second <h1> element with the text 1*

At this point, we have had an introduction to Flask, which is good enough to enable us to start deploying pretrained models. In the next sections, the pretrained models against the Fruits 360 and CIFAR10 datasets will be deployed to the web server to enable accessing them by Flask applications for classifying uploaded images by clients.

Deploying Trained Model Using Fruits 360 Dataset

The first model we are going to deploy is the trained model in Chapter 5 using the Fruits 360 dataset and optimized using the GA. The Flask application consists of two main pages.

The first page is the homepage. It has an HTML form that allows the user to select an image file. That file is uploaded to the server. The second page accomplishes most of the work. It follows the same steps in Chapter 5. It reads the image after being uploaded to the server, extracts its features, filters features using STD, predicts the image class label using the pretrained ANN, and finally allows the user to return back to the homepage to select another image for classification. The application has the structure defined in Figure 7-19. Let's discuss the application in detail.

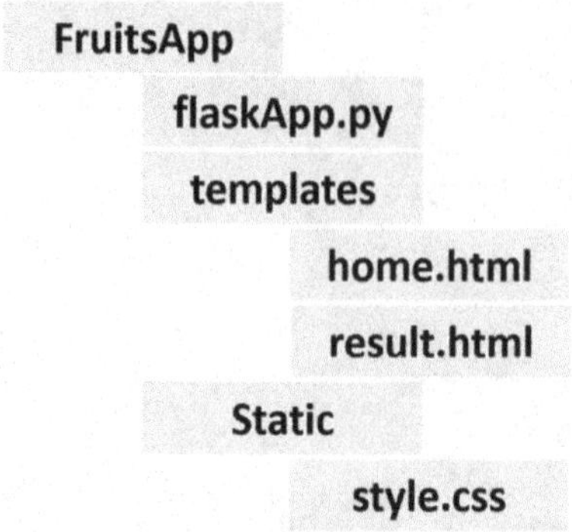

FruitsApp

flaskApp.py

templates

home.html

result.html

Static

style.css

Figure 7-19. *Fruits 360 recognition application structure*

Listing 7-20 starts the first step toward building the application. All required modules for the entire application are imported. An instance of the Flask class is created with the import_name argument of the constructor set to the name of the parent directory, which is FruitsApp. A single rule is created up to the current time. That rule binds the URL of the homepage / to the view function homepage. The application runs using host 127.0.0.5, port number 6302, and active debug mode.

Listing 7-20. Basic Structure of the Fruits 360 Recognition Application

```
import flask, werkzeug, skimage.io, skimage.color, numpy, pickle

app = flask.Flask(import_name="FruitsApp")

def homepage():
    return flask.render_template(template_name_or_list="home.html")
app.add_url_rule(rule="/", view_func=homepage, endpoint="homepage")

app.run(host="127.0.0.5", port=6300, debug=True)
```

When the user visits the home page http://127.0.0.5:6302, the view function homepage() renders the home.html template using the render_template() method. The associated endpoint used is homepage, which is identical to the name of the view function. Note that omitting this endpoint will not change anything because the default endpoint actually equals to the view function name. The content of the home.html page is given in Listing 7-21.

Listing 7-21. Implementation of the `home.html` Page

```html
<html>
<header>
<title>Select Image</title>
<link rel="stylesheet" href="{{url_for(endpoint='static', filename='style.
css')}}">
</header>
<body>

<h1>Select an Image from the Fruits 360 Dataset</h1>
<form enctype="multipart/form-data" action="{{url_
for(endpoint='extract')}}" method="post">
<input type="file" name="img"><br>
<input type="submit">
</form>

</body>
</html>
```

That page creates an HTML form with an input named `img` representing the file to be uploaded. Remember that the encryption type attribute `enctype` of the form is set to `multipart/form-data` and the method is `post`. The action represents the page to which the form data will be submitted. After submitting the form, its data are sent to another page to classify the image file uploaded. To avoid hard-coding the URLs, the endpoint of the target rule, which is set to `extract`, is used to fetch its URL using the `url_for()` method. To enable running this expression from within the HTML page, it is enclosed between `{{...}}`.

In the page header, the stylesheet static file `style.css` is linked to the page by using an expression that accepts the `endpoint` and the `filename` arguments for the `url_for()` method. Remember that the `endpoint` for static files is set to `static`. The `filename` argument is set to the target static file name. The content of the CSS file is discussed later. Figure 7-20 presents the screen of the homepage after selecting an image file. After submitting the form, the selected file details are sent to the view function `extractFeatures`, which is associated with the endpoint `extract` for further processing.

319

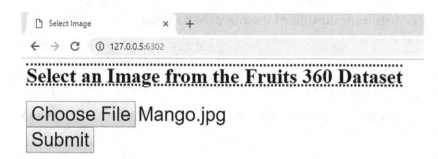

Figure 7-20. *Screenshot of the homepage for uploading an image from the Fruits 360 dataset*

Listing 7-22 gives the code for the `extractFeatures` view function associated with the `/extract` rule. Note that this rule is made to listen only to POST HTTP methods. The `extractFeatures` view function responds to the form submitted previously. It returns the uploaded image file using the dictionary `flask.request.files`. The file name is returned using the `filename` property of the image file. To make saving the file more secure, the secure file name is returned using the `secure_filename()` function, which accepts the original file name and returns a secure name. The image is saved according to this secure name.

Listing 7-22. Python Code for the `extractFeatures` View Function

```python
def extractFeatures():
    img = flask.request.files["img"]
    img_name = img.filename
    img_secure_name = werkzeug.secure_filename(img_name)
    img.save(img_secure_name)
    print("Image Uploaded successfully.")

img_features = extract_features(image_path=img_secure_name)
    print("Features extracted successfully.")

    f = open("weights_1000_iterations_10%_mutation.pkl", "rb")
    weights_mat = pickle.load(f)
    f.close()
    weights_mat = weights_mat[0, :]

    predicted_label = predict_outputs(weights_mat, img_features,
    activation="sigmoid")
```

```
    class_labels = ["Apple", "Raspberry", "Mango", "Lemon"]
    predicted_class = class_labels[predicted_label]
    return flask.render_template(template_name_or_list="result.html",
    predicted_class=predicted_class)
app.add_url_rule(rule="/extract", view_func=extractFeatures,
methods=["POST"], endpoint="extract")
```

After uploading the image to the server, its features are extracted using the extract_
features function defined in Listing 7-23. It accepts the image path and follows the
steps in section **Fruits 360 Dataset Feature Mining** of Chapter 3 from reading the image
file, extracting the hue channel histogram, filtering features using STD, and finally to
returning the filtered set of features. The features are filtered according to the indices of
the selected elements based on the experiment done on the training data. The number
of these elements is 102. The feature vector is then returned into a row NumPy vector of
shape 1×102. This makes it ready for matrix multiplication. After returning the feature
vector, we can continue executing the extractFeatures view function.

Listing 7-23. Extracting Features from the Uploaded Image

```
def extract_features(image_path):
    f = open("select_indices.pkl", "rb")
    indices = pickle.load(f)
    f.close()

    fruit_data = skimage.io.imread(fname=image_path)
    fruit_data_hsv = skimage.color.rgb2hsv(rgb=fruit_data)
    hist = numpy.histogram(a=fruit_data_hsv[:, :, 0], bins=360)
    im_features = hist[0][indices]
    img_features = numpy.zeros(shape=(1, im_features.size))
    img_features[0, :] = im_features [:im_features.size]
    return img_features
```

According to Listing 7-23, the next step in receiving the feature vector into the
img_features variable is to restore the set of weights learned by the ANN trained
using GA. The weights are returned to the weights_mat variable. Note that these weights
represent all solutions of the population returned after the last generation. We just need
to find the first solution in the population. This is why the index 0 is just returned from
the weights_mat variable.

321

After preparing the image features and the learned weights, the next step is to apply them on the ANN for producing the prediction label using the `predict_outputs()` function according to Listing 7-24. It accepts the weights, features, and activation functions. The activation functions are identical to what we implemented before. The `predict_outputs()` function goes through a loop that performs matrix multiplication between the inputs and the weights of each layer in the ANN. After reaching the result of the output layer, the predicted class index is returned. It corresponds to the class with the maximum score. This index is returned by this function.

Listing 7-24. Predicting the Class Label for the Uploaded Image

```
def predict_outputs(weights_mat, data_inputs, activation="relu"):
    r1 = data_inputs
    for curr_weights in weights_mat:
        r1 = numpy.matmul(a=r1, b=curr_weights)
        if activation == "relu":
            r1 = relu(r1)
        elif activation == "sigmoid":
            r1 = sigmoid(r1)
    r1 = r1[0, :]
    predicted_label = numpy.where(r1 == numpy.max(r1))[0][0]
    return predicted_label
```

After returning the predicted class index, we come back to Listing 7-22. The returned index is then converted into the string label of the corresponding class. All labels are saved into the `class_labels` list. The predicted class label is returned to the `predicted_class` variable. The `extractFeatures` view function finally renders the `result.html` template using the `render_template()` method. It passes the predicted class label to such a template. The code of this template is available in Listing 7-25.

Listing 7-25. Content of the `result.html` Template

```
<html>
<header>
<title>Predicted Class</title>
<link rel="stylesheet" href="{{url_for(endpoint='static', filename='style.
css')}}">
```

```
</header>
<body>

<h1>Predicted Label</h1>
<h1>{{predicted_class}}</h1>
<a href="{{url_for(endpoint='homepage')}}">Classify Another Image</a>
</body>
</html>
```

The template creates an expression to be able to render the predicted class label within the <h1> element. An anchor is created to let the user return back to the homepage to classify another image. The URL of the homepage is returned based on its endpoint. The screen of the result.html file after printing the class label is shown in Figure 7-21.

Figure 7-21. *The result of classifying an uploaded image*

Note that the application just has a single static file named style.css implemented according to Listing 7-26. It simply change the font size of both the <input> and <a> elements. It also adds decorations to the text of <h1> elements by adding a line over and under the text.

Listing 7-26. Static CSS File for Adding Styles

```
a, input{
font-size: 30px;
color: black;
}
```

```
h1 {
text-decoration: underline overline dotted;
}
```

After discussing each part of the application, the complete code is available in Listing 7-27.

Listing 7-27. Complete Code of Flask Application for Classifying Fruits 360 Dataset Images

```
import flask, werkzeug, skimage.io, skimage.color, numpy, pickle

app = flask.Flask(import_name="FruitsApp")

def sigmoid(inpt):
    return 1.0/(1.0+numpy.exp(-1*inpt))

def relu(inpt):
    result = inpt
    result[inpt<0] = 0
    return result

def extract_features(image_path):
    f = open("select_indices.pkl", "rb")
    indices = pickle.load(f)
    f.close()

    fruit_data = skimage.io.imread(fname=image_path)
    fruit_data_hsv = skimage.color.rgb2hsv(rgb=fruit_data)
    hist = numpy.histogram(a=fruit_data_hsv[:, :, 0], bins=360)
    im_features = hist[0][indices]
    img_features = numpy.zeros(shape=(1, im_features.size))
    img_features[0, :] = im_features[:im_features.size]
    return img_features

def predict_outputs(weights_mat, data_inputs, activation="relu"):
    r1 = data_inputs
    for curr_weights in weights_mat:
        r1 = numpy.matmul(a=r1, b=curr_weights)
```

```python
        if activation == "relu":
            r1 = relu(r1)
        elif activation == "sigmoid":
            r1 = sigmoid(r1)
    r1 = r1[0, :]
    predicted_label = numpy.where(r1 == numpy.max(r1))[0][0]
    return predicted_label

def extractFeatures():
    img = flask.request.files["img"]
    img_name = img.filename
    img_secure_name = werkzeug.secure_filename(img_name)
    img.save(img_secure_name)
    print("Image Uploaded successfully.")

    img_features = extract_features(image_path=img_secure_name)
    print("Features extracted successfully.")

    f = open("weights_1000_iterations_10%_mutation.pkl", "rb")
    weights_mat = pickle.load(f)
    f.close()
    weights_mat = weights_mat[0, :]

    predicted_label = predict_outputs(weights_mat, img_features,
    activation="sigmoid")

    class_labels = ["Apple", "Raspberry", "Mango", "Lemon"]
    predicted_class = class_labels[predicted_label]
    return flask.render_template(template_name_or_list="result.html",
    predicted_class=predicted_class)
app.add_url_rule(rule="/extract", view_func=extractFeatures,
methods=["POST"], endpoint="extract")

def homepage():
    return flask.render_template(template_name_or_list="home.html")
app.add_url_rule(rule="/", view_func=homepage)

app.run(host="127.0.0.5", port=6302, debug=True)
```

Deploying Trained Model Using CIFAR10 Dataset

The steps we discussed for deploying the model trained with the Fruits 360 dataset will be repeated but for a model created using TensorFlow trained using CIFAR10 dataset. There are some enhancements compared to the previous application. The structure of the application is given in Figure 7-22.

Figure 7-22. *Application structure for deploying the pretrained model using CIFAR10 dataset*

We will discuss each part of the application later. Let's start with the code in Listing 7-28. The libraries required across the entire application are imported. It is preferred to make the prediction step in a separate module. This is why the `CIFAR10Predict` module is used. It has all required functions to predict the class label of an image from the CIFAR10 dataset. This makes the Python file of the Flask application focused on the view functions.

Listing 7-28. Preparing a Flask Application for Deploying the Pretrained Model Using CIFAR10 Dataset

```
import flask, werkzeug, os, scipy.misc, tensorflow
import CIFAR10Predict

app = flask.Flask("CIFARTF")

def redirect_upload():
```

```
      return flask.render_template(template_name_or_list="upload_image.html")
app.add_url_rule(rule="/", endpoint="homepage", view_func=redirect_upload)

if __name__ == "__main__":
    prepare_TF_session(saved_model_path='\\AhmedGad\\model\\')
    app.run(host="localhost", port=7777, debug=True)
```

Before running the application, it is good practice to ensure it is the main file executed and not referenced from another file. If the file is running as the main file, the __name__ variable inside it will be equal to __main__. Otherwise, the __name__ variable is set to the module from which the file is called. The file should run only if it is the main file. This is why the if statement is used.

A TF session is created in order to restore the pretrained model using the prepare_ TF_session function implemented according to Listing 7-29. This function receives the path of the saved model in order to restore the graph and prepare the session by initializing the variables in the graph before making predictions.

Listing 7-29. Restoring the Pretrained TF Model

```
def prepare_TF_session(saved_model_path):
    global sess
    global graph

    sess = tensorflow.Session()

    saver = tensorflow.train.import_meta_graph(saved_model_path+'model.
    ckpt.meta')
    saver.restore(sess=sess, save_path=saved_model_path+'model.ckpt')

    sess.run(tensorflow.global_variables_initializer())

    graph = tensorflow.get_default_graph()
    return graph
```

After preparing the session, the application runs with localhost as the host, port number 7777, and active debug mode.

There is a rule created that binds the homepage URL / to the view function redirect_upload(). This rule has the endpoint homepage. When the user visits the homepage http://localhost:777, the view function uses the render_template() method to render the upload_image.html template defined in Listing 7-30.

Listing 7-30. HTML File for Uploading an Image from the CIFAR10 Dataset

```
<!DOCTYPE html>
<html lang="en">
<head>
<link rel="stylesheet" type="text/css" href="{{url_for(endpoint='static',
filename='project_styles.css')}}">
<meta charset="UTF-8">
<title>Upload Image</title>
</head>
<body>
<form enctype="multipart/form-data" method="post" action="http://
localhost:7777/upload/">
<center>
<h3>Select CIFAR10 image to predict its label.</h3>
<input type="file" name="image_file" accept="image/*"><br>
<input type="submit" value="Upload">
</center>
</form>
</body>
</html>
```

This HTML file creates a form that allows the user to select the image to get uploaded to the server. A screenshot of this page is shown in Figure 7-23.

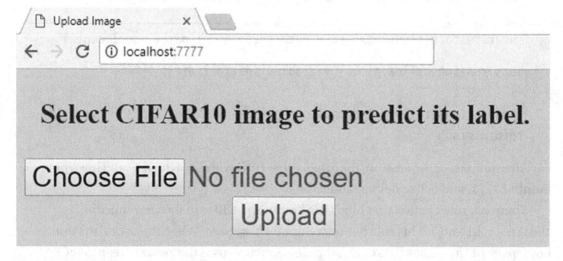

Figure 7-23. *Screenshot of the HTML page used to upload a CIFAR10 image*

This page is very similar to the form created for the Fruits 360 application. After submitting the form, the data will be sent to the page associated with the rule specified by the action attribute, which is /upload. The rule in addition to its view function is given in Listing 7-31.

Listing 7-31. Uploading a CIFAR10 Image to the Server

```
def upload_image():
    global secure_filename
    if flask.request.method == "POST"
        img_file = flask.request.files["image_file"]
        secure_filename = werkzeug.secure_filename(img_file.filename
        img_file.save(secure_filename)
        print("Image uploaded successfully.")
        return flask.redirect(flask.url_for(endpoint="predict"))
    return "Image upload failed."
app.add_url_rule(rule="/upload/", endpoint="upload", view_func=upload_
image, methods=["POST"])
```

The /upload rule is given an endpoint named upload and just responds to the HTTP messages of type POST. It is associated with the upload_image view function. It retrieves the secure file name from the original file name and saves the image to the server. If the image is successfully uploaded, then it redirects the application using the redirect() method to the URL associated with the predict endpoint. That endpoint belongs to the /predict rule. The rule and its view function are given in Listing 7-32.

Listing 7-32. View Function to Predict the Class Label for CIFAR10 Image

```
def CNN_predict():
    global sess
    global graph

    global secure_filename

    img = scipy.misc.imread(os.path.join(app.root_path, secure_filename))
```

```
    if(img.ndim) == 3:
        if img.shape[0] == img.shape[1] and img.shape[0] == 32:
            if img.shape[-1] == 3:
                predicted_class = CIFAR10Predict.main(sess, graph, img)
                return flask.render_template(template_name_or_
                list="prediction_result.html", predicted_class=predicted_
                class)
            else:
                return flask.render_template(template_name_or_list="error.
                html", img_shape=img.shape)
        else:
            return flask.render_template(template_name_or_list="error.
            html", img_shape=img.shape)
    return "An error occurred."
app.add_url_rule(rule="/predict/", endpoint="predict", view_func=CNN_
predict)
```

The function reads the image file and checks if it already belongs to the CIFAR10 dataset based on its shape and size. Each image in such a dataset has three dimensions; the first two dimensions are equal in their size, which is 32. Moreover, the images are RGB and thus the third dimension has three channels. If these specifications are not found, then the application will get redirected to the error.html template implemented according to Listing 7-33.

Listing 7-33. Template for Indicating That the Uploaded Image Does Not Belong to the CIFAR10 Dataset

```
<!DOCTYPE html>
<html lang="en">
<head>
<link type="text/css" rel="stylesheet" href="{{url_for(endpoint='static',
filename='project_styles.css')}}">
<meta charset="UTF-8">
<title>Error</title>
</head>
<body>
<center>
```

```
<h1 class="error">Error</h1>
<h2 class="error-msg">Read image dimensions {{img_shape}} do not match the
CIFAR10 specifications (32x32x3).</h2>
<a href="{{url_for(endpoint='homepage')}}"><span>Return to homepage</
span>.</a>
</center>
</body>
</html>
```

It uses expressions to print the size of the uploaded image in addition to the standard size of the CIFAR10 dataset. When uploading an image of different shapeCIFAR10 dataset:shape and size, uploaded images, the error looks like what is shown in Figure 7-24.

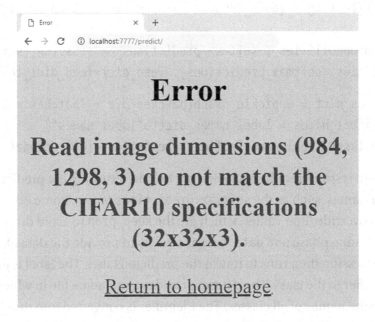

Figure 7-24. *Error when uploading an image with different shape or size from the CIFAR10 images*

If the shape and size of the uploaded images match those of the CIFAR10 images, then it is likely a CIFAR10 image and its label will be predicted using the module CIFAR10Predict. As shown in Listing 7-34, it has a function called main, which accepts the image after being read and returns its class label.

Listing 7-34. Predicting the Class Label of the Image

```python
def main(sess, graph, img):

    patches_dir = "\\AhmedGad\\cifar-10-python\\cifar-10-batches-py\\"
    dataset_array = numpy.random.rand(1, 32, 32, 3)
    dataset_array[0, :, :, :] = img

    softmax_propabilities = graph.get_tensor_by_name(name="softmax_
    probs:0")
    softmax_predictions = tensorflow.argmax(softmax_propabilities, axis=1)
    data_tensor = graph.get_tensor_by_name(name="data_tensor:0")
    keep_prop = graph.get_tensor_by_name(name="keep_prop:0")

    feed_dict_testing = {data_tensor: dataset_array, keep_prop: 1.0}


    softmax_propabilities_, softmax_predictions_ = sess.run([softmax_
    propabilities, softmax_predictions], feed_dict=feed_dict_testing)

    label_names_dict = unpickle_patch(patches_dir + "batches.meta")
    dataset_label_names = label_names_dict[b"label_names"]
    return dataset_label_names[softmax_predictions_[0]].decode('utf-8')
```

The function restores required tensors that help in returning the prediction label based on their names, such as the softmax_predictions tensor. Some other tensors are restored to override their values, which are the keep_prop to avoid dropping any neuron in the testing phase and data_tensor tensors to provide the data of the image file uploaded. The session then runs to return the predicted label. The label is just a number that is an identifier to the class. The dataset provides a metadata file in which there is a list containing the names of all classes. The identifier is converted into the class string label by indexing the list.

After prediction completes, the CNN_predict() view functions sends the predicted class to the prediction_result.html template for rendering. This template is implemented as given in Listing 7-35. It is very simple. It just uses an expression to print the predicted class within a <span> element. The page provides a link to return to the homepage based on the endpoint to select another image for classification. The rendered page after uploading an image is given in Figure 7-25.

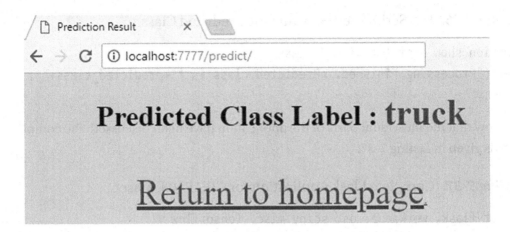

Figure 7-25. *The rendered result after predicting the class label*

Listing 7-35. Rendering Predicted Class

```
<!DOCTYPE html>
<html lang="en">
<head>
<link rel="stylesheet" type="text/css" href="{{url_for(endpoint='static',
filename='project_styles.css')}}">
<script type="text/javascript" src="{{url_for(endpoint='static',
filename='result.js')}}"></script>
<meta charset="UTF-8">
<title>Prediction Result</title>
</head>
<body onload="show_alert('{{predicted_class}}')">
<center><h1>Predicted Class Label : <span>{{predicted_class}}</span></h1>
<br>
<a href="{{url_for(endpoint='homepage')}}"><span>Return to homepage</
span>.</a>
</center>
</body>
</html>
```

Note that when loading the <body> element of Listing 7-35, there is a call to a
JavaScript function named show_alert(). It accepts the predicted class label and shows
an alert. Its implementation is given in Listing 7-36.

Listing 7-36. JavaScript Alert Showing the Predicted Class

```
function show_alert(predicted_class){
alert("Processing Finished.\nPredicted class is *"+predicted_class+"*.")
}
```

Now that the individual parts of the application have been discussed, the complete code is given in Listing 7-37.

Listing 7-37. Complete Flask Application for CIFAR10 Dataset

```
import flask, werkzeug, os, scipy.misc, tensorflow
import CIFAR10Predict#Module for predicting the class label of an input
image.

#Creating a new Flask Web application. It accepts the package name.
app = flask.Flask("CIFARTF")

def CNN_predict():
    """

    Reads the uploaded image file and predicts its label using the saved
    pretrained CNN model.
    :return: Either an error if the image is not for the CIFAR10 dataset or
    redirects the browser to a new page to show the prediction result if no
    error occurred.
    """

    global sess
    global graph

# Setting the previously created 'secure_filename' to global.
# This is because to be able to invoke a global variable created in another
function, it must be defined global in the caller function.

    global secure_filename
    #Reading the image file from the path it was saved in previously.
    img = scipy.misc.imread(os.path.join(app.root_path, secure_filename))

# Checking whether the image dimensions match the CIFAR10 specifications.
```

CIFAR10 images are RGB (i.e. they have 3 dimensions). Its number of dimensions was not equal to 3, then a message will be returned.

```
    if(img.ndim) == 3:
```

Checking if the number of rows and columns of the read image matched CIFAR10 (32 rows and 32 columns).

```
        if img.shape[0] == img.shape[1] and img.shape[0] == 32:
```

Checking whether the last dimension of the image has just 3 channels (Red, Green, and Blue).

```
            if img.shape[-1] == 3:
```

Passing all preceding conditions, the image is proved to be of CIFAR10.
This is why it is passed to the predictor.

```
                predicted_class = CIFAR10Predict.main(sess, graph, img)
```

After predicting the class label of the input image, the prediction label is rendered on an HTML page.
The HTML page is fetched from the /templates directory. The HTML page accepts an input which is the predicted class.

```
                return flask.render_template(template_name_or_
                list="prediction_result.html", predicted_class=predicted_
                class)
        else:
                # If the image dimensions do not match the CIFAR10
                specifications, then an HTML page is rendered to show the
                problem.
                return flask.render_template(template_name_or_list="error.
                html", img_shape=img.shape)
    else:
```

```
            # If the image dimensions do not match the CIFAR10
            specifications, then an HTML page is rendered to show the
            problem.
            return flask.render_template(template_name_or_list="error.
            html", img_shape=img.shape)
    return "An error occurred."#Returned if there is a different error
    other than wrong image dimensions.


# Creating a route between the URL (http://localhost:7777/predict) to a
viewer function that is called after navigating to such URL.
# Endpoint 'predict' is used to make the route reusable without hard-coding
it later.

app.add_url_rule(rule="/predict/", endpoint="predict", view_func=CNN_
predict)


def upload_image():
    """

    Viewer function that is called in response to getting to the 'http://
    localhost:7777/upload' URL.
    It uploads the selected image to the server.
    :return: redirects the application to a new page for predicting the
    class of the image.
    """

    #Global variable to hold the name of the image file for reuse later in
    prediction by the 'CNN_predict' viewer functions.
    global secure_filename
    if flask.request.method == "POST":#Checking of the HTTP method
    initiating the request is POST.
        img_file = flask.request.files["image_file"]#Getting the file name
        to get uploaded.
        secure_filename = werkzeug.secure_filename(img_file.
        filename)#Getting a secure file name. It is a good practice to use
        it.
        img_file.save(secure_filename)#Saving the image in the specified
        path.
        print("Image uploaded successfully.")
```

```
# After uploading the image file successfully, next is to predict the class
label of it. The application will fetch the URL that is tied to the HTML
page responsible for prediction and redirects the browser to it.
# The URL is fetched using the endpoint 'predict'.

        return flask.redirect(flask.url_for(endpoint="predict"))
    return "Image upload failed."

# Creating a route between the URL (http://localhost:7777/upload) to a
viewer function that is called after navigating to such URL.
# Endpoint 'upload' is used to make the route reusable without hard-coding
it later. The set of HTTP method the viewer function is to respond to is
added using the 'methods' argument. In this case, the function will just
respond to requests of the methods of type POST.

app.add_url_rule(rule="/upload/", endpoint="upload", view_func=upload_
image, methods=["POST"])


def redirect_upload():
    """

    A viewer function that redirects the Web application from the root to
    an HTML page for uploading an image to get classified.
    The HTML page is located under the /templates directory of the
    application.
    :return: HTML page used for uploading an image. It is 'upload_image.
    html' in this example.
    """

    return flask.render_template(template_name_or_list="upload_image.html")

# Creating a route between the homepage URL (http://localhost:7777) to a
viewer function that is called after getting to such a URL.
# Endpoint 'homepage' is used to make the route reusable without hard-
coding it later.

app.add_url_rule(rule="/", endpoint="homepage", view_func=redirect_upload)
```

```python
def prepare_TF_session(saved_model_path):
    global sess
    global graph

    sess = tensorflow.Session()

    saver = tensorflow.train.import_meta_graph(saved_model_path+'model.
    ckpt.meta')
    saver.restore(sess=sess, save_path=saved_model_path+'model.ckpt')

    #Initializing the variables.
    sess.run(tensorflow.global_variables_initializer())

    graph = tensorflow.get_default_graph()
    return graph

# To activate the web server to receive requests, the application must run.
# A good practice is to check whether the file is called from an external
Python file or not.
# If not, then it will run.

if __name__ == "__main__":

# In this example, the app will run based on the following properties:
# host: localhost
# port: 7777
# debug: flag set to True to return debugging information.

    #Restoring the previously saved trained model.
    prepare_TF_session(saved_model_path='\\AhmedGad\\model\\')
    app.run(host="localhost", port=7777, debug=True)
```

CHAPTER 8

Cross-Platform Data Science Applications

There are releases from the current DL libraries that support building applications for mobile devices. For example, TensorFlowLite, Caffe Android, and Torch Android are all releases from TF, Caffe, and Torch, respectively, to support mobile devices. These releases are based on their parents. There must be an in-between step in order to make the original model work on mobile devices. For example, the process of creating an Android application that uses TensorFlowLite has the following summarized steps:

1. Prepare the TF Model.

2. Convert the TF Model to TensorFlowLite Model.

3. Create an Android Project.

4. Import the TensorFlowLite Model Within the Project.

5. Call the Model Within Java Code.

It is tiresome to go through these steps for building a model suitable for running on mobile devices. The challenging step is the second one.

TensorFlowLite is a release compatible with mobile devices. Thus, it is simplified compared to its ancestor TF. This means it does not support everything in its parent library. Some operations in TF such as tanh, image.resize_bilinear, and depth_to_space are not supported in TensorFlowLite to date. This adds restrictions when preparing a model that works on mobile devices. Moreover, the model developer has to use languages in order to create an Android application running a trained CNN model. Using Python, the model will be created using TF. After optimizing the model using the TF optimizing converter (TOCO), a project is created using Android Studio. Inside such a project, the model will be called using Java. As a result, the process is not

© Ahmed Fawzy Gad 2018
A. F. Gad, *Practical Computer Vision Applications Using Deep Learning with CNNs*,
https://doi.org/10.1007/978-1-4842-4167-7_8

straightforward, and it is challenging to create the application. For more information about building mobile applications using TensorFlowLite, read the documentation at this link (`www.tensorflow.org/lite/overview`). In this chapter, we will use Kivy (KV) for building applications running cross-platform with minimal effort.

Kivy is an abstract and modular open source cross-platform Python framework used to create natural user interfaces (UIs). It decouples the developer from complex details by using back-end libraries for low-level access to graphics hardware and handling both audio and video. It just gives the developer simple APIs for doing the tasks.

This chapter gives an introduction to Kivy using a number of simple examples to help explain its basic program structure, UI widgets, structuring of the widgets using KV language, and handling actions. Kivy supports the execution of the same Python code on Window, Linux, Mac, and also mobile devices, which makes it cross-platform. Using Buildozer and Python-4-Android (P4A), the Kivy application is converted into an Android package. Not only executes native Python code; Kivy also supports some libraries to be executed on mobile devices such as NumPy and PIL (Python Image Library). By the end of this chapter, a cross-platform application is built to execute the CNN implemented in Chapter 5 using NumPy. Ubuntu is used in this chapter because Buildozer is currently available on Linux.

Introduction to Kivy

In this section, Kivy basics are discussed in detail based on some examples. This helps us to put our hands on the way to build our own applications. Remember from Chapter 7 that Flask application starts to create an application by instantiating the Flask class; then the application runs by calling the `run()` method. Kivy is similar but with some changes. We can assume that the `Flask` class corresponds to the `App` class in Kivy. There is a method called `run()` inside both Kivy and Flask. The Kivy application is created not by instantiating the class App but by instantiating a child class extending the App class. The application then runs by calling the `run()` method using an instance created from the child class.

Kivy is used to build a UI that consists of a set of visual elements called widgets. Between instantiating the class and running it, we have to specify which widgets are used and their layout. The App class supports a method called `build()`, which returns the layout widget containing all other widgets in the UI. This method can be overridden from the parent App class.

Basic Application Using BoxLayout

Let's make things clearer by discussing a basic Kivy application in Listing 8-1. At first, the required modules from Kivy are imported. The kivy.app contains the App class. This class is used as the parent of our defined class FirstApp. The second statement imports kivy.uix.label, which has the label widget. This widget just displays text on the UI.

Inside the build() method, the label widget is created using the kivy.uix.label. Label class. The class constructor accepts an argument named text, which is the text to be displayed on the UI. The returned label is saved as a property of the FirstApp object. Adding widgets as properties for the class object makes it easy to retrieve them later compared to saving them in separate variables.

Listing 8-1. Basic Kivy Application

```
import kivy.app
import kivy.uix.label
import kivy.uix.boxlayout

class FirstApp(kivy.app.App):
    def build(self):
        self.label = kivy.uix.label.Label(text="Hello Kivy")
        self.layout = kivy.uix.boxlayout.BoxLayout()
        self.layout.add_widget(widget=self.label)
        return self.layout

firstApp = FirstApp()
firstApp.run()
```

Widgets in Kivy are grouped into a root widget. In Listing 8-1, the BoxLayout is used as the root widget, which contains all other widgets. This is why the kivy.uix.boxlayout is imported. Based on the constructor of the kivy.uix.label.BoxLayout class, the BoxLayout object is saved as a property of the FirstClass object. After creating both the label and the layout objects, the label is added to the layout using the add_widget() method. This method has an argument named widget, which accepts the widget to be added to the layout. After adding the label into the root widget (layout), the layout is returned by the build() method.

After creating the child class `FirstApp` and preparing its `build()` method, an instance from that class is created. The `run()` method is then called by that instance and the application window is displayed according to Figure 8-1.

Figure 8-1. *Simple Kivy application with a text label*

Kivy Application Life Cycle

By just running the application, the widgets defined inside the `build()` method are rendered on the screen. Note that the Kivy life cycle is illustrated in Figure 8-2. It is similar to the Android application life cycle. The life cycle starts by running the application using the `run()` method. After that, the `build()` method is executed, which returns the widgets to be displayed. After executing the `on_start()` method, the application runs successfully. Also, the application might get paused or stopped. If paused, then the `on_pause()` method is called. If the application resumed, then the `on_resume()` method is called. If not resumed, then the app stops. The app might get stopped directly without being paused. If this case, the `on_stop()` method is called.

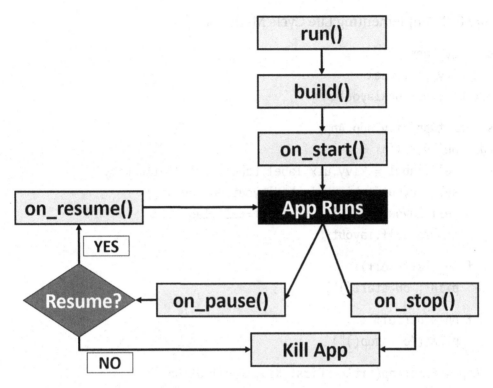

Figure 8-2. *Kivy application life cycle*

The title at the top of the Figure 8-1 has the word First. What is that? The child class is named FirstApp. When the class is named with the word App at the end, Kivy uses the work before it as the application title. Naming the class MyApp, then the title is My. Note that the word App must start with a capital letter. If the class is named Firstapp, then the title will be also Firstapp. Note that we have the ability to set a custom name using the title argument of the class constructor. The constructor also accepts an argument named icon, which is the path of an image.

Listing 8-2 sets the application title to a custom title and also implements the on_start() and on_stop() methods. The window is shown in Figure 8-3. When the application starts, the on_start() method is called to print a message. This is the same for the on_stop() method.

Listing 8-2. Implementing Life Cycle Methods

```
import kivy.app
import kivy.uix.label
import kivy.uix.boxlayout

class FirstApp(kivy.app.App):
    def build(self):
        self.label = kivy.uix.label.Label(text="Hello Kivy")
        self.layout = kivy.uix.boxlayout.BoxLayout()
        self.layout.add_widget(widget=self.label)
        return self.layout

    def on_start(self):
        print("on_start()")

    def on_stop(self):
        print("on_stop()")

firstApp = FirstApp(title="First Kivy Application.")
firstApp.run()
```

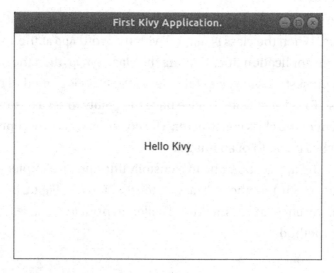

Figure 8-3. *Channing the application title*

We can add more than one widget inside the BoxLayout. This layout widget arranges its child widgets either vertically or horizontally. Its constructor has an argument named orientation to define the arrangement. It has two values: horizontal and vertical. It defaults to horizontal.

If the orientation is set to vertical, then the widgets are stacked on top of each other, where the first widget added appears at the bottom of the window and the last widget added appears on the top. In this case, the window height is divided equally across all child widgets.

If the orientation is horizontal, then the widgets are added side by side, where the first widget added is the leftmost widget on the screen, while the last widget added is the rightmost widget on the screen. In this case, the width of the window is divided equally across all child widgets.

Listing 8-3 uses five button widgets with their text set to Button 1, Button 2, up to Button 5. These widgets are added horizontally inside a BoxLayout widget. The result is given in Figure 8-4.

Listing 8-3. Kivy Application using BoxLayout as the Root Widget with Horizontal Orientation

```
import kivy.app
import kivy.uix.button
import kivy.uix.boxlayout

class FirstApp(kivy.app.App):
    def build(self):
        self.button1 = kivy.uix.button.Button(text="Button 1")
        self.button2 = kivy.uix.button.Button(text="Button 2")
        self.button3 = kivy.uix.button.Button(text="Button 3")
        self.button4 = kivy.uix.button.Button(text="Button 4")
        self.button5 = kivy.uix.button.Button(text="Button 5")
        self.layout = kivy.uix.boxlayout.BoxLayout(orientation=
        "horizontal")
        self.layout.add_widget(widget=self.button1)
        self.layout.add_widget(widget=self.button2)
        self.layout.add_widget(widget=self.button3)
        self.layout.add_widget(widget=self.button4)
        self.layout.add_widget(widget=self.button5)
```

```
        return self.layout
```

```
firstApp = FirstApp(title="Horizontal BoxLayout Orientation.")
firstApp.run()
```

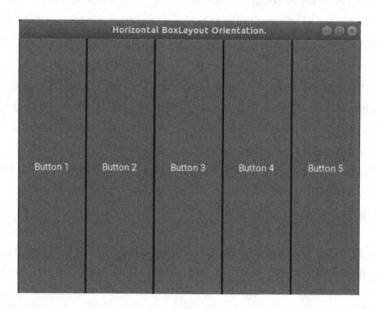

Figure 8-4. *The horizontal orientation of the* BoxLayout *widget*

Widget Size

The BoxLayout divides the screen equally across all widgets. Adding five widgets, then it splits the screen into five equal parts in both width and height. It assigns each widget a part of equal size. We can make the part size assigned to a widget larger or smaller using the size_hint argument of the widgets. It accepts a tuple with two values defining the width and height relative to the window size. By default, the tuple is (1,1) for all widgets. This means equal sizes. If this argument is set to (2, 1) for a widget, the widget width will be doubled compared to the default width. If it is set to (0.5,1), then the widget width will be half the default width.

Listing 8-4 changes the size_hint argument for some widgets. Figure 8-5 shows the result where the text of each button reflects its widths relative to the window size. Note that the widgets make a hint to the parent widget that it would like its size to be according to the values specified by the size_hint argument. The parent might accept or reject the request. This is why it has the word hint in the argument name.

For example, setting the col_force_default or row_force_default properties of the widget makes the parent completely ignore the size_hint argument. Note that the size_hint is an argument to the widget constructor and also available as a property for the instances from the widgets.

Listing 8-4. Using the size_hint Argument with theIf added "with" not OK, please clarify listing caption. Widgets to Change Their Relative Size

```python
import kivy.app
import kivy.uix.button
import kivy.uix.boxlayout

class FirstApp(kivy.app.App):
    def build(self):
        self.button1 = kivy.uix.button.Button(text="2", size_hint = (2, 1))
        self.button2 = kivy.uix.button.Button(text="1")
        self.button3 = kivy.uix.button.Button(text="1.5", size_hint =
        (1.5, 1))
        self.button4 = kivy.uix.button.Button(text="0.7", size_hint =
        (0.7, 1))
        self.button5 = kivy.uix.button.Button(text="3", size_hint = (3, 1))
        self.layout = kivy.uix.boxlayout.BoxLayout(orientation="horizontal")
        self.layout.add_widget(widget=self.button1)
        self.layout.add_widget(widget=self.button2)
        self.layout.add_widget(widget=self.button3)
        self.layout.add_widget(widget=self.button4)
        self.layout.add_widget(widget=self.button5)
        return self.layout

firstApp = FirstApp(title="Horizontal BoxLayout Orientation.")
firstApp.run()
```

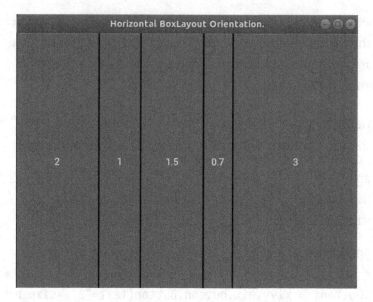

Figure 8-5. *Changing the width of the widgets using size_hint argument*

GridLayout

There are also layouts other than the BoxLayout. For example, the GridLayout divides the screen into a grid based on the specified number of rows and columns. According to Listing 8-5, a grid layout is created with two rows and three columns in which six buttons are added. The number of rows and columns are set according to the rows and cols properties, respectively. The first widget added appears on the top left corner, while the last widget added appears on the bottom right corner. The result is illustrated in Figure 8-6.

Listing 8-5. Dividing the Window into a Grid of Size 2×3 Using GridLayout

```
import kivy.app
import kivy.uix.button
import kivy.uix.gridlayout

class FirstApp(kivy.app.App):
    def build(self):
        self.button1 = kivy.uix.button.Button(text="Button 1")
        self.button2 = kivy.uix.button.Button(text="Button 2")
        self.button3 = kivy.uix.button.Button(text="Button 3")
        self.button4 = kivy.uix.button.Button(text="Button 4")
```

```
        self.button5 = kivy.uix.button.Button(text="Button 5")
        self.button6 = kivy.uix.button.Button(text="Button 6")
        self.layout = kivy.uix.gridlayout.GridLayout(rows=2, cols=3)
        self.layout.add_widget(widget=self.button1)
        self.layout.add_widget(widget=self.button2)
        self.layout.add_widget(widget=self.button3)
        self.layout.add_widget(widget=self.button4)
        self.layout.add_widget(widget=self.button5)
        self.layout.add_widget(widget=self.button6)
        return self.layout

firstApp = FirstApp(title="GridLayout with 2 rows and 3 columns.")
firstApp.run()
```

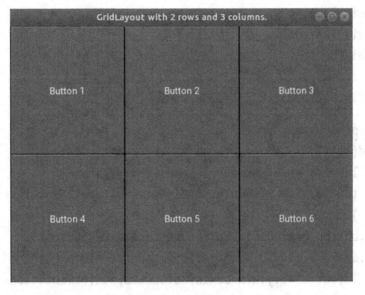

Figure 8-6. *GridLayout with two rows and three columns*

Another layout that is suitable for mobile devices is the PageLayout. It actually builds several pages within the same layout. At the page borders, the user can drag the page left or right in order to navigate to another page. Creating such a layout is simple. Just create an instance of the kivy.uix.pagelayout.PageLayout class, which is similar to what we did before. Then, add widgets into the layout exactly as we did using the add_widget() method.

More Widgets

There are multiple widgets to use in the UI. For example, the Image widget is used to display an image based on its source. The TextInput widget allows the user to type inputs into the application. Others include CheckBox, RadioButton, Slider, and more.

Listing 8-6 gives an example with Button, Label, TextInput, and Image widgets. The TextInput class constructor has a property named hint_text that shows a hint message inside the widget to help the user know what input to enter. The image widget uses the source property to specify the image path. Figure 8-7 shows the result. Later, we will handle the actions of these widgets such as button click, changing label text, and more.

Listing 8-6. BoxLayout with Label, TextInput, Button, and Image Widgets

```
import kivy.app
import kivy.uix.label
import kivy.uix.textinput
import kivy.uix.button
import kivy.uix.image
import kivy.uix.boxlayout

class FirstApp(kivy.app.App):
    def build(self):
        self.label = kivy.uix.label.Label(text="Label")
        self.textinput = kivy.uix.textinput.TextInput(hint_text="Hint
        Text")
        self.button = kivy.uix.button.Button(text="Button")
        self.image = kivy.uix.image.Image(source="im.png")
        self.layout = kivy.uix.boxlayout.BoxLayout(orientation="vertical")
        self.layout.add_widget(widget=self.label)
        self.layout.add_widget(widget=self.textinput)
        self.layout.add_widget(widget=self.button)
        self.layout.add_widget(widget=self.image)
        return self.layout

firstApp = FirstApp(title="BoxLayout with Label, Button, TextInput, and
Image")
firstApp.run()
```

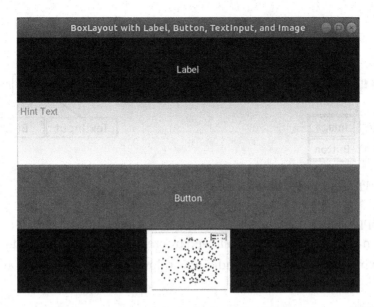

Figure 8-7. *Vertical* `BoxLayout` *with* `Label`, `TextInput`, `Button`, *and* `Image`
widgets

Widget Tree

In the previous examples, there is a root widget (layout) with several children directly
connected to it. The widget tree of Listing 8-6 is illustrated in Figure 8-8. The tree has
just one level. We can create a deeper tree like the one in Figure 8-9, in which the root
`BoxLayout` widget with vertical orientation has two layouts as children. The first one is
a `GridLayout` widget with two rows and two columns. The second child is a horizontal
`BoxLayout` widget with horizontal orientation. These child `GridLayout` widgets have
their own child widgets.

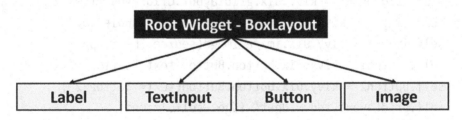

Figure 8-8. *Widget tree of the Kivy application in Listing 8-6*

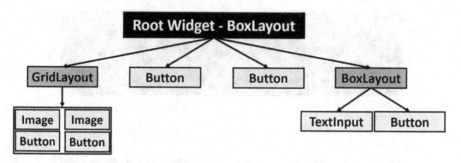

Figure 8-9. *Widget tree with nested layouts*

The Kivy application with the widget tree defined in Figure 8-9 is given in Listing 8-7. The application creates each parent followed by creating its children and finally adding these children into the parent. The rendered window of the application is available in Figure 8-10.

Listing 8-7. Kivy Application with Nested Widgets in the Widget Tree

```
import kivy.app
import kivy.uix.label
import kivy.uix.textinput
import kivy.uix.button
import kivy.uix.image
import kivy.uix.boxlayout
import kivy.uix.gridlayout

class FirstApp(kivy.app.App):
    def build(self):
        self.gridLayout = kivy.uix.gridlayout.GridLayout(rows=2, cols=2)
        self.image1 = kivy.uix.image.Image(source="apple.jpg")
        self.image2 = kivy.uix.image.Image(source="bear.jpg")
        self.button1 = kivy.uix.button.Button(text="Button 1")
        self.button2 = kivy.uix.button.Button(text="Button 2")
        self.gridLayout.add_widget(widget=self.image1)
        self.gridLayout.add_widget(widget=self.image2)
        self.gridLayout.add_widget(widget=self.button1)
        self.gridLayout.add_widget(widget=self.button2)
```

```
        self.button3 = kivy.uix.button.Button(text="Button 3")
        self.button4 = kivy.uix.button.Button(text="Button 4")

        self.boxLayout = kivy.uix.boxlayout.BoxLayout(orientation=
        "horizontal")
        self.textinput = kivy.uix.textinput.TextInput(hint_text="Hint
        Text.")
        self.button5 = kivy.uix.button.Button(text="Button 5")
        self.boxLayout.add_widget(widget=self.textinput)
        self.boxLayout.add_widget(widget=self.button5)

        self.rootBoxLayout = kivy.uix.boxlayout.BoxLayout(orientation=
        "vertical")
        self.rootBoxLayout.add_widget(widget=self.gridLayout)
        self.rootBoxLayout.add_widget(widget=self.button3)
        self.rootBoxLayout.add_widget(widget=self.button4)
        self.rootBoxLayout.add_widget(widget=self.boxLayout)

        return self.rootBoxLayout

firstApp = FirstApp(title="Nested Widgets.")
firstApp.run()
```

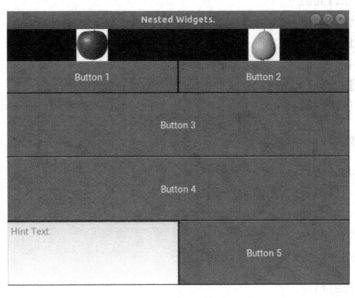

Figure 8-10. *Nested widgets*

Handling Events

We can handle the events generated by the Kivy widgets using the bind() method. This method accepts an argument specifying the target event to be handled. This argument is assigned a function or method to be called for handling such an event. For example, when a button is pressed, the on_press event is fired. As a result, the argument used with the bind() method will be named on_press. Assume that we want to handle this event using a method called handle_press, then the on_press argument of the bind() method will be assigned this method name. Note that the method handling an event accepts an argument representing the widget that fired the event. Let's see how things work using the application in Listing 8-8.

The application has two TextInput widgets, one Label, and a Button. The user enters a number in each of the TextInput widgets. When the button is pressed, the numbers are fetched and added, and then the result is rendered on the Label. Everything in the application is familiar to us based on the previous examples except for calling the bind() method for handling the press event using the add_nums() method.

Listing 8-8. Application for Adding Two Numbers and Showing Their Results on a Label

```
import kivy.app
import kivy.uix.label
import kivy.uix.textinput
import kivy.uix.button
import kivy.uix.image
import kivy.uix.boxlayout
import kivy.uix.gridlayout

class FirstApp(kivy.app.App):

    def add_nums(self, button):
        num1 = float(self.textinput1.text)
        num2 = float(self.textinput2.text)
        result = num1 + num2
        self.label.text = str(result)

    def build(self):
```

```
        self.boxLayout = kivy.uix.boxlayout.BoxLayout(orientation=
        "horizontal")
        self.textinput1 = kivy.uix.textinput.TextInput(hint_text="Enter
        First Number.")
        self.textinput2 = kivy.uix.textinput.TextInput(hint_text="Enter
        Second Number.")
        self.boxLayout.add_widget(widget=self.textinput1)
        self.boxLayout.add_widget(widget=self.textinput2)

        self.label = kivy.uix.label.Label(text="Result of Addition.")
        self.button = kivy.uix.button.Button(text="Add Numbers.")
        self.button.bind(on_press=self.add_nums)

        self.rootBoxLayout = kivy.uix.boxlayout.BoxLayout(orientation=
        "vertical")
        self.rootBoxLayout.add_widget(widget=self.label)
        self.rootBoxLayout.add_widget(widget=self.boxLayout)
        self.rootBoxLayout.add_widget(widget=self.button)

        return self.rootBoxLayout

firstApp = FirstApp(title="Handling Actions using Bind().")
firstApp.run()
```

The button calls the bind() method, which is a property of any widget. For handling the on_press event, the method will use it as an argument. This argument is set equal to the custom function created with the name add_nums. This means the add_nums() method will be executed each time the on_press event is fired. The on_press itself is a method. Because it is empty by default, we need to add some logic to it. That logic may be a method we defined in the Python file, such as the add_nums method. Note that we created a method, not a function for handling the event to have access to all widgets within the object. If a function is used, then we have to pass the properties of the widgets needed for handling the event.

Inside the add_nums() method, the text inside the two TextInput widgets is returned using the text property into the num1 and num2 variables. Because the result returned by the text property is a string, we have to convert it into a number. This is done using the float() function. The two numbers are added together and the result is returned to the result variable. Adding two numbers will return a number. Thus, the data type of the result variable is numeric. Because the text property only accepts strings, we have to convert the result variable into a string using the str() function in order to display its value on the label. Figure 8-11 shows the application UI after adding two numbers and rendering the result on the Label widget.

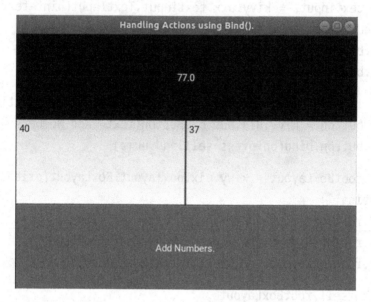

Figure 8-11. *Application UI that adds two numbers and displays the result on a* Label *widget*

KV Language

Enlarging the widget tree by adding more widgets makes the Python code harder to debug. Similar to what we did in Chapter 7 by separating the HTML code from the logic inside the Flask application, in this chapter we will separate the UI code from the application logic.

The UI will be created using a language called KV language (kvlang or Kivy language). This language creates files with extension .kv holding the UI widgets. Thus, there will be a .py file for the application logic such as handling the events, and another .kv file for holding the UI of the application. The KV language builds the widget tree in a simple way that is well read compared to adding it inside the Python code. KV language makes it easy to debug the UI because it is clear what children belong to a given parent.

The KV file consists of a set of rules similar to the CSS rule that defines the widgets. A rule consists of the widget class and a set of properties with their values. A colon is added after the widget class name to indicate the beginning of the widget content. The content under a given widget is indented just the same as what Python does for defining the content of blocks. There is a colon between the property name and its value. For example, Listing 8-9 creates a rule for building a button widget.

The button widget is written followed by a colon. Everything indented after the colon belongs to that widget. The number of indentation spaces is not fixed to just four. It is similar to Python in that we can use any number of spaces. We find that there are three properties that are indented. The first one is the text property, which is separated from the value using a colon. Going to a new indented line, we can write the new property background_color, which is separated from its value using a colon. By the way, the color is defined using the RGBA color space, where A represents the alpha channel. Color values are between 0.0 and 1.0. For the third property, the same process is repeated by writing its name separated from its value using a colon. The color property defines the text color.

Listing 8-9. Preparing the Button Widget with Some Properties Using KV Language

```
Button:
    text: "Press Me."
   background_color: (0.5, 0.5, 0.5, 1.0)
    color: (0,0,0,1)
```

We can create a simple Kivy application that uses a KV file for building the UI. Assume we want to build a UI with the BoxLayout widget as the root with vertical orientation. That root widget has three children (Button, Label, and TextInput). Note that the KV language has only one root widget, which is defined by typing it without any indentation. The children of this root widget will be indented equally. The KV language file is given in Listing 8-10. The Button, Label, and TextInput widgets are indented by four spaces after the root widget. The root widget itself can have properties. The properties of each child widget are indented behind their widgets. It is simple enough, but how can we use this KV file inside the Python code?

Listing 8-10. Simple UI Created Using KV Language

```
BoxLayout:
    orientation: "vertical"
    Button:
        text: "Press Me."
        color: (1,1,1,1)
```

```
Label:
    text: "Label"
TextInput:
    hint_text: "TextInput"
```

There are two ways of loading the KV file inside the Python code. The first way is to specify the path of the file inside the load_file() method of the kivy.lang.builder. Builder class. This method uses its filename argument to specify the path of the file. The file can be located anywhere and is not required to be in the same directory as the Python file. Listing 8-11 shows how to locate the KV file this way.

Previously, the return of the build() method is the root widget defined within the Python file. Now it returns the result of the load_file() method. The Python code is clearer after separating the logic inside the Python file from the presentation, which is now inside the KV file.

Listing 8-11. Locating the LV File Using Its Path

```
import kivy.app
import kivy.lang.builder

class FirstApp(kivy.app.App):

    def build(self):
        return kivy.lang.builder.Builder.load_file(filename='ahmedgad/
        FirstApp/first.kv')

firstApp = FirstApp(title="Importing UI from KV File.")
firstApp.run()
```

The code can be made clearer by using the second way of loading the KV file. This way depends on the name of the child class inheriting the App class. If this class is named FirstApp, then Kivy will look for a KV file named first.kv. That is, the App word is removed and the remaining text First is converted into lowercase. If there is a file named first.kv inside the same directory at which the Python file exists, then this file will be loaded automatically.

When this method is used, the Python code will be as given in Listing 8-12. The code is now clearer than before and simpler to debug. The pass statement is added inside the FirstApp class to avoid leaving it empty. Note that if Kivy could not locate a file named according to first.kv, the application will still run but it will show a blank window.

Listing 8-12. Loading the KV File Named According to the Child Class Name

```
import kivy.app

class FirstApp(kivy.app.App):
    pass

firstApp = FirstApp(title="Importing UI from KV File.")
firstApp.run()
```

We can separate the UI in Listing 8-8 from the Python code and bind the event handler to the button inside the KV file. The KV file is given in Listing 8-13.

There are some further points worth mentioning. A widget can be given an ID inside the KV file using the id property. Its value does not need to be enclosed between quotes. The ID can be used to retrieve properties of widgets inside both the KV file and the Python file. According to the code, IDs are given to the elements Label and the two TextInput widgets. The reason is that these are the widgets we are looking to retrieve or change in terms of their properties.

Listing 8-13. UI of Listing 8-8 for Adding Two Numbers Separated into KV File

```
BoxLayout:
    orientation: "vertical"
    Label:
        text: "Result of Addition."
        id: label
    BoxLayout:
        orientation: "horizontal"
        TextInput:
            hint_text: "Enter First Number."
            id: textinput1
        TextInput:
            hint_text: "Enter Second Number."
            id: textinput2
    Button:
        text: "Add Numbers."
        on_press: app.add_nums(root)
```

The button widget has the on_press property. It is used to bind the event handler to the on_press event. The event handler is the add_nums() method found inside the Python code in Listing 8-14. Thus, we want to call a Python method from the KV file. How can we do that?

The KV language has three helpful keywords: app, referring to the application instance; root, referring to the root widget in the KV file; and self, which refers to the current widget. The suitable keyword for use in order to call a method from the Python code is the app keyword. Because it refers to the entire application, then it will be able to refer to the methods inside the Python file. Thus, we can use it to call the add_nums() method using app.add_nums().

Listing 8-14. Kivy Python File for Handling the on_press Event

```python
import kivy.app

class FirstApp(kivy.app.App):

    def add_nums(self, root):
        num1 = float(self.root.ids["textinput1"].text)
        num2 = float(self.root.ids["textinput2"].text)
        result = num1 + num2
        self.root.ids["label"].text = str(result)

firstApp = FirstApp(title="Importing UI from KV File.")
firstApp.run()
```

Inside this method, we want to refer to the TextInput and label widgets in order to fetch the numbers entered and print the result on the label. Because the self argument refers to what called it, which is the instance about the entire application, we can use it to refer to the root widget using self.root. This returns the root of the widgets, which can be used to access any of its child widgets based on their IDs.

All IDs inside the KF file are saved inside the ids dictionary. We can use this dictionary to retrieve whatever widget we want as long as it has an ID. After retrieving the widget itself, we can fetch its properties. This way we can return the entered numbers within the TextInput widgets, convert their values from string to float, add them, and assign the text property of the Label widget the result after being converted into a string.

P4A

At this point, we have a good overview of Kivy. We can go forward toward a building Android applications using Kivy. We will start by packaging the Kivy application in Listing 8-13 and Listing 8-14.

Without any change in the previous applications, they will run on Android after packaging them. The simplified steps of converting the Kivy application into an Android application are illustrated in Figure 8-12.

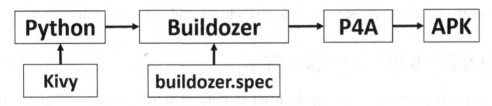

Figure 8-12. *Steps for building Android applications from Kivy applications*

After completing the Kivy Python application, the Buildozer tool prepares the required tools for creating the APK file. The most important tool is called P4A. The Buildozer tool creates a file named buildozer.spec for each Kivy application before being converted into an Android application. This file holds details about the application that will be discussed later in section **Preparing buildozer.spec File**. Let's start by installing the Buildozer tool.

Installing Buildozer

The Buildozer tool is used in this section to package the Kivy applications as Android applications. Once installed, Buildozer automates the process of building the Android applications. It prepares the environment by all requirements in order to build the applications successfully. These requirements include P4A, Android SDK, and NDK. Before installing Buildozer, some dependencies are required. They can be downloaded and installed automatically using the following Ubuntu commands:

```
ahmed-gad@ubuntu:~$ sudo pip install --upgrade cython==0.21
ahmed-gad@ubuntu:~$ sudo dpkg --add-architecture i386
ahmed-gad@ubuntu:~$ sudo apt-get update
ahmed-gad@ubuntu:~$ sudo apt-get install build-essential ccache git
libncurses5:i386 libstdc++6:i386 libgtk2.0-0:i386 libpangox-1.0-0:i386
```

libpangoxft-1.0-0:i386 libidn11:i386 python2.7 python2.7-dev openjdk-8-jdk
unzip zlib1g-dev zlib1g:i386

After installing these dependencies successfully, Buildozer can be installed
according to this command:

ahmed-gad@ubuntu:~$ sudo install --upgrade buildozer

In case Buildozer is currently installed on your machine, the --upgrade option makes
sure it is upgraded to the latest version. After installing Buildozer successfully, let us
prepare the buildozer.spec file in order to build the Android application.

Preparing buildozer.spec File

The project structure to be packaged into an Android application is given in Figure 8-13.
There is a folder named FirstApp, which contains three files. The first file is named main.
py, which is the Kivy application that was named FirstApp.py previously. The reason
it has been renamed is that when building the Android application, there must be a file
named main.py, which is the entrance of the application. This will not change anything
in the application.

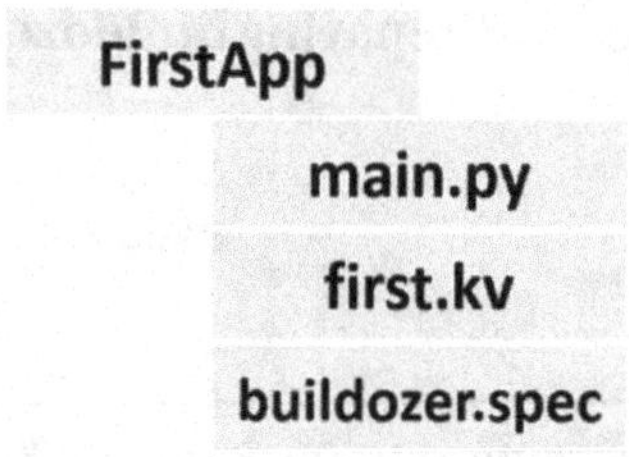

FirstApp

main.py

first.kv

buildozer.spec

Figure 8-13. *Project structure*

It is preferred to check whether the Kivy application runs successfully before
proceeding the next steps. Just activate the Kivy virtual environment on your machine
and run the main.py Python file according to Figure 8-14. It is expected to work as in
Figure 8-11.

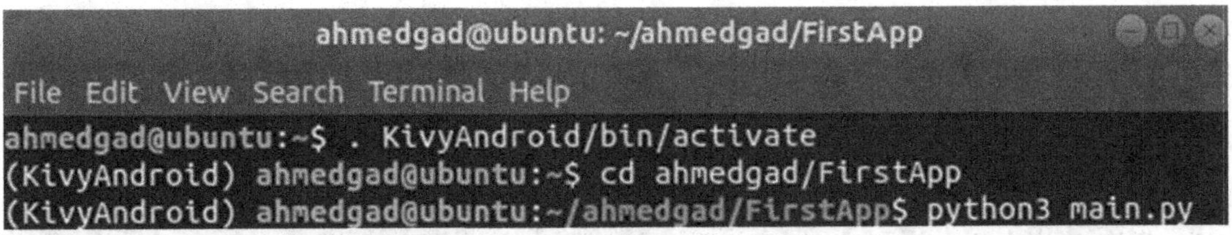

```
                ahmedgad@ubuntu: ~/ahmedgad/FirstApp
File  Edit  View  Search  Terminal  Help
ahmedgad@ubuntu:~$ . KivyAndroid/bin/activate
(KivyAndroid) ahmedgad@ubuntu:~$ cd ahmedgad/FirstApp
(KivyAndroid) ahmedgad@ubuntu:~/ahmedgad/FirstApp$ python3 main.py
```

Figure 8-14. *Activating the Kivy virtual environment for running the Kivy application*

By this point, a Kivy desktop application has been created successfully. We can now start preparing the missing file `buildozer.spec` and build an Android application.

The `buildozer.spec` file can be simply and automatically generated using Buildozer. After opening the Ubuntu terminal and navigating to the `FirstApp` directory in which the application Python and KV files exist, issue the following command:

```
ahmed-gad@ubuntu:~/ahmedgad/FirstApp$ buildozer init
```

After issuing this command, a confirmation message appears, as shown in to Figure 8-15. Some of the important fields of that file are listed in Listing 8-15. For example, the `title` represents the application title; `source` directory refers to the root directory of the application in which the `main.py` file exists, which is set in this case as the current directory; app version; Python and Kivy versions; `orientation`, that is, whether the application appears in full screen or not; and application `requirements`, which is just set to kivy. If we use a library supported by P4A such as NumPy, then we need to list it beside kivy in order to load it into the application. The `permissions` property represents the requested permissions by the application. You can also hard-code the paths of both SKD and NDK if they already exist on your machine to save time downloading them. Note that the # character before a line indicates it is a comment. The `presplash.filename` property is used to specify the image path that appears when loading the application before being started. The `icon.filename` property is assigned the file name of an image to be used as the application icon.

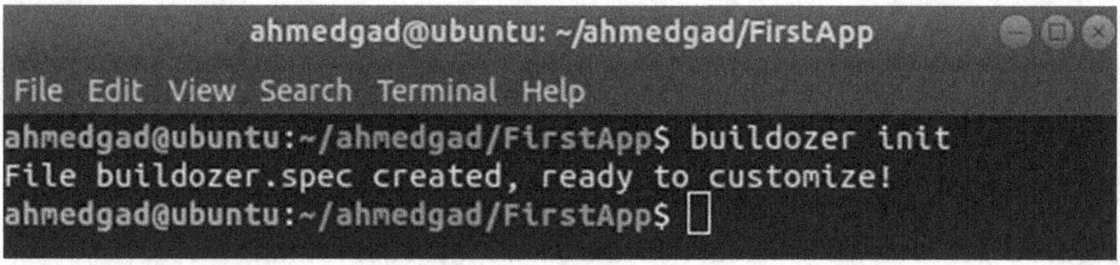

Figure 8-15. *Creating the* buildozer.spec *file successfully*

These fields are inside the [app] section of the specification file. You can also edit the specification file to change whatever fields you see as worth modifying. The package.domain property is by default set to org.test, which is used just for testing, not production. If this value is left as is, it will prevent the building of the application.

Listing 8-15. Some Important Fields from the buildozer.spec File

```
[app]
title = Simple Application
package.name = firstapp
package.domain = gad.firstapp
source.dir = .
source.include_exts = py,png,jpg,kv,atlas
version = 0.1
requirements = kivy
orientation = portrait
osx.python_version = 3
osx.kivy_version = 1.10.1
fullscreen = 0
presplash.filename = presplash.png
icon.filename = icon.png
android.permissions = INTERNET
android.api = 19
android.sdk = 20
android.ndk = 9c
android.private_storage = True
#android.ndk_path =
#android.sdk_path =
```

After preparing the required files to build the Android application, the next step is to build it using Buildozer.

Building Android Application Using Buildozer

After preparing all project files, Buildozer uses them to produce the APK file. For development, we can produce a debug version of the application using the following command:

```
ahmed-gad@ubuntu:~/ahmedgad/FirstApp$ buildozer android release
```

Figure 8-16 shows the response when the command is entered. When building the application for the first time, Buildozer has to download all of the required dependencies such as SDK, NDK, and P4A. Buildozer saves a lot of effort by downloading and installing them automatically. Based on your Internet connection, the process might take time before everything is up and running; be patient.

Figure 8-16. *Installing dependencies required by Buildozer to build the Android application*

After the installation has been done successfully, there are two folders created. The first one is named .buildozer; it represents all files downloaded by Buildozer necessary for building the application. The second folder is named bin; it stores the APK files produced after building the application. We can transfer the APK file to an Android device to install and test it. The screen of the Android application is shown in Figure 8-17.

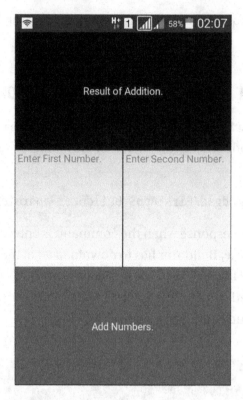

Figure 8-17. *Running the Android application*

If an Android device is connected and recognized by the machine, Buildozer could both produce the APK file and install it once produced on the machine according to this command:

```
ahmed-gad@ubuntu:~/ahmedgad/FirstApp$ buildozer android debug deploy run
```

After building a basic Android application based on the Python Kivy application, we can start building more advanced applications. Not all Kivy applications running on desktops can work directly on mobile devices. Some libraries might not be supported to be packaged into the mobile application. For example, P4A only supports a set of libraries that could be used in the Android application. If you used an unsupported library, the application crashes.

Kivy is supported by P4A, which can build the application UI exactly the same as we discussed previously. P4A also supported other libraries such as NumPy, PIL, dateutil, OpenCV, Pyinius, Flask, and more. The restriction when building an Android application using Python is to only use the set of supported libraries by P4A. In the next section, we will discuss how to build an Android application from the application created in Chapter 3 for recognizing the Fruits 360 dataset images.

Image Recognition on Android

The application created in Chapter 3 extracts features from the Fruits 360 dataset, which used for training an ANN. In Chapter 7, a Flask application was created to access it from the Web. In this chapter, we will discuss how to package it into an Android application that runs offline where features are extracted on device.

The first thing to think about is whether the libraries used in this application are supported by P4A. The libraries used are as follows:

- `scikit-image` for reading the original RGB image and converting it into HSV.

- NumPy for extracting the features (i.e., hue histogram), building the ANN layers, and making predictions.

- `pickle` for restoring the best weights for the network trained using GA and indices of the selected feature elements.

From the used libraries, P4A only supports NumPy. Neither `scikit-image` and `pickle` are supported. As a result, we have to find alternative libraries supported by P4A to replace these two libraries. The available choices for replacing `scikit-image` are OpenCV and PIL. We just need a library to read the image file and convert it to HSV and no more. OpenCV has more features than the two required ones. Packaging this library into the Android application will increase its size. For this reason, PIL is used because it is simpler.

Regarding `pickle`, we can replace it with NumPy. NumPy can save and load variables in a file with the `.npy` extension. For this reason, the weights and selected element indices will be saved into `.npy` files in order to read them using NumPy.

The project structure is illustrated in Figure 8-18. The `Fruits.py` file contains the function required for extracting features from the test image, and predicting its label. These functions are almost identical to the previous ones in Chapter 3 except for using NumPy rather than `pickle` and PIL rather than `scikit-image`. The implementation of this file is given in Listing 8-16.

The `extract_features()` function has an argument representing the image file path. It reads it using PIL and converts it into HSV color space using the `convert` method. This method accepts the HSV string specifying that the image is to be converted into HSV. After that, the `extract_features()` method extracts the features, filters the feature elements based on the selected indices' .npy file, and finally returns them. The `predict_outputs()` function is made to accept the weights .npy file path and then read it using NumPy, classify the image based on the ANN, and return the classification label.

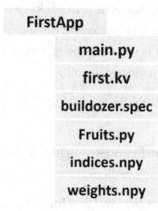

Figure 8-18. *Project structure for recognizing Fruits 360 dataset images on Android*

Listing 8-16. `Fruits.py` Module for Extracting Features and Classifying Images

```
import numpy
import PIL.Image

def sigmoid(inpt):
    return 1.0/(1.0+numpy.exp(-1*inpt))

def relu(inpt):
    result = inpt
    result[inpt<0] = 0
    return result

def predict_output(weights_mat_path, data_inputs, activation="relu"):
    weights_mat = numpy.load(weights_mat_path)
    r1 = data_inputs
    for curr_weights in weights_mat:
```

```
        r1 = numpy.matmul(a=r1, b=curr_weights)
        if activation == "relu":
            r1 = relu(r1)
        elif activation == "sigmoid":
            r1 = sigmoid(r1)
    r1 = r1[0, :]
    predicted_label = numpy.where(r1 == numpy.max(r1))[0][0]
    return predicted_label

def extract_features(img_path):
    im = PIL.Image.open(img_path).convert("HSV")
    fruit_data_hsv = numpy.asarray(im, dtype=numpy.uint8)

    indices = numpy.load(file="indices.npy")

    hist = numpy.histogram(a=fruit_data_hsv[:, :, 0], bins=360)
    im_features = hist[0][indices]
    img_features = numpy.zeros(shape=(1, im_features.size))
    img_features[0, :] = im_features[:im_features.size]
    return img_features
```

The KV file first.kv responsible for building the UI of the application is given in
Listing 8-17. It's worth mentioning that the font size of both the label and button widgets
is increased using the font_size property. Also, the classify_image() method is called
in response to the button widget on_press event.

Listing 8-17. KV File of the Fruits Recognition Application

```
BoxLayout:
    orientation: "vertical"
    Label:
        text: "Predicted Class Appears Here."
        font_size: 30
        id: label
    BoxLayout:
        orientation: "horizontal"
```

```
        Image:
            source: "apple.jpg"
            id: img
    Button:
        text: "Classify Image."
        font_size: 30
        on_press: app.classify_image()
```

The implementation of the classify_image() method is available inside the main.
py file according to Listing 8-18. This method loads the path of the image to be classified
from the source property of the image widget. This path is passed to the extract_
features() function inside the Fruits module as an argument. The predict_output()
function accepts both the extracted features, ANN weights, and the activation function.
It returns the classification label after matrix multiplication between the inputs of each
layer and its weights. The label is then printed on the label widget.

Listing 8-18. Implementation of the main.py File of the Fruits Recognition
Application

```
import kivy.app
import Fruits

class FirstApp(kivy.app.App):
    def classify_image(self):
        img_path = self.root.ids["img"].source

        img_features = Fruits.extract_features(img_path)

        predicted_class = Fruits.predict_output("weights.npy", img_
        features, activation="sigmoid")

        self.root.ids["label"].text = "Predicted Class : " + predicted_
        class

firstApp = FirstApp(title="Fruits 360 Recognition.")
firstApp.run()
```

Before starting to build the APK file, we can ensure that everything works as expected by running the Kivy application. After running the application and pressing the button, the image is classified; the result is shown in Figure 8-19. After making sure the application is running successfully, we can start building the Android application.

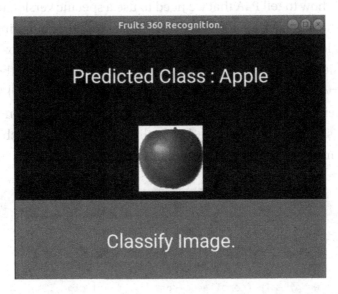

Figure 8-19. *The result of running the Kivy application after classifying an image*

Before building the application using Buildozer, the buildozer.spec file must be generated. You can use the buildozer init command to create it automatically. It is important to note that inside the application, we use two .npy files representing the filtered element indices and the weights. We need to include them into the APK file. How can we do that? Inside the buildozer.spec file, there is a property named source. include_exts. It accepts the extensions of all files we need to include into the APK file separated by commas. These files are located at the root of the application. For example, to add the files with extensions py, npy, kv, png, and jpg, the property will be as follows:

```
source.include_exts = py,png,jpg,kv ,npy
```

Two critical steps for the successful execution of the application are converting the RGB image into HSV using the PIL and matrix multiplication using the matmul() function inside NumPy. Take care to use the versions of the libraries that offer these functionalities.

Regarding the conversion from RGB to HSV, make sure to use the new version of PIL called Pillow. It is just an extension to PIL that could be imported and used with no difference. Regarding the matrix multiplication, it is only supported in NumPy version 1.10.0 and higher. Take care not to use a lower version. This leaves an additional question, which is how to tell P4A that we need to use a specific version of a library. One way is to specify the required version inside the P4A recipe corresponding to NumPy. These recipes are located in the P4A installation directory under Buildozer installation. For example, version 1.10.1 is used according to Figure 8-20. Based on the specified version, the library will be downloaded from Python package index (PyPI) and installed automatically when building the application. Note that preparing the environment of Kivy for Android is harder than its usage. We are living in an era in which preparing the development environment is harder than the development itself.

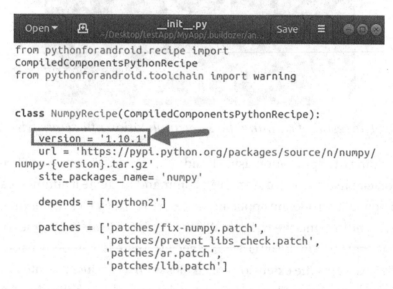

Figure 8-20. *Specifying the version of NumPy to be installed*

Now we are ready to build the Android application. We can use the command `buildozer android debug deploy run` for building, installing, the running the application on a connected Android device to the development machine. We can also use the `logcat` tool to print debugging information about the device. Just add this word at the end of the command. After the building has been done successfully, the Android application UI will be as shown in Figure 8-21.

Figure 8-21. *UI of the Android application used to classify images of the Fruits 360 dataset*

CNN on Android

In section **Building a CNN using NumPy from Scratch** of Chapter 5, we created a project for building CNN from scratch using NumPy. In this section, this project will be packaged into an Android application to execute the CNN on the device. The project structure is illustrated in Figure 8-22. The numpycnn.py file holds all functions discussed in Chapter 5 for building the CNN layers. The main application file named main.py has its child class named NumPyCNNApp. This is why the KV file should be named numpycnn. kv. The buildozer.spec file is similar to what we discussed previously. We will just discuss the main file and its KV file briefly. It is expected that most of this part of the project will be clear based on the previous discussion across the chapter.

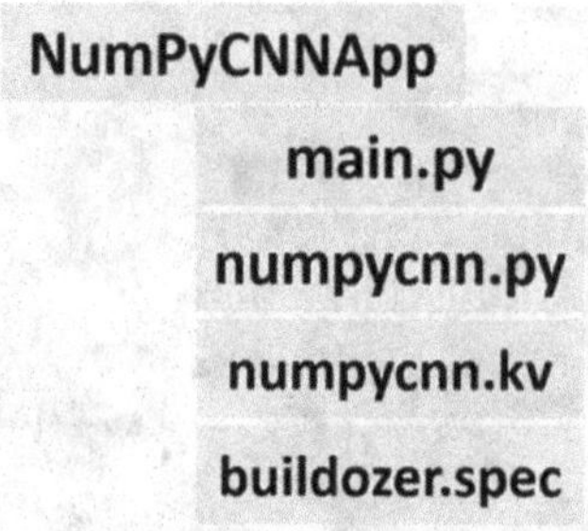

NumPyCNNApp

main.py

numpycnn.py

numpycnn.kv

buildozer.spec

Figure 8-22. *Project structure for running CNN on Android*

We will start by the KV file in Listing 8-19. The root widget is a vertical BoxLayout that has two child GridLayout widgets. The first GridLayout widget displays both the original image and the result of the last layer in the CNN. It is divided equally to hold two vertical child BoxLayout widgets. Each layout has label and image widgets. The label just makes it indicate where the original and result images are.

The second child of the root widget, GridLayout, has three widgets. The first one is a Button that executes the CNN when pressed by calling the start_cnn() method inside the main Python file. The second one is a Label that prints the size of the result after executing all CNN layers. Finally, the third child is a TextInput widget, which allows the user to specify the architecture of the CNN as a text. For example, conv2,pool,relu means that the network consists of three layers: the first one is a conv layer with four filters, the second one is an average pooling layer, and the third one is a ReLU layer. When the application runs, it has the UI shown in Figure 8-23.

Listing 8-19. KV File of the CNN Kivy Application

```
BoxLayout:
    orientation: "vertical"
    GridLayout:
        size_hint_y: 8
        cols: 3
        spacing: "5dp", "5dp"
        BoxLayout:
            orientation: "vertical"
            Label:
                id: lbl1
                size_hint_y: 1
```

```
                font_size: 20
                text: "Original"
                color: 0, 0, 0, 1
            Image:
                source: "input_image.jpg"
                id: img1
                size_hint_y: 5
                allow_stretch: True
        BoxLayout:
            orientation: "vertical"
            Label:
                id: lbl2
                size_hint_y: 1
                font_size: 20
                text: ""
                color: 0, 0, 0, 1
            Image:
                id: img2
                size_hint_y: 5
                allow_stretch: True
    GridLayout:
        cols: 3
        size_hint_y: 1
        Button:
            text: "Run CNN"
            on_press: app.start_cnn()
            font_size: 20
            id: btn
        Label:
            text: "Click the button & wait."
            id: lbl_details
            font_size: 20
            color: 0, 0, 0, 1
```

```
TextInput:
    text: "conv4,pool,relu"
    font_size: 20
    id: cnn_struct
```

The implementation of the main.py file is given in Listing 8-20. The entry point for this file is the start_cnn() method. It reads the image path from the Image widget and reads it using PIL as we discussed in the previous example. For simplicity, the image is converted into gray using the convert() method. The character L converts the image into gray. After pressing the Button widget, this function runs a background thread that executes the CNN according to the structure specified in the TextInput. The result of the last layer is returned to the refresh_GUI() method. This method displays the first matrix of the result on the UI window.

Figure 8-23. *The main window of the Kivy application executing CNN*

Listing 8-20. Implementation of the Main File of the Kivy Application Executing CNN

```
import kivy.app
import PIL.Image
import numpy
import numpycnn
import threading
```

```python
import kivy.clock

class NumPyCNNApp(kivy.app.App):

    def run_cnn_thread(self):
        layers = self.root.ids["cnn_struct"].text.split(",")
        self.root.ids["lbl_details.text"] = str(layers)
        for layer in layers:
            if layer[0:4] == "conv":
                if len(self.curr_img.shape) == 2:
                    l_filter = numpy.random.rand(int(layer[4:]), 3, 3)
                else:
                    l_filter = numpy.random.rand(int(layer[4:]), 3, 3,
                        self.curr_img.shape[-1])
                self.curr_img = numpycnn.conv(self.curr_img, l_filter)
                print("Output Conv : ", self.curr_img.shape)
            elif layer == "relu":
                self.curr_img = numpycnn.relu(self.curr_img)
                print("Output RelU : ", self.curr_img.shape)
            elif layer == "pool":
                self.curr_img = numpycnn.avgpooling(self.curr_img)
                print("Output Pool : ", self.curr_img.shape)
            elif layer[0:2] == "fc":
                num_outputs = int(layer[2:])
                fc_weights = numpy.random.rand(self.curr_img.size, num_
                outputs)
                print("FC Weights : ", fc_weights.shape)
                self.CNN_FC_Out = numpycnn.fc(self.curr_img, fc_weights=fc_
                weights, num_out=num_outputs)
                print("FC Outputs : ", self.CNN_FC_Out)
                print("Output FC : ", self.CNN_FC_Out.shape)
            else:
                self.root.ids["lbl_details"].text = "Check input."
                break
        self.root.ids["btn.text"] = "Try Again."
        self.refresh_GUI()
```

```
def start_cnn(self):
    img1 = self.root.ids["img1"]#Original Image
    im = PIL.Image.open(img1.source).convert("L")
    img_arr = numpy.asarray(im, dtype=numpy.uint8)
    self.curr_img = img_arr

    im_size = str(self.curr_img.shape)
    self.root.ids["lbl_details"].text = "Original image size
    " + im_size

    threading.Thread(target=self.run_cnn_thread).start()
    self.root.ids["btn"].text = "Wait."

@kivy.clock.mainthread
def refresh_GUI(self):
    im = PIL.Image.fromarray(numpy.uint8(self.curr_img[:, :, 0]))
    layer_size = str(self.curr_img.shape)
    im.save("res.png")
    self.root.ids["img2"].source = "res.png"
    self.root.ids["lbl2"].text = "Last Layer Result"
    self.root.ids["lbl_details"].text = "Out size "+layer_size

if __name__ == "__main__":
    NumPyCNNApp().run()
```

The thread executes the run_cnn_thread() method. That method starts by splitting the text retrieved from the TextInput to return each layer separately. Based on if statements, the suitable function from the numpycnn.py file is called to build the specified CNN layer. For example, if the current string is relu, then the relu function will be called. The number appended to the conv string is used as an argument specifying the number of filters. The shape of all filters is 3×3. They are filled randomly. If there is an unrecognized string, the application displays a message on the Label to indicate there is something wrong with the inputs. After this function finishes execution, it returns to the refresh_ GUI() method. It displays the first matrix returned and prints its size on the Label.

A modified version of this application allows running all three successive conv, pool, and ReLU layers and shows results returned by all of them. Based on the first three layers (two filters, conv layer with two filters followed by pooling and then ReLU), all returned results are given in Figure 8-24.

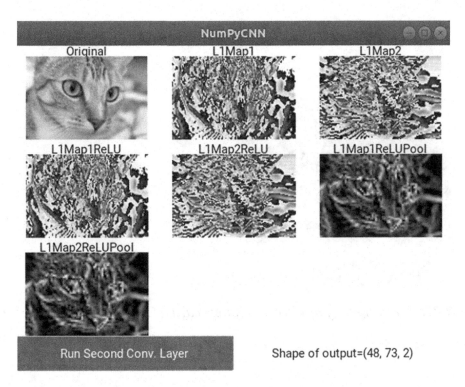

Figure 8-24. *The result of all layers based on three layers CNN (conv2,pool,relu)*

After making sure the application runs well on the desktop, the only file remaining to build the application is the `buildozer.spec` file. It can be prepared according to our previous discussion. After creating it successfully, we can start building it using Buildozer as we did previously. The UI of the application after running it on an Android device is given in Figure 8-25.

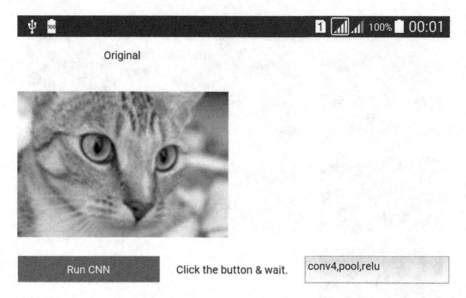

Figure 8-25. *Running Kivy application for executing CNN on Android devices*

APPENDIX A

Installing Your Own Projects Using pip Installer

Most of us have worked with several languages such as Java, C++, and Python and created a number of projects, but unfortunately, these projects are possibly buried and no one knows about them. Why not make these projects live online? Distributing projects is very easy with Python. We can benefit from the implementation of CNN using NumPy in Chapter 5 to make it available for everyone looking to do the same job.

This appendix discusses the steps required to package your Python projects, distribute them in distribution formats using setuptools, upload them into the PyPI repository using twine, and finally install them using Python installers such as pip and conda. This appendix starts with a very simple Python project called "printmsg", which has a simple function to print a message when called.

We are going to discuss the following points:

- Creating a Simple Python Project.

- How Does Python Locate Libraries?

- Manual Installation by Copying Project Files to **site-packages.**

- How Do Python Installers Locate Libraries?

- Preparing the Package and Its Files (**__init__.py** and **setup.py**).

- Distributing the Package.

- Uploading the Distribution Files Online to Test PyPI.

- Installing the Distributed Package from Test PyPI.

- Importing and Using the Installed Package.

- Using PyPI Rather Than Test PyPI.

381

© Ahmed Fawzy Gad 2018
A. F. Gad, *Practical Computer Vision Applications Using Deep Learning with CNNs*,
https://doi.org/10.1007/978-1-4842-4167-7

The platform used is Linux Ubuntu 18.04 with Python 3.6.5, but you can use other platforms such as Windows with little or no difference in the commands used. Let's see how things work.

Creating a Simple Python Project

Let us create a very simple project and distribute it. To be able to package and distribute any Python project, there must be an associated folder containing all of the required files for the project. The folder name will later be the project name.

Project Structure

This project will have just a single level containing a single Python file. The project structure is available in Figure A-1.

```
/printmsg
    print_msg_file.py
```

Figure A-1. Simple project structure

The used project/folder name is "printmsg" to reflect its use. The Python file inside it is named "print_msg_file.py". The Python file contains a function and a variable. The function is named "print_msg_func", and it will print a message once called. Because most of the existing projects contain some variables to reflect their properties such as the version, there is a variable named "version" that holds the version of the project.

Project Implementation

The implementation of the "print_msg_file.py" file is given in Listing A-1. The first line defines the version of the project using a variable named "__version__". The "print_msg_func()" function prints a hello message when called. It is good practice to handle the situations at which the Python file is called as the main file or not. This is the job of the "if" statement at the end of the file using the built-in special variable "__name__".

When a Python file is executed as the main program, then the "__name__" variable is set equal to "__main__". In case that file is used within a module, the "__name__" variable is set to the module name. The if statement ensures that the file is not imported within another module and then calls the "print_msg_func()" to print the hello message.

Listing A-1. Implementation of print_msg_file.py

```
__version__ = "1.0"

def print_msg_func():
    print("Hello Python Packaging")

if __name__ == "__main__":
    print_msg_func()
```

Running the Project

After completing such a simple project, the next step is to execute it to ensure that everything is running well. A Python file is to be executed from either the Linux terminal or Windows command prompt by issuing the Python command followed by the location of the file. Figure A-2 shows how to run the Python file using both Windows and Ubuntu. Note that the project folder is saved into the Desktop.

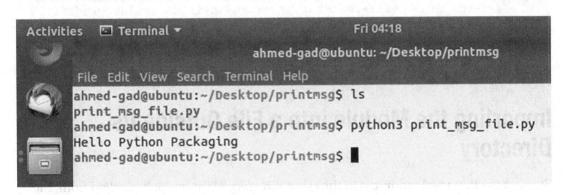

Figure A-2. *Running the module as the main program*

The CMD/terminal are opened in the "printmsg" directory. Its content is displayed using the "ls" command. Just the target file "print_msg_file.py" exists there. The Python command is issued to run the file.

Importing the Module into a File Inside Its Directory

After making sure everything is working well, it is possible to import that project into another Python file in order to be able to call its content. If a file to be imported into another, a legacy way for doing this is to create another file inside the same directory of that file. Note that it is not required to be in the same directory, but it will be simple in this case to avoid long paths. For example, another Python file named "inside_project.py" imports the project and calls its function according to Listing A-2.

Listing A-2. Importing a Module and Calling Its Functions

```
import print_msg_file
print_msg_file.print_msg_func()
```

The project is imported as in line 1. Then, it is used to call its function in line 2. After opening the terminal and setting its current directory to the "printmsg" folder, the new file "inside_project.py" can be executed as in Figure A-3. The function got called successfully.

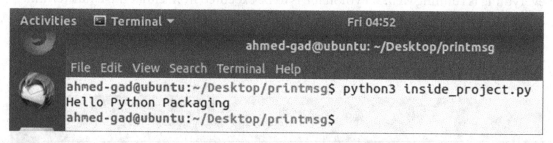

Figure A-3. *Importing the module successfully inside another file*

Importing the Module into a File Outside Its Directory

Because the imported module is in the same directory of the script it is called from, the process is straightforward. Just type the name of the module in an import statement. But an important question now arises: What if the script calling the file is in a different directory than the module it would like to import? Let us try to create another Python file not located in the same directory of the imported module and try to import the module again. The file is named "**outside_project.py**" and is located in the desktop. In other words, that file is located one level up compared to the module. It has the same code used in the previous file, **"inside_project.py"**. After running this file from the terminal, the result is shown in Figure A-4.

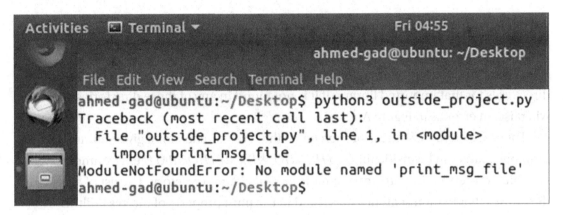

Figure A-4. *Unable to locate the module in a different directory*

The module is not found because the file and the module to be imported are in different directories. The file is located in the "~/**Desktop**/" directory, and the module is located in "~/**Desktop/printmsg**/" directory. To solve that issue, the **printmsg** is appended to the name of the module to make the interpreter know where it can find the module as given in Listing A-3.

Listing A-3. Appending Module Name When Importing the Function

```
import printmsg.print_msg_file
printmsg.print_msg_file.print_msg_func()
```

The result of executing the "**outside_project.py**" file is shown in Figure A-5.

Figure A-5. *Successfully locating the module after locating it correctly within the import statement*

But appending the folder name in the path from the file to the module it imports is tiresome, especially if the file is away from the module in more than one level. To solve this issue, let's learn how the Python interpreter locates its imported libraries.

How Does Python Locate Libraries?

When the Python interpreter encounters an import statement, it searches in some of its directories for that imported library. If it is not found in any of those directories, then it will raise an error as in Figure A-4.

There are multiple sources of such paths that are searched for a given library. For example, paths can be inside the *PYTHONHOME* or *PYTHONPATH* environment variables, current script directory, and the **site-packages** directory. The list of all directories that Python searches in is listed in the **path** property of the **sys** built-in module. It can be printed according to Listing A-4.

Listing A-4. Printing List of Search Directories

```
import sys
print(sys.path)
```

The sys.path list is printed using the terminal, and the result is shown in Figure A-6.

```
ahmed-gad@ubuntu:~/Desktop/printmsg$ python3
Python 3.6.5 (default, Apr  1 2018, 05:46:30)
[GCC 7.3.0] on linux
Type "help", "copyright", "credits" or "license" for more information.
>>> import sys
>>> sys.path
['', '/usr/lib/python36.zip', '/usr/lib/python3.6', '/usr/lib/python3.6/lib-dyn
load', '/home/ahmed-gad/.local/lib/python3.6/site-packages', '/usr/local/lib/py
thon3.6/dist-packages', '/usr/lib/python3/dist-packages']
>>> []
```

Figure A-6. *Search paths that Python uses to locate a module*

In our example, the module is not located in any of the directories listed in **sys.path**, and this is why an exception is thrown. We can fix that by moving the library into one of these paths. The directory that will be used is the **site-packages** directory. The reason is that the installed libraries using **pip** or **conda** are added to that directory. Let us see how to add our project into that directory manually.

Manual Installation by Copying Project Files to Site-Packages

In Figure A-5, the site-packages directory is listed as a search path for imported libraries. By simply copying and pasting the project directory "**printmsg**" inside the site-packages directory, the **print_msg_file** module can be imported. Figure A-7 shows that the **printmsg** project is copied into site-packages.

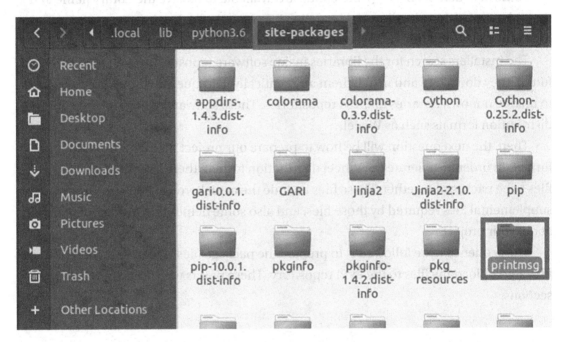

Figure A-7. *Copying the project into the site-packages directory to make it locatable by Python*

Based on the previous two lines in Listing A-3, the "**outside_project.py**" file can now successfully import the project and print the output as in Figure A-5. In this case, the imported module **print_msg_file** is prepended by the directory of the project "**printmsg**", but this will be valid wherever the "**outside_project.py**" file is located.

How Do Python Installers Locate Libraries?

Up to this point, in order to import the project successfully, it should be copied manually inside the **site-packages** directory. Before doing that, the project must be copied to the machine in some way, such as by being downloaded from any file hosting server. But all of the work is manual. Some users will find such work tiresome to do for every library they are to install. As a result, there is an alternative way of installing libraries.

Some installers such as pip and conda are available to receive the library name and they take care of downloading and installing it automatically. **But how can we make our own libraries accessible by these installers?**

The installers search for the libraries inside software repositories such as PyPI. Once found, they download and install them automatically. Our question now should be how to upload our own libraries to these repositories. These software repositories accept distribution formats such as Wheel.

Then, the next question will be how to prepare our project into Wheel distribution format. In order to generate the Wheel distribution format, there are a number of files to be packaged together. These files include the actual project Python files, any supplemental files required by those files, and also some helper files to give some details about your project.

The sequence to be followed is to prepare the package files, generate the distribution files, and upload the files to the PyPI repository. These points will be covered in the next sections.

Preparing the Package and Its Files (__init__.py and setup.py)

The first step is to structure the package and its files. The structure of the package will be as shown in Figure A-8.

```
/root
    /printmsg
        __init__.py
        print_msg_file.py
    setup.py
```

Figure A-8. *Project structure prepared for use by the Python installers*

There is a root directory holding all files and directories of the package. Inside that root directory, there is another directory named "**printmsg**" that holds the Python file to be imported later after being installed.

For our simple example, the minimal files required will be used; these are **__init__.py** and **setup.py** in addition to the actual project file **print_msg_file.py**. The next step is to prepare these files.

__init__.py

The first file to prepare is the **__init__.py** file. The main use of this file is to allow Python to treat the directory as a package. When the package has the **__init__.py** file, the package can be imported as a regular library after being installed by either installer. Just its existence is enough even if empty. You might wonder why it is now required despite being not when the library installed manually in the "Manual Installation by Copying Project Files to Site-Packages" section. The answer is that the installer will not know that the directory is a package without the **__init__.py** file. That is why it will not fetch the library Python files (**print_msg_file.py**).

Assuming that the library is now accessible by Python installers and we successfully installed it in Windows, there are two folders generated in the site-packages directory ("**printmsg-1.4.dist-info**" and "**printmsg**") as in Figure A-9 in the case of using the **__init__.py** file.

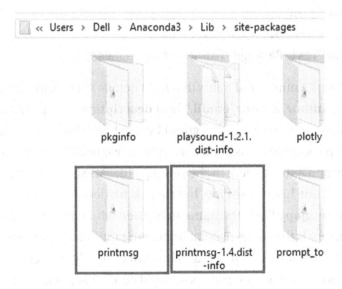

Figure A-9. *Project directories created within the site-packages directory*

The "**printmsg**" folder is what holds the Python files to be imported later. If the __ init__.py file is not used, then the "**printmsg**" folder will not be found. As a result, it will become impossible to use the Python code because it will be missing.

Besides telling Python that the directory is a Python package, the __init__.py file is the first file to be loaded when the module is imported and thus can do initializations.

setup.py

After marking the directory as a package using the __init__.py file, the next step is to add more details about the package. This is why the **setup.py** file is used. The **setup.py** script is what gives details about your project, such as what dependencies are required to make your project run. This script uses the **setuptools** distribution tool for building the distribution files to be uploaded later to PyPI. Listing A-5 has the content of the setup.py file in order to distribute the project.

Listing A-5. Content of setup.py File

```
import setuptools

setuptools.setup(
    name="printmsg",
    version="1.6",
    author="Ahmed Gad",
    author_email="ahmed.f.gad@gmail.com",
    description="Test Package for Printing a Message")
```

That file contains a number of fields that hold details such as the **name** of the package, **version**, **author**, **author_email**, short **description** to appear on PyPI, and others. There are many other fields that could be used based on your needs.

Note that the package name is used currently in two positions. One time for the module directory and another here in the setup.py file. Must they be equivalent? The answer is **NO**. Each one has its own job, but there is no dependency between them. The name used in the **setup.py** file is the name to be used when installing the package. The name of the directory is the name used to import the module. If they are different, then the package will be installed by a name and imported by a different name. There should be consistency between these two names to avoid confusing package users.

Distributing the Package

After preparing the package, we are ready to distribute it. Before actual distribution, we should make sure that the dependencies required are already existing. To distribute the project, **setuptools** and **wheel** projects are required to be installed. The **wheel** project is used to generate the **wheel** distribution format. Make sure they are installed and updated as in Figure A-10 according to this command:

ahmed-gad@ubuntu:~/Desktop/root$ pip install --user --upgrade setuptools wheel

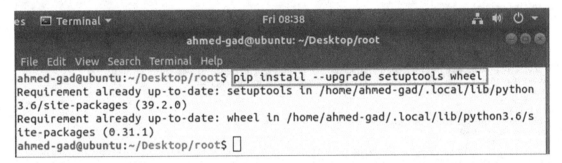

Figure A-10. *Install the required packages for packaging the project*

Then we can distribute the package by running the **setup.py** file as in Figure A-11. After opening the terminal, make the root of the package the current directory and then execute the **setup.py** file.

ahmed-gad@ubuntu:~/Desktop/root$ python3 setup.py sdist bdist_wheel

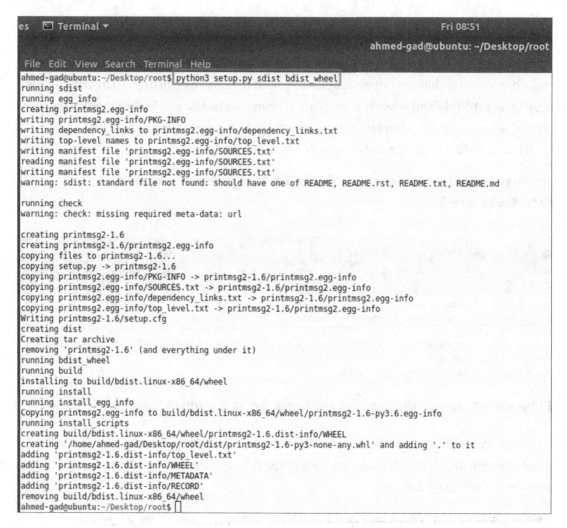

Figure A-11. *Generating source and wheel distributions of the project*

sdist is used to generate a source distribution format, while **bdist_wheel** generates the wheel built distribution format. Both of these distributions are provided for compatibility with different users.

After executing the **setup.py** file, you can expect to get some new directories inside the root of the package. The files and directories inside the root are shown in Figure A-12.

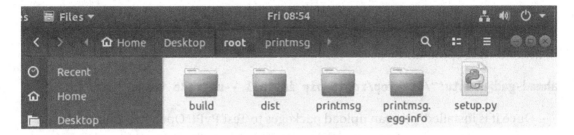

Figure A-12. *Generated files and directories of the project*

The most important folder is the **dist** folder, because it contains the distribution files that will be uploaded to PyPI. Its content is presented in Figure A-13. It contains the **.whl** file, which is the build distribution, and also the source distribution **.tar.gz** file.

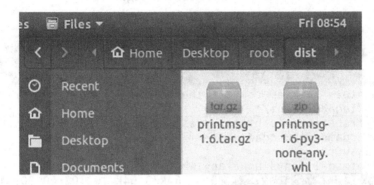

Figure A-13. *Source and wheel distribution files of the project*

After preparing the distribution files, the next step is to upload them to PyPI.

Uploading the Distribution Files Online to Test PyPI

There are two Python package repositories to use. One of them, Test PyPI (**test.pypi. org**), is for testing and experimentation, and the other, PyPI (**pypi.org**), is for real index. Their uses are similar, but we can start using Test PyPI.

Before uploading to Test PyPI, you should register yourself to get a username and password for uploading your packages. Just register by your active e-mail address, where a confirmation will be received to activate your account. The registration link is https:// test.pypi.org/account/register/.

After registration is complete, we can use the **twine** utility for uploading package distributions to Test PyPI. You should make sure it is installed and upgraded according to the following command:

`ahmed-gad@ubuntu:~/Desktop/root$ pip install --upgrade twine`

Once it is installed, you can upload packages to Test PyPI. Open the terminal, make sure you are currently on the root of the package, and issue the following command:

`ahmed-gad@ubuntu:~/Desktop/root$ twine upload --repository-url https://test.pypi.org/legacy/ dist/*`

You will be asked to enter your Test PyPI username and password. Once you are verified, the upload will start. The result is shown in Figure A-14.

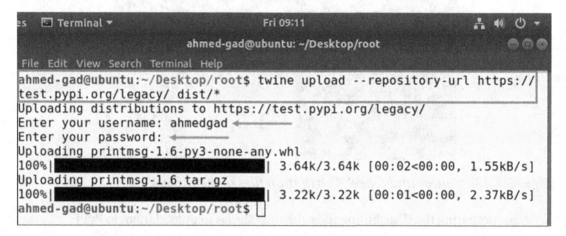

Figure A-14. *Uploading the project into Test PyPI using twine*

After uploading the files successfully, you can open your profile at Test PyPI to see your uploaded projects. Figure A-15 shows that the **printmsg** project successfully becomes live. Note that the value used for the description field inside the **setup.py** file is now appearing on the repository.

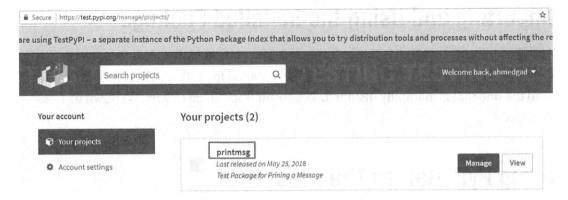

Figure A-15. *The project is successfully uploaded to Test PyPI.*

Installing the Distributed Package from Test PyPI

By this point, you have successfully packaged and distributed your Python project. It is available now for download by any user connected to the Internet. To install the project using pip, just issue the following command. The result is shown in Figure A-16.

ahmed-gad@ubuntu:~/Desktop/root$ pip install --index-url https://test.pypi. org/simple/ printmsg

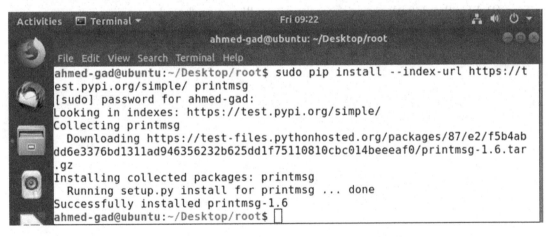

Figure A-16. *Installing the project uploaded to Test PyPI using pip*

Importing and Using the Installed Package

After installing the project, it can be imported. The code in Listing A-3 can now be executed. The difference is using the package installed from Test PyPI repository rather than the one that is manually installed. The result is identical to what is shown in Figure A-4.

Using PyPI Rather Than Test PyPI

If you decided to put your project into the real PyPI, then you will just repeat the previous steps with few changes. At first, you have to register at `https://pypi.org/` and get a username and a password. I hate to say so, but you will have to register **AGAIN** because registration in Test PyPI is different from registration in PyPI.

The first change is not using the **--repository-url** option with **twine** because PyPI is the default repository for uploading packages. So, the command required will be as follows:

```
ahmed-gad@ubuntu:~/Desktop/root $ twine upload dist/*
```

Similarly, the second change is omitting the **--index-url** option with **pip** for the same reason (PyPI is the default repository when installing a package):

```
ahmed-gad@ubuntu:~/Desktop/root$ pip install printmsg
```

Index

© Ahmed Fawzy Gad 2018
A. F. Gad, *Practical Computer Vision Applications Using Deep Learning with CNNs*,
https://doi.org/10.1007/978-1-4842-4167-7